Purchasing Costing and Control

FOR HOTEL AND CATERING OPERATIONS

*This book is dedicated to my daughter Alexis
who was born during its writing and to Jo
without whom neither would have been possible.*

Purchasing Costing and Control

FOR HOTEL AND CATERING OPERATIONS

Peter Odgers FHCIMA. Cert. Ed.
Senior Lecturer, Westminster College

STANLEY THORNES (PUBLISHERS) LTD

First published in 1985 by Gale Odgers Publications
Reprinted in 1987, 1989

Reprinted in 1990 by
Stanley Thornes (Publishers) Ltd
Ellenborough House
Wellington Street
CHELTENHAM GL50 1YW
United Kingdom

96   97   98   99   00   /   10   9   8   7   6

British Library Cataloguing in Publication Data

Odgers, Peter
    Purchasing, costing and control for hotel and
    catering operations.
    1. Hotel, taverns, etc — Great Britain —
    Finance   2. Hotel management — Great Britain
    3. Caterers and catering — Great Britain — Finance
    4. Food service management — Great Britain
    I. Title
    647'.94'0681   TX911.3.F5

    ISBN 0 7487 0324 1

Printed and bound in Great Britain by
T. J. Press (Padstow) Ltd, Cornwall

PREFACE

Any study of hotel and catering operations must, inevitably, include the element of purchasing, costing and financial control

The financial investment involved in setting up and running such an operation will demand optimum profitability from any such investment and, therefore, be blended with an approach that satisfies customer demands for the product or service offered for sale. The materials used in hotel and catering operations are either of an essential or attractive nature to both staff and customers alike. This linked with the demands previously stated emphasises the need for the control of materials used, in both their standard and their security. A hotel or catering operation will also need to ascertain its financial efficiency at any given time, in order to monitor its progress towards achieving targets it has been set.

The material in this book covers these aspects of purchasing, costing and control with a supervisory and managerial approach, it is intended to provide students at all levels with an understanding of all that is involved in dealing with these aspects of hotel and catering operations. The specific range that the study book is intended to cover may be outlined in the following way. The content is structured in such a way that they may be relevant and useful for students at BTEC Certificate level, BTEC Diploma level and taking the bridging span of Higher BTEC Diplomas. Considerable attention has been paid, in writing the book, to the structure and content of the new BTEC programmes being introduced in 1985. The book has additional relevance to students taking HCIMA examinations Parts A & B and, in particular, Food and Liquor Studies together with the accounting elements in the recently restructured Part A in addition to aspects of Food and Beverage Management (B204) and Financial Management (B205).

The study book not only provides students with a relevant and comprehensive set of texts but also with a wide range of learning aids. These take the form of student activities, assessment questions and suggestions for further reading and research. These approaches are intended to assist teachers and students alike. In this context the study book is also designed to be used by students on Open Tech or formal 'top up' learning schemes and those taking more traditional correspondence type courses. At all stages the study books are structured with the learning objectives of the various units in mind.

The method used to express various formulae for calculations of percentages and other ratios in this book is by using traditional arithmetical signs rather than fractions. The purpose being to assist students in understanding these calculations at each stage and to facilitate the use of calculator and computer keyboards. It should also be emphasised that the examples used in figures or specimen forms etc. are only a guide as to their content, each establishment designing their own to meet their own specific needs and systems.

The author would like to thank the 'Caterer and Hotelkeeper' for its permission to use extracts from their Food Prices Index and Surveys and the HCIMA for their permission to use and adapt case studies from their B204 'Food and Beverage Management' examination papers.

Appreciative thanks are also offered to my wife Jo, Ken and Loobs, Dave and Pam for their advice and time in assisting with the writing and setting up of this project.

Peter Odgers

CONTENTS

STUDY BOOK THREE

page

Note:

Each section contains Student Activities at the end of each sub-section with further reading recommendations and assessment questions at the end of each section.

Purchasing Costing and Control

STUDY BOOK ONE

Principles of Purchasing

THE CONTRIBUTION OF THE PURCHASING FUNCTION TO EFFECTIVE BUSINESS MANAGEMENT

Effective business management stems from the creation of a business policy which in turn is created by a business organisation setting itself objectives that it wishes to achieve. These objectives in a broad sense are twofold, to make sufficient profits in order to make an investment worthwhile and to provide an adequate product or service that satisfies the needs of the market aimed at. The role of management is to carry out the policy of the business organisation, an essential ingredient of successful management is to carry out such policies effectively. In a hotel and catering operation the purchasing of materials and equipment would be included in the company's policy and the purchasing function would have an important role in its day to day operation.

The purchasing function in any hotel and catering operation extends from: —

- the identification of the best sources of supply
- making arrangements with suppliers
- liaison with the departments of an operation regarding purchasing requirements and specifications
- placing orders
- liaison with the accounting function of an operation for payment of purchases.

Principles of Purchasing

The basic principles of purchasing may be defined as having four main characteristics.

 (i)   Establishing who is responsible for purchasing.
 (ii) Establishing standards and quality of materials or equipment to be purchased.
 (iii) Establishing the quantities required.
 (iv) Establishing the most favourable prices.

Each of the four characteristics will be expanded as we continue through this section of the book.

Aims of Effective Purchasing

The aims of effective purchasing are closely linked to the aims and objectives of the hotel or catering operation. Purchasing must be

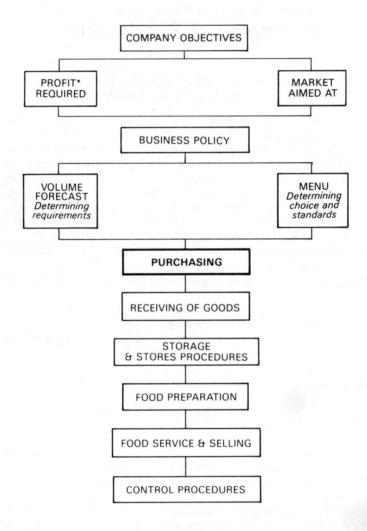

Fig. 1   *The Function of Purchasing in a Food Operation*

*In Institutional or Industrial Operations Profit Required may be substituted by Cost Restrictions or Allocations.

carried out with the overall aim of supplying the materials and equipment necessary to provide for the choice and standards set down in the company's objectives and to achieve the desired profits through any cost restrictions set down by such objectives.

Example
The aims of purchasing for a 1st Class 'Haute Cuisine' Restaurant with an à la carte menu which is catering for the most expensive end of the market would be more concerned with higher grades of quality and availability of foods, rather than the cost which would be more easily recovered by greater flexibility in its pricing policy. Whereas a café operating at the cheaper end of the market would limit its menu to foods more readily available, of a lower grade and smaller portions as costs will be of greater importance. Each market in the examples given will have their respective demands on the food provided, which will be reflected by the different establishments in their purchasing aims.

Responsibility for Purchasing
It is important in all types of establishment that there are persons who are responsible for purchasing. The essential qualities and knowledge required of purchasing officers or those responsible may be briefly listed as.
  (i)   A knowledge of materials used and their uses, which may be gained from some form of general catering education.
  (ii)   An ability to communicate and co-operate with other people.
  (iii) The ability to make sound judgements and quick decisions.
  (iv)   Organisational abilities to prepare and carry out efficient systems of work.
  (v)   Honesty and integrity.
The person or persons responsible for purchasing will vary from establishment to establishment, according to the type and size. Establishments which are part of a group may well have central purchasing policies which will differ from individually or privately owned business organisations. In Figure 2 a selection of different catering establishments are listed showing the member(s) of staff who would be responsible for purchasing.

Duties of Purchasing Officer
The duties of the purchasing officer will not be the same in any particular establishment, except in those which are part of a large group and which are uniform in their operation. In general, however, the duties are usually similar and will involve the following:
  (i)   Selecting the sources of supply of materials and constantly reviewing them, as well as finding new materials to maintain standards and reduce costs.
  (ii)   The purchasing of all materials for the establishment and maintaining the required level of stocks.

3

Type	Size	Person Responsible For Purchasing
5 Star City Centre Luxury Hotel	Rooms: 150-200 Banqueting Facilities for 300-400	Purchasing Officer
3/4 Star City Hotel	Rooms: 150-120 Banqueting Facilities for 300-400	Food & Beverage Manager in liason with Chef de Cuisine — Departmental Heads
2/3 Star Holiday or Town Centre Hotel	Rooms: 50	Manager/Chef
Guest House — Small Restaurants	20-50 Covers Daily	Proprietor/Manager
1st Class Restaurant	60-150 Covers Daily	Chef de Cuisine
Fast Food Operation	300-1000 Covers Daily	Manager
Hospitals	Part of Group	Group Supplies Officer with assistance of Catering Officers
Industrial Canteen	50-200 Meals Daily	Supervisor
	200 Meals Daily	Catering Manager
Colleges	500 Meals Daily	Catering Manager or Bursar

Fig. 2 *Persons responsible for purchasing in different types and sizes of catering operations*

(iii) The receiving and checking of all materials.

(iv) The issuing of materials to all departments in the operation.

(v) Maintaining the necessary records to control the purchasing, receiving and issuing of materials.

(vi) Co-operating with all departments to standardise materials, avoiding unnecessary duplication of materials.

(vii) Liaison with all departments to ensure that materials are to the standard and quality required.

(viii) Liaison with the accounting function to ensure prompt settlement of accounts.

Student Activity   No. 1.1

(i) Identify a catering establishment in your location which produces more than 300 meals each day.

(ii) Discuss who would be responsible for purchasing within that establishment.

(iii) List the duties of the purchasing officer within that establishment.

(iv) Discuss the responsibilities the purchasing officer will have.

BASIS FOR THE SELECTION OF SOURCES OF SUPPLY

The person responsible for purchasing should, in the first instance, circulate a description of the goods or commodities required to a number of suppliers, both nationally and locally. When considering responses to this information he should check the availability of the products from potential suppliers as this may vary from area to area, according to the particular location of his business. In more remote areas it may be necessary to consider more than one supplier as local supplies may be limited in the range available. On checking availability the purchaser must take into consideration the following points and questions:

(i)   Are prices quoted competitive for the goods specified in relation to the quality specified?

(ii) Are the goods available meeting the purchaser's specification by size, weight, grade etc? It may be necessary to request samples of such goods from suppliers.

(iii) Does the delivery service offered meet the requirements of your establishment and the nature of the product in order to maintain quality? An advantage of local suppliers may be the availability of supply six or seven days a week in emergency circumstances.

(iv) The minimum practical ordering quantities from suppliers.

(v)   What are the financial terms available in relation to discounts offered and the period of credit given before settlement of any accounts?

On considering the information received from potential suppliers the purchaser may decide to visit these suppliers in order to discuss and check relevant points. It may also be worthwhile to check with other customers of such suppliers regarding their reliability on prices and quality of supplies and of the service given by them.

Selection should be made of at least two suppliers for each group (eg. meat, fish, vegetables, dry goods etc) in order to maintain continuity of supplies. This may not apply in the case of specialist supplies such as confectionary or unusual foods. In the case of goods obtained by contract this will obviously not apply.

Purchasing Systems Available

Purchasing By Contract

This method of purchasing is most commonly used by large institutions such as hospital catering and local authorities when catering for schools, colleges etc. It is also fairly common in non-profit making organisations such as industrial catering. However in commercial catering organisations contract purchasing may only be used by large companies, usually for basic supplies and furnishings.

The two most common forms of contract purchasing are either over a period of time, or for a specified quantity of goods which may be spread over a period of time. Firstly we will consider contract purchasing over a period of time; the length of time may range from three months to a year, when a supplier agrees to supply certain goods for that period, at a fixed price. This type of contract is used for items which remain fairly stable in price, such as dairy and bakery produce. For items which have fluctuating prices such as meats and fish, due to national or international trade agreements, provisions should be made in the contract for rising and falling prices. The second type of contract purchasing concerns specific quantities of food over a trading period. This is used most commonly for frozen foods and dry goods and involves the purchaser agreeing to buy a set quantity of goods during the trading period with delivery phased at weekly, fortnightly or monthly intervals according to their needs. A contract is a legal document and great care should be taken when it is negotiated and drawn up to avoid any possible dispute. In study 2 we shall examine more closely the content of contracts and the details that are necessary to protect both the purchaser and the supplier.

The advantages of contract purchasing may be listed as follows:
   (i)   Continuity of supply at a fixed price.
   (ii)   Time saving by eliminating price and supply negotiations.
   (iii) Avoiding the need to hold high stocks to gain bulk buying discounts.
   (iv)   Avoiding over ordering of items.
   (v)   Regular ordering and delivery procedures are set up.

The disadvantages of contract purchasing may be listed as follows:
   (i)   Inflexibility in the choice of suppliers and in some cases the commodities available.
   (ii)   Advantage of special offers or price cuts may be eliminated.
   (iii) Suppliers may take the customer for granted.
   (iv)   In the case of specific quantity contracts, for certain items it may lead to high stock holding, should there be a change in customer demands.
   (v)   The difficulties involved in changing suppliers should a supplier prove inconsistent in the service or goods provided.

Centralised Purchasing

Centralised purchasing is used mainly by chain operations or groups and occasionally by small groups of independent operators who have similar needs. Under such a centralised purchasing system the requirements of individual units within the group are relayed to a central office, which would determine the total requirements of all units within the group and purchase that total. Delivery is made either directly to the unit, or to a central location for distribution by the group themselves.

The advantages of centralised purchasing are:
  (i) Price reductions due to bulk buying.
 (ii) Wider choice of markets due to volume of trade.
(iii) Greater range of stock items available.
 (iv) Specifications of purchases may be more precise.
  (v) Supply and quality are easier to control due to volume of trade.
 (vi) Control over dishonesty by unit managers.

The disadvantages of centralised purchasing are:
  (i) Units do not have freedom to purchase stock items which may be peculiar to their particular need.
 (ii) Standardisation of menus and products limits the freedom of units to change.
(iii) The advantage of localised price reductions cannot benefit the unit.
 (iv) Centralised delivery may cause distribution problems.

Purchasing by Market List or Quotation
This method of purchasing is practised by large establishments either on a daily basis for perishable foods or on a weekly, fortnightly or monthly basis for any goods and grocery commodities. In basic terms the person responsible for purchasing will telephone the suppliers and request a price quotation for the goods required, according to the purchase specification previously sent to the supplier. The supplier who offers the most competitive price against the quantity required will be given the order to supply the goods. In some cases where groceries, for example, are required on a less regular, say monthly, basis then suppliers are requested to submit written quotations. Once again the order is given to the most competitive price. Some establishments send their own quotation sheets for suppliers to complete.

The advantages of this system or purchasing are:
  (i) The purchaser is able to select the most competitive price from different suppliers.
 (ii) It makes the suppliers' price quotations more competitive.
(iii) It ensures the availability of supplies.
 (iv) Suppliers only quote against your purchase specification.
  (v) It assists the purchaser in selecting the most economic ordering quantity.

The disadvantages of market quotations are:
  (i) It may be time consuming.
 (ii) It is impracticable for small establishments due to the volume of supplies required, making it uneconomic for suppliers to quote or offer such a service.
(iii) Suppliers who offer a better service than others may not be as

7

competitive in price, thus the establishment may not benefit from such service.

Purchasing from Wholesalers

Wholesalers are most common in the supply of liquor and may be better described as shippers in the supply of wine or breweries in the supply of beers, wines and spirits. Shippers specialise in the sale of wine usually from one country or region; they purchase the wine in its country of origin and arrange its 'shipping' to the country of sale. Breweries or other wine and spirit companies supply all types of liquor in addition to their own proprietory brands or those of their subsidiary companies.

The advantages and disadvantages of using shippers or breweries are best explained separately due to the different services they have to offer. The advantages of shippers are:

(i)   The ability to offer good quality products.
(ii) The ability to offer specialist advice, being a known expert on the region or country of the wine they supply.

The disadvantages of shippers are:

(i)   They offer a limited range of products.
(ii) They only deal with large organisations due to economical ordering quantities being high and most establishments would not have sufficient storage space nor capital available to hold large stocks.
(iii) Less frequent delivery service and after sales services.

The advantages of using breweries or wine and spirit merchants are:

(i)   Regular local deliveries.
(ii) Wide range of products available.
(iii) Good after sales service and promotional materials such as bar cloths, beer mats, glassware etc are generally available.
(iv) Minimum orderable quantities are less, thus suiting the smaller business.

The disadvantages are:

(i)   Less competitive prices.
(ii) Lack of specialist knowledge across the range of their products.

One feature of using breweries or wines and spirits merchants is that they will often supply a cellar stock for an establishment and suspend payment, only invoicing the purchaser for replacement stocks, the cellar stock will remain the property of the supplier unless paid for. This will obviously tie the purchaser to the supplier which may be a disadvantage but is compensated for by the fact that the purchaser does not have to finance his own liquor stock holding.

Purchasing from Cash and Carry

This method of purchasing supplies has developed over the last ten years and is most commonly used by small businesses, where the purchaser can visit a local wholesale warehouse to carry out his purchasing requirements. These cash and carry establishments have restricted entry to traders only and carry a whole range of food stuffs, hardware products, liquor and tobacco and it is possible for a caterer to purchase all his requirements from them. The caterer is able to see all the products available and compare prices between them, he then pays by cash or cheque and transports the goods to his own establishment.

The advantages of cash and carry purchasing are:
  (i)   Prices are competitive.
 (ii)   There are no minimum order levels.
(iii)   Their accessibility means that caterers can make frequent visits according to their own requirements.
(iv)   Stock levels can be kept to a minimum.
 (v)   The caterer can see a range of products available to him and experiment with them.

The disadvantages of cash and carry purchasing are:
  (i)   In most cases there is no delivery service.
 (ii)   Credit is not available to purchasers.
(iii)   On occasions availability of products may be restricted.

Purchasing from Van Sales

This method of purchasing is used in more rural areas, by smaller establishments in general. Local suppliers and in a few cases, national companies, use vans or lorries carrying a range of their products and visit establishments on a regular basis for the caterer to make his purchases direct from the van and pay on a monthly account. The most common types of traders who supply this service are fruit and vegetable merchants, bakeries, dairies and frozen food traders.

The advantages of using this method of purchasing are:
  (i)   The caterer is able to see the goods available and any alternatives.
 (ii)   Special offers can be taken immediate advantage of.
(iii)   Fluctuations in levels of business can be easily coped with.
(iv)   Stock holding can be easily controlled.

The disadvantages of van sales are:
  (i)   Products may on occasions not be available.
 (ii)   Prices may not be as competitive as wholesalers or market prices.
(iii)   It may limit the choice of supplier.

ESTABLISHMENT GOODS	Hospital Independent 1000 meals daily	Factory Canteen Independent 500 meals daily	Luxury Hotel Group Owned 600 covers (300 rooms)	Small Hotel/Restaurant Privately Owned 40 covers (20 rooms)	Steak House Franchised 200 covers daily
WET FISH	—Contract —Local Supplier	—Market Quotation —Local Supplier	—Market Quotation & Supplier	—Market/Local Supplier Quotation	—Market Quotation —Local Supplier if frozen —Centralised Purchasing
FLOUR	—Contract —Wholesaler	—Market Quotation —Wholesaler	—Centralised Purchasing	—Cash 'n' Carry	—Centralised Purchasing
FROZEN VEGETABLES	—Contract —Local/National Wholesaler	—Market Quotation —Local/National Wholesaler	—Centralised Purchasing	—Cash 'n' Carry —Local Wholesaler —Van Sales	—Centralised Purchasing
FRESH VEGETABLES	—Contract —Market	—Market Quotation —Local Supplier	—Market Quotation & Supplier	Van Sales	—Local Market Quotation and Supplier or Van Sales
BREAD/ROLLS	—Contract —Local/National Supplier	—Contract —Local/National Supplier	—If not self made —Contract —Local/National Supplier	—Van Sales	—Van Sales
HOUSE WINE	Infrequent use Local Supplier	—Brewery Local Wholesaler	—Centralised Purchasing —Shipper	—Brewery or —Wine and Spirit Merchant	—Centralised Purchasing Shipper or Wholesaler
PAPER SERVIETTES	—Contract —National Supplier	—Contract —National Supplier	—Centralised Purchasing	—Cash 'n' Carry	—Centralised Purchasing
LIGHT BULBS	—Contract —National Supplier	—Local Supplier	—Centralised Purchasing	—Cash 'n' Carry	—Local Wholesaler or Supplier

Fig. 3 Chart showing appropriate sources of Supply/Purchasing System for specific goods in different types & sizes of establishments

Examples of Appropriate Purchasing Policies and Systems

The chart shown in figure 3 shows appropriate sources of supply and purchasing systems for different goods in a variety of establishments. It can be seen that some different goods by their very nature, ie. perishables and their method of distribution, fall into the same method of purchase whatever the size and ownership of an operation. For example Wet Fish purchases will in most cases be purchased depending on market price quotation and availability from local suppliers. Whereas paper serviettes in most cases will be purchased from national suppliers, usually under some form of contract. This will even apply to cash and carries who will also be supplied by a national supplier for these products. With regard to purchasing policies adopted by different organisations or establishments, fig 3 illustrates the reliance of hospital catering on contract purchasing with the exception of items that are infrequently used. Group owned and franchised establishments will use centralised purchasing for most goods except those of a fresh nature, leaving purchasing to the individual establishment which will rely on local market price quotations applicable to the company's purchase specification. The purchasing policy adopted by industrial catering units will depend on whether or not the unit is independently operated or the unit is contracted out to a company specialising in the provision of catering services. Independent units will adapt their purchasing systems according to their own policy and requirements whereas catering services companies will rely on centralised purchasing for the majority of their goods. Small establishments are limited in their sources of supply by nature of the volume of purchases required, the cost of stock and its storage and their location. We can see from fig 3 that in most cases the smaller establishment relies on local suppliers and markets or cash and carry organisations. It can therefore be said that the purchasing system adopted by establishments, will be greatly influenced by the form of ownership of the operation, its size and location in relation to the sources of supply.

Student Activity No. 1.2

Identify the purchasing system that may be used for buying fresh vegetables, poultry, coffee, wines, dish washing machine detergent and teaspoons in the following establishments:

(i)   36 cover 'bistro', privately owned.
(ii) 200 bedroom city centre hotel, company owned.
(iii) A college refectory serving 800 meals daily.

PURCHASE SPECIFICATIONS

In the previous section we introduced Purchase Specifications into the purchasing system, let us now look at them more closely. A purchase specification is the main requirement for successful purchasing and

regarded as essential for establishments that wish to supply a standard product. Different writers have defined purchase specifications in their own way and a combination of their definitions describes them as:
- the weight, quality and origin of a product
- the weight, size and content of its packaging

A purchased specification should be prepared by all those concerned with its use in an establishment; those being the purchasing officer, a representative of management and the head chef or another person directly concerned with the products' use. In some cases it is also advisable to include the supplier in order that he is aware of any specific requirements. This is especially important in meat products as to where on a carcass certain cuts start and finish eg. best end of lamb. The specification should be set out in clear terms so as to avoid any misunderstandings. Where brand names are involved it is better to use them so that inferior or more expensive products are not sent in their place, this would apply in particular to liquor products.

Purchase specifications are useful in several ways:
  (i)   They ensure that persons responsible for purchasing and the use of commodities and products determine precise requirements.
  (ii) They eliminate the possibility of any misunderstandings between the purchaser and supplier.
  (iii) They may be distributed to different suppliers, thus enabling them to make competitive price quotations.
  (iv) They speed up the ordering procedure as suppliers are aware of specific requirements.
  (v)   They enable deliveries to be checked more easily when they are received.

The format and layout of purchase specifications will vary from establishment to establishment, as well as from product to product, this is shown in the examples below. The essential feature of any specification is that the precise requirements are conveyed to the supplier in the most easily understood method. With most fresh meats and vegetables, specifications as to standard, size and quality have been set down by government departments and the European Economic Community in liaison with the commodities markets and these specifications are protected by legislation. Where available, it is best that these gradings and classifications are used in the preparation of such specifications.

In figures 4 and 5 the supplier is informed of both product and packaging requirements to meet the demands of the particular establishment. Details of price quotation and delivery instructions are also shown to make the supplier aware of the quantity to be quoted for and the time span between ordering and delivery. Figure 4 shows a more formal layout that would be sent to suppliers, whereas figure 5 shows a layout for internal use within an establishment. Specifications should be dated when issued to suppliers, any changes in the specification would then naturally be updated using the normal procedure with a fresh specification being distributed.

P&O CATERERS LIMITED
249 Queens Road, London SE1 4PX
Tel: 01-546 5555

STANDARD PURCHASE SPECIFICATION   No. 26

COMMODITY:	Fresh tomatoes
SIZE:	50 gms/2 oz each
QUALITY:	Firm, well formed, good red colour
ORIGIN:	English preferred
WEIGHT:	6 kilo/12 lb net per box
COUNT:	90-100 per box
QUOTE:	per box
DELIVERY:	Day following order
DATE:	31 March 198__

Fig. 4   *Standard purchase specification for fresh tomatoes*

CANNED PEACHES
Yellow cling halves
US Grade A (Fancy)
Heavy Syrup
2 kilo/66 oz per A10 can
30-35 count per A10 can
Price quotation per case of 6
Certification of grade required
Delivery within 4 days per order
Specification distributed to:
1.
2.
3.

Fig. 5   *Standard purchase specification for canned peaches*

P&O CATERERS LIMITED
249 Queens Road, London SE1 4PX
Tel: 01-546 5555

STANDARD PURCHASE SPECIFICATION   No. 47

COMMODITY:	Fresh apples (Golden Delicious)
SIZE:	
QUALITY:	As per EEC standards
ORIGIN:	for fresh apples
WEIGHT:	Class 1
COUNT:	
QUOTE:	Per box
DELIVERY:	Day following order
DATE:	31 March 198__

Fig. 6   *Standard purchase specification for fresh apples*

In figure 6, showing a purchase specification for fresh apples, the details concerning the product and packaging have been taken directly from the EEC standard for fresh apples and pears which gives very concise details as to the requirements for different grades. The supplier will obviously be aware of such grades, the information being available from Her Majesty's Stationery Office in their standard publications. The only additional information needed on the specification being that which applies to quotation and delivery.

P&O CATERERS LIMITED
249 Queens Road, London SE1 4PX
Tel: 01-546 5555

STANDARD PURCHASE SPECIFICATION   No. 62

COMMODITY:	Frozen chicken
SIZE:	3 lb 6 oz — 3 lb 10 oz
QUALITY:	All chicken to be plump, free from bruising and scars. All chicken to be drawn, cleaned, trimmed and trussed. Giblets to be separately packed. Not exceeding 6 ozs.
ORIGIN:	British
WEIGHT:	28 lb approx per case
COUNT:	8 birds
QUOTE:	Per case
DELIVERY:	Day following order
DATE:	31 March 198__

Fig. 7   *Standard purchase specification for frozen chicken*

In figure 7 the specification for meat products shows a more detailed description of quality and preparation, these will be specific to the requirements of different establishments. In this example chickens of 3 lb 8 oz weight are ideally required, but some tolerance must be allowed to ensure continuity of supply and price consistency. Whilst frozen chicken are regarded as standard in the quality of supply, fresh meat specifications shown in figure 8, need to be more specific for reasons previously discussed.

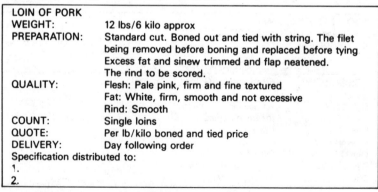

LOIN OF PORK	
WEIGHT:	12 lbs/6 kilo approx
PREPARATION:	Standard cut. Boned out and tied with string. The filet being removed before boning and replaced before tying. Excess fat and sinew trimmed and flap neatened. The rind to be scored.
QUALITY:	Flesh: Pale pink, firm and fine textured. Fat: White, firm, smooth and not excessive. Rind: Smooth
COUNT:	Single loins
QUOTE:	Per lb/kilo boned and tied price
DELIVERY:	Day following order
Specification distributed to:	
1.	
2.	

Fig. 8   *Standard purchase specification for loin of pork (internal use)*

Purchase specifications must be regarded as an essential means of communication between purchasers and suppliers for effective purchasing and standardisation of products sold by the caterer. They ensure that all persons know what is expected, they enable accurate price comparisons and prevent any variation in the quality of the product. This has and will be referred to throughout this area of study on purchasing. It must also be remembered that the purchase specification is part of the overall purchasing procedure and cannot be used in isolation. Standard specifications play an important role in providing a standard product.

Student Activity   No. 1.3
Discuss the specifications the following establishments would have in the purchase of paper serviettes:
  (i)   Self service café.
  (ii)   Take-away hamburger bar.
  (iii) 50 cover steakhouse.
  (iv) 80 room town centre hotel.

Student Activity   No. 1.4
From your college or local library find out the EEC standards for fresh apples and pears.

Purchasing Information
There is a great amount of purchasing information available today; this information is readily available to the caterer and comes from a variety of sources

Trade and Professional Directories
The most common Trade Directory for purchasers to find sources of supply of commodities is the Yellow Pages classification, supplied to all British Telecom subscribers. Other local and national directories such as Thompsons Directory and Kelly's give similar information, they differ in being more specialist in terms of location and products or services respectively. There are specialist directories for the hotel and catering industry published occasionally by trade journals such as Caterer and Hotel Keeper and Catering and Hotel Management. The Hotel, Catering and Institutional Management Association (HCIMA) publishes an annual directory of equipment and food suppliers which is distributed to its members. Other professional associations have lists of suppliers which are distributed to their members occasionally eg Chambers of Commerce.

Trade and Professional Journals
There are a variety of journals published, either weekly or monthly, giving caterers information on products available to them. They review existing and new products, give sources of supply throughout the

country and also act as advertising media for companies wishing to publicise their products. Journals also offer their advertisers additional services such as 'freepost', further information collection services and directory entries. Local associations of caterers also publish their own journals occasionally which include reviews and advertising of a more local nature. As well as specialist publications for their industry, caterers can also gain purchasing information from the various trade journals published for the food retail industry eg. The Grocer.

Suppliers Brochures and Price Lists
Most suppliers of products to the industry have brochures prepared advertising and giving further details and specifications of their products. These are usually prepared to support media advertising as well as being sent direct to caterers. They are often supported by sample packs for the caterer to test. Wholesalers distribute regular price lists to both existing and potential customers, giving details of latest price changes and special offers that may be available.

Exhibitions and Displays
Suppliers are able to display and advertise their products at Catering Exhibitions held throughout the country annually, or at the National Catering Exhibition 'Hotelympia' every two years. Suppliers at these exhibitions rent stands and are able to display their products, give samples and have their salesmen available to discuss their products and negotiate sales agreements or entertain potential and existing customers. Exhibitions serve the dual purpose of introducing new products as well as carrying out a public relations exercise. Some suppliers also arrange promotional functions to introduce new products. Displays at Cash and Carry's are particularly useful for small business owners to sample and discuss products; they can also be used in more remote locations which may not have the benefit of local exhibitions. Cash and Carry companies themselves often arrange displays or promotional functions for customers within their catchment area.

Other sources of supply information can be obtained from recommendations by other traders, although it must be realised that whilst one supplier may suit one caterer it may not suit another's requirements. Caterers themselves should also be aware of new product developments through reading the national press or through television and radio programmes directed at the public.

Student Activity   No. 1.5
List the publications and journals which are available to the hotel and catering industry giving purchasing information.

ORDERING PROCEDURES

It is important for all catering establishments to establish rigid ordering procedures with their suppliers, these procedures must be regarded as essential in any purchasing function. In this section we examine the four main functions involved in ordering procedures, those being enquiries, quotations, purchase orders and acknowledgements.

Firstly it is important that suppliers are made aware of ordering procedures and are informed in writing of any instructions. These should include the following points:

(i) Delivery times and any special delivery requirements.
(ii) Up to date information regarding prices and availability are given at regular intervals.
(iii) Variation in supplies or prices must have previous consent.
(iv) No alteration between quoted and invoiced prices.
(v) Goods supplied will be as ordered.
(vi) Names of persons who are authorised to make orders.
(vii) Names of persons who are authorised to receive deliveries.

Enquiries

Enquiries regarding sources of supply should be made in writing to several potential suppliers of the product. The enquiry must be accompanied by a purchase specification of the product or products required and the potential supplier asked to provide the following details regarding the service he can offer:

(i) Delivery service he is able to offer on both a regular and an emergency basis.
(ii) Ordering procedure for telephone and written orders.
(iii) Advance notice of orders required for delivery, both minimum and maximum times.
(iv) Minimum ordering quantities of products and minimum value of each order for delivery.
(v) Accounting procedures, to include periods of credit given and any discounts given.
(vi) References by other customers of the supplier receiving a similar service.
(vii) Back up service, after sales service and promotional materials available, (these services are considered in the purchase of alcoholic liquor).

Quotations

Quotations from suppliers must be considered in an organised manner. The service offered by different suppliers, as set out in the previous section about enquiries should be compared against each other. Primary consideration must also be given to their ability to supply products according to the Purchase Specifications as previous mentioned in the section on the Selection of Sources of Supply.

Price quotations need to be considered on a regular basis and would be best organised by drawing up price quotation sheets as illustrated in figure 9. In this illustration the suppliers have made their quotation according to the specification and quantities required. This enables the purchaser to select the most competitive price. The cheapest need not necessarily be selected, in the example the supplier Skinner is quoting the lowest price for most beef products and Small for most other products. Perry is quoting the lowest price for gammon and the same price as Skinner for mince, therefore to make up a balanced order for Perry, he has been given the mince order. Using this system for suppliers quotes makes comparison simple, as well as keeping suppliers' prices competitive. Suppliers must be made aware that the price quoted is adhered to when delivery is made.

HAYMARKET STEAKHOUSE			PRICE QUOTATION LIST Week/Month commencing 01 March 8__			
Commodity	Size	Quantity Required	Suppliers Quotations			Quotation Accepted
			Skinners	Perrys	Smalls	
T Bone Steak	16oz	120	£2.20	£2.25	£2.25	Skinner
Rump Steak	12oz	120	£1.65	£1.70	£1.68	Skinner
Rump Steak	8oz	120	£1.10	£1.13	£1.12	Skinner
Sirloin Steak	10oz	80	£1.40	£1.30	£1.35	Perry
Gammon Steak	8oz	60	£0.90	£0.95	£0.90	Small
Pork Chops	8oz	80	£0.62	£0.60	£0.61	Small
Lamb Chops	6oz	40	£0.51	£0.50	£0.51	Small
Chuck Steak	lb	40lb	£1.10 lb	£1.15 lb	£1.06 lb	Small
Kidney	lb	10lb	£0.56 lb	£0.60 lb	£0.52 lb	Small
Mince 'A' Grade	lb	16lb	£1.02 lb	£1.02 lb	£1.04 lb	Perry
Filet Steak	6oz	80	£1.35	£1.40	£1.40	Skinner

Fig. 9   *Comparative Weekly Price Quotation Sheet for a Steak House (80 covers)*

Student Activity   No. 1.6

(i)   Draw up a price quotation form for the supply of the following commodities:
Grapefruit (fresh)
Middle cut of Bacon (lb)
Eggs (size 3)
Pork Sausages (lb)
Tomatoes (lb)
Bread (thick sliced)
New Zealand Butter (250 gms)

(ii)   Visit 3 supermarkets and record the prices of the commodities listed on to your quotation form.

(iii)   Prepare a report showing which supermarket has the cheapest price per commodity and which supermarket has the most economic price overall.

Ordering

Suppliers should be given their orders and other instructions, such as delivery time or date, as soon as practically possible prior to delivery. In most cases a supplier will require a minimum period of notice to prepare orders before delivery can be made. Orders should be made in writing, or if made by telephone written confirmation despatched to them as soon as possible. It is better for establishments to have standard ordering forms or books, these being numbered and set out according to control and accounting needs. Duplicate copies should be kept for internal purposes; the number of copies will vary according to the organisation of the establishment or company. An establishment which is part of a large group may well have to send copies to Head Office, Accounts Department, Food and Beverage Controller and the Head of Department concerned, whereas smaller individually owned establishments may only require one copy to satisfy their requirements. There are certain essential details which must be included on order forms, these are as follows:

(i)   Order Number.
(ii)   Date of Order.
(iii) Date of Delivery.
(iv)   Name and Address of Supplier.
(v)   Quantity, Size and Description of goods ordered.
(vi)   Price Quoted by Supplier.
(vii) Total Price of Order.
(viii) Signature of Purchasing Officer.

In Figure 10 the illustration shows the order form sent from the Haymarket Steakhouse, to the supplier 'Skinner', from the quotation sheet shown in Figure 9.

PURCHASE ORDER

HAYMARKET STEAKHOUSE
47 Haymarket
London WC1
Tel: 01-822 1477

ORDER NO. 142
To: Skinners Wholesale Meat
Smithfield
London EC1

Quantity	Description	Unit Size	Price Quoted	Total Value
120	T Bone Steak	16oz	2.20	264.00
120	Rump Steak	12oz	1.65	198.00
120	Rump Steak	8oz	1.10	132.00
80	Filet Steak	6oz	1.35	108.00
				£702.00

Date of Order 03 Mar 8__	Signed
Date of Delivery 05 Mar 8__	Purchasing Officer

Fig. 10 *Purchase Order sent to Suppliers*

Order forms should be made out for all orders and despatched to suppliers; this may be impractical for items that are delivered daily and in such cases, eg. milk and bread a system must be devised and maintained. A method of dealing with such tradesmen may be to issue an order at the time of delivery, this is essential when the tradesman's order is to stock up a particular commodity to a certain level each day, as is the case in many establishments. Without the use of purchase orders problems regarding quantity, description or prices of goods may be in dispute and cause the first phase of control to breakdown.

Student Activity No. 1.7
Design an order form and enter on it the details of the total commodities required with regard to dry stores for your group's most recent practical lesson.

When large or expensive orders are placed, not only for food and drink commodities, but also for furniture or equipment, it is advisable for purchasers to request an acknowledgment of the order from the supplier. This acknowledgment should state that the supplier is able to supply the goods ordered at the time and price requested, some suppliers have a standard procedure for this by issuing special forms or slips.

Purchasing may be regarded as the first stage of any control system and is essential for establishments that wish to produce a constant supply of a standard product. The purchasing function of a large group will spend millions of pounds a year and without proper procedures it would be easy for the whole function to break down. Proportionately, this has the same effect in smaller, individually owned establishments, although the function and procedures may be less complex or formal, they should still exist. We have examined such functions in this section and whilst there are further considerations to be made regarding purchasing in books two and three, the basis for purchasing has been set out. We are now able to continue this study by examining the receiving of purchases made, their storage and issuing.

Student Activity No. 1.8
Compare two cash and carry operators in your area with regard to:
   (i)   Distance from your home or college.
   (ii) Opening hours and days.
   (iii) Restrictions placed on types of customer.
   (iv) Availability of alchololic beverages.
   (v)   Availability of fresh meats.
   (vi) Availability of fresh vegetables.
   (vii) Availability of small items of catering equipment.
   (viii) Availability of painting and decorating materials.
   (ix) Café or snack facilities available to customers.
   (x)   Any form of delivery service to customers.

Further Reading

Food and Beverage Control: *Kotas and Davis* Chapter 5
Catering Costs and Control: *Paige* Chapter 7
Professional Kitchen Management: *Fuller* Chapter 16

ASSESSMENT QUESTIONS

1. Explain the purchasing function in hotel and catering operations.
2. List the principles that are involved in purchasing.
3. Explain the qualities and knowledge required of purchasing officers.
4. List the duties that a purchasing officer will have within the normal scope of his job.
5. Explain the basis of how sources of supply are selected.
6. Describe the purchasing systems that are used in the hotel and catering industry.
7. List the advantages and disadvantages of the different purchasing systems available with regard to the size and ownership of catering establishments.
8. Describe the purchasing system that would be used for the purchase of tea in the following establishments.
    (i) 300 bed hospital.
    (ii) 10 bedroom privately owned guest house.
    (iii) Independently operated factory canteen serving 250 meals and 1000 snacks daily.
9. Define 'Purchase Specifications' and describe their use.
10. Design a purchase specification suitable for a large hotel to send to potential suppliers for the supply of lamb cutlets.
11. Explain where the owner of a seaside hotel would be most likely to obtain purchasing information.
12. List the details that would be asked of potential suppliers regarding the service they would be able to offer.
13. List the instructions that would be given to suppliers regarding all orders given to them.
14. Explain the purpose of preparing price quotation forms.
15. List the essential details that must be included on a purchase order.

Section B

Storage and Stores Procedures

In this section we will examine the requirements for efficient storage of raw materials and equipment used in hotel and catering establishments and the procedures used for effective stores control. If we refer to Figure 1 in the previous section it shows storage and stores procedures as an integral part of any food and beverage control system. Therefore no matter how efficient an organisation's purchasing procedure may be, bad storage conditions and procedures would have an adverse affect on the standard of food or drink sold. Eventually this would result in the organisation failing to achieve their required cost and profit targets.

STORAGE OF MATERIALS AND EQUIPMENT

The purpose of efficient storage conditions is to maintain materials or commodities in the condition in which they were purchased and for them to be safe until they are issued to the appropriate department for use or sale to the customer. We must therefore examine the conditions in which different types of commodities are stored, the legal requirements of the storage of some commodities, the layout and situation of the stores giving regard to efficient operation and security.

Correct storage requirements of commodities

The different types of commodities will require separate storage conditions in order to maintain or improve their condition and quality. These commodities are split up into the general categories of meats, fish, fresh fruit and vegetables, dairy produce, frozen foods, tinned foods, dry goods and cleaning materials.

Meats

All sides, quarters or whole carcasses of meat should be hung in a cold room at a temperature of 0-1°C with a space between them to allow free circulation of air with drip trays placed underneath in order to collect any blood. According to the type of meat this period will vary from 2-10 days, permitting a chemical change to take place to produce more tender meat.

Poultry and game if undrawn should be hung at a temperature of 0-1°C with the exception of venison or hares and rabbits which should be hung at a temperature of 3-4°C. Drawn or eviscerated poultry should be stored on slatted shelves at 0-1°C and game placed on metal trays at the same temperature.

Fish

Wet fish should be stored in a separate, special type of refrigerator with perforated non-rust trays allowing the fish to drain and permitting easy cleaning of the refrigerator. The fish should be placed on crushed ice on a wet cloth, covered with another cloth and crushed ice being stored at a temperature of 1°C. Shell fish should be placed in boxes covered with a wet sack and crushed ice, being stored at a temperature of not lower than 3°C. Both wet fish and shell fish should be stored for the minimum period of time possible.

Fresh fruits and vegetables

All types of fresh fruits and vegetables need careful storage, preferably in a northerly facing room or where there is no sunlight. The room should be dry, cool and well ventilated with bins for root vegetables and racking for other types. Fruit and vegetables deteriorate quickly and space should therefore be available to enable easy stock rotation (ie. old stocks are used first) and to identify any rotten items for their quick removal as they will affect others. Bananas and pineapples should be hung in a cool room, soft fruits and melons should be refrigerated at 1-2°C.

Dairy produce

Most dairy products with the exception of cheeses should be stored in a refrigerator or cold room at a temperature of 0-4°C. Milk should be stored in the container in which it is delivered and kept covered because it will absorb strong smells. Butter and eggs also absorb strong smells, especially those of fish, onions and cheese. Cheese should be stored in a cool place which is dry and well ventilated. Because of its strong smell cheese should be kept away from other items, if whole cheeses are to be stored for a period of time they should be rotated occasionally.

Frozen foods

There is a great variety of frozen foods in either an uncooked or cooked state and these should be stored at a temperature of at least -10°C. The lower the temperature of a freezer means foods can be kept for a longer time, -17°C for one year and -28°C for two years. All foods should be kept frozen until needed but time must be allowed for defrosting before issuing. Foods should be kept on plastic coated trays in upright deep freezers and in plastic coated baskets in the chest type of deep freeze.

Tinned foods

Tinned foods should be stored in a dry, well ventilated store to prevent them from rusting. They should be unpacked from their cases and inspected for bulges (ie. blown tins) caused by gases from either bacteria or the tin plating being attacked by the food. When this happens they must be thrown away or returned to the supplier for a refund. Dented tins should be used immediately before they rust and eventually puncture through corrosion.

Dry goods
Dry goods are sugar, flour, pulses, cereals, preserved foods such as jams, pickles, canned and bottled foods, cakes, dried fruits, tea, coffee, and bread etc. The conditions of the store should be cool, dry and well ventilated with all commodites being kept in bins with lids. Some dry goods require air-tight lids eg. tea, coffee, rice and nuts without shells. Other items such as bread, flour or sugar should have loose fitting lids. Goods with strong aromas should be stored away from other items that are likely to absorb their flavour.

Cleaning materials
A separate store is necessary for all cleaning materials because of their strong smells and the possibility of confusion or mistakes being accidentally made in their issue. The store should be dry, well ventilated with slatted racks used for storage purposes.

Liquor store and Wine/Beer cellars
All drinks should be stored in a room which has a constant temperature, this is best maintained by automatically controlled air-conditioning systems. Wines should be racked in order to preserve their quality and to facilitate easy stock taking. Spirits and liqueurs should be stored upright on deep shelves. Bottled beers are stored in their crates in a separate area of the store or in larger establishments in their own store. It is important to provide extra space for the storage of empty bottles and crates because of their high value. Draught and keg beers should be kept in a separate area of the liquor store which is accessible from dispense areas because of the need to change barrels or kegs during service times. This area is often totally separate from other liquor stores to maintain the security of other liquor products, kegs and barrels of beer being cumbersome and not so likely to be stolen.

Equipment stores
Most hotel and catering establishments have a separate storage area for small equipment such as crockery, cutlery, glassware, linen, stationery, small items of kitchen and food service equipment and any necessary maintenance supplies such as light bulbs and fittings etc. Cleaning materials may also be stored in this area, according to the size of the establishment. The storage area should be comprised of racked shelving of differing heights, be dry and well secured.

Student Activity   No. 1.8
List the raw materials you would expect to find in the dry store of an Industrial Catering establishment which caters for 300 main meals daily.

Stores operation and layout

An essential feature of any catering establishment is an efficiently organised and clean store, to enable storekeeping staff to check materials entering and leaving the store and to maintain a continuity of supply of such materials in their best condition. It has become apparent in this section that the varying types of materials and commodities require different storage conditions. Most catering operations will require a dry store, vegetable store, cold room, refrigeration and deep freeze equipment. When considering the design and stores operation of an establishment the principal considerations are hygiene, security, efficient flow of goods in and out of the store and the storage requirements of commodities.

A high standard of hygiene is essential therefore all walls, floors, shelving etc must be easy to clean and designed to prevent the accumulation of dirt, with sufficient lighting and space for this to be carried out. Spacing of shelves should be varied according to the amount of stocks to be held and to facilitate easy movement of them. The layout of the stores should be considered, with regard to the different storage conditions necessary, with separate rooms or areas for vegetables and goods that require differing temperatures. As shown in the requirements of the different categories of materials the stores should be dry and well ventilated with a cold room for meats etc, with special refrigerators for fish and dairy produce and deep freeze facilities for frozen goods.

The positioning of the store is equally important in order to facilitate easy receiving and issuing of stores. The ideal position would be close to the external entrance of the kitchen, enabling deliveries to be made without passing through other areas of the establishment, whilst also being close to the kitchen for issues. This location would also be a good security factor in that goods would be delivered directly into the store which would minimise any possibility of them being left where unauthorised persons might have access to them. Security is an important aspect of stores control, the storekeeper and his staff, or in smaller establishments the person responsible for the stores, should be the only persons who have access to the store.

The layout and design of the stores must also incorporate security, goods should come into the store through a separate entrance direct from the loading bay. A counter should be provided for issuing goods and to keep unauthorised personnel out of the store to minimise any risks of pilfering. Doors should have very secure locks and windows barred as a preventative measure against burglary. Liquor stores and wine cellars will need extra physical security systems due to the high value of liquor stock. Some large establishments use closed circuit television surveillance techniques for this purpose. Further considerations regarding security in stores operation are also discussed later in this section.

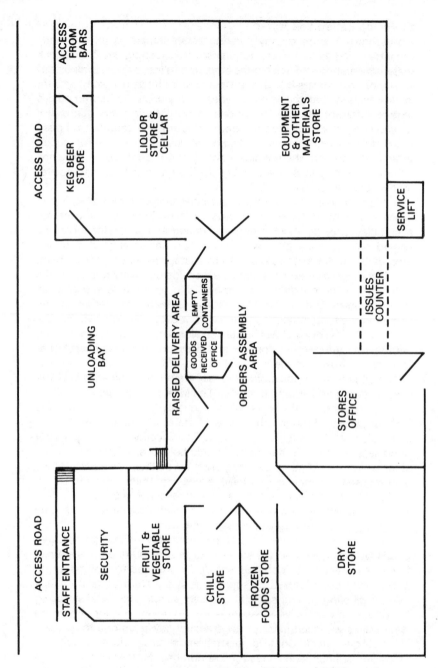

Fig. 1.11 Stores layout suitable for a 400 bedroom hotel

26

The actual layout of stores will vary according to the structure and design of the establishment, consideration being given to access routes and the supply of services within the building. In figure 1.11 a suggested plan for the storage facilities of a large hotel are shown. The illustration shows the location of the store with convenient access for suppliers delivering goods and consideration being given for goods being distributed around the establishment by the placement of the issues counter close to the service lift. The security office should be situated close to delivery areas and staff entrances separated from them. Goods Received and Stores Offices should be centrally placed for efficiency and security purposes. In the illustration emergency access to the keg beer store is permitted without creating a security risk. Space is also available for stores requisitioned by departments to be assembled prior to issuing.

Small establishments by their very size will have a much more limited storage space, will also require less stocks of materials and may well have to improvise their storage facilities. A secure store room which is dry and well ventilated may well contain the dry store, equipment, chest type freezers, spirits and liqueurs. Refrigerators which may be accessible to staff should be of a locking type, vegetables should be kept in outside stores and such things as cleaning materials kept in the housekeeper's office or separate store cupboard.

When considering all types of storage facilities for establishments of different sizes and types the important factors to remember are the flow of goods throughout the establishment, accessibility regarding stocktaking, issuing, replacing and security.

Student Activity 1.9
Discuss the layout of storage facilities suitable for either:
 (i)   your college refectory *or*
 (ii) your department's teaching kitchens *or*
 (iii) an establishment where you have worked.
Special consideration must be made to the access and structure of the existing building and services provided such as lifts.

Legal constraints on storage
There are certain legal constraints concerning the storage of foods and other materials which establishments must adhere to; failure to do so would leave 'them liable to prosecution. Legislation set down by government is in two specific areas; that which applies to the storage of food by The Food and Hygiene (General) Regulations in 1970 and that which applies to dangerous materials by The Fire Precautions Act 1971 and subsequently by The Health and Safety At Work Act 1974.

Storage of food
The Food Hygiene (General) Regulations 1970 sets out in Section 27 the temperatures at which certain foods must be stored or kept. This

regulation applies to foods consisting of meat, fish, gravy, imitation cream, egg or milk with certain exceptions such as those for preserved foods or when eggs and milk are used prior to cooking and butter, cheese, bacon etc. The storage requirements for such foods are that they are kept at a temperature of not less than 62.7°C (145°F) and not more than 10°C (50°F) until they are required for consumption. The regulations also state that cooked foods and raw foods should not be stored in the same area because of the risk of cross contamination. It is the responsibility of the establishment to provide storage facilities which comply with these regulations and is an obvious influence on the design, layout and provision of food storage areas.

Storage of other materials
Dangerous materials such as those which are inflammable and stored in quantity must be notified to the fire authority in compliance with the Fire Precautions Act 1971. Adequate safe storage facilities must be provided and be approved by them. The Health and Safety At Work Act 1974 passed legislation regarding the safety of employees at work, making employers responsible for providing safe working conditions and the employee responsible for carrying them out. Materials which are likely to be dangerous eg. chemicals and inflammable materials must be adequately stored in proper containers or bins.

The storage of alcoholic beverages, especially spirits is considered when premises are inspected by the fire authority for the granting of liquor licences. Applications for licences have been refused because of inadequate safe storage for spirits. The licensee should store spirits in steel cupboards away from areas where there may be a fire risk, eg. boiler rooms or electrical installations.

All legislation which has been passed regarding the storage of food and materials is concerned with the health and safety of staff and the general public coming into contact with them.

Student Activity   No. 1.10
List items that may be found in the stores of a hotel which are controlled by legislation.

Stores security
We considered at some length the security of storage areas, regarding their design and layout earlier in this section. Whilst having secure premises is most important, an establishment must also have good security procedures in its operations and organisation systems to be totally effective. When materials are stolen or go astray it is in most cases a fault in the security procedures of the operation.

Employees access
All employees working in an establishment must be made aware of any conditions of their employment regarding their being searched and proper procedures set down for this. Employees must also be made

aware of any rules and regulations regarding access to the stores. Accessibility to the stores should be restricted to stores personnel and designated management only. Access should be limited to the minimum number of staff as is practically possible and persons who are not employed by the establishment should not be allowed into storage areas. Exceptions to this may be equipment maintenance contractors who should be accompanied at all times if this is practical. Employees working in storage areas should be closely vetted with regard to their trustworthiness by taking up references from past employers.

Opening hours

In large establishments where specific stores personnel are employed it is possible for the stores to be open most of the day. All staff should be informed of opening hours and be made aware that issues are only made during these times. Emergency procedures must also exist for the issuing of stores, should the need arise. These procedures should specify who is responsible for opening the stores and issuing goods, the person responsible being made aware of the system for issuing goods. Suppliers should also be informed of times at which goods may be delivered and of any procedure when this is not possible. Smaller establishments may only open their stores for short periods of time, which should be at the most convenient time to ensure the smooth running of the establishment. Emergency issue procedures should also be set up and staff made aware of who is responsible. Stores should never be left open for staff to help themselves as and when they need supplies. Keys to stores should never leave the premises and staff who are responsible should be required to sign for keys each time they are issued in an official key log book.

Receiving and issuing procedures

Security is an important factor in the control of receiving and issuing goods. We examine these procedures in the next part of this section. Where security is concerned, goods should not be received into the store without the proper documentation and goods should not be issued without proper documentation. All standard forms should be closely controlled and securely stored, they should also be numbered or coded and spoiled forms should be kept for continuity purposes. Duplicate copies should be made where necessary and should accompany any issues from the store to their user department.

Security of stores and materials used is a very important aspect of food and beverage control and it must be emphasised that it is a combination of the physical aspect of storage (ie. the premises) and the operational aspect (ie. the systems used) for effective storage to take place.

Student Activity   No. 1.11

Prepare a list of security considerations that must be made in the layout of the stores and their day to day operations.

STORES CONTROL PROCEDURES

We have examined storage facilities and the demands placed on them by different commodities and materials, the various legal requirements and different aspects of security. Physical storage is an important aspect of food and beverage control and we must now examine the control procedures used in the stores that are necessary for effective storage. We must look at systems for receiving goods into the store, maintaining levels of stock and stores records, methods of stock-taking, calculating stock value and systems for issuing stores to the different departments in a hotel or catering operation.

Receiving goods

All establishments must have set down procedures for receiving, checking and accepting goods which have been delivered by suppliers. These goods must be checked against the purchase specification applicable to them and the order made to the supplier as described in the previous section of this book. Large organisations will have a Goods Received Clerk or Officer on whom this responsibility falls, whereas in smaller establishments the responsibility may fall on the departmental head, manager or proprietor.

The procedure involved in checking goods delivered will vary in different establishments; the receiver of goods needs to be competant and have knowledge of purchase specifications. The goods should be inspected, counted and weighed to check against:

  (i)   Commodities received not reaching the required specification, eg. New Zealand lamb delivered instead of English or incorrect sizes.

 (ii)   Inferior or damaged products, eg. stale vegetables or blown cans.

(iii)   Short weight or quantity.

Goods should then be stored as soon as possible to minimise the risk of deterioration and the possibility of pilfering taking place. The Goods Received area should have sufficient space and be adequately lit; to enable the procedure to be carried out quickly and efficiently, scales and other equipment should be provided. The goods receiver should have a copy of the order sent to the supplier and should check this off against the delivery note from the supplier.

The necessary documentation must then be completed; this documentation will vary according to the size and control needs of particular establishments. Small establishments may file the delivery note once it has been checked against the delivery and may use it at a later stage when checking against the Invoice or Statement for payment. (Examples of suppiers' documents such as Delivery Notes, Invoices and Statements are shown later in this section).

Signing of Delivery Notes

Most suppliers will require their copy of the delivery note to be signed by the receiver as proof of delivery and that the goods are satisfactory.

In situations where goods are not checked on receipt the delivery note should be marked 'contents unknown' and signed by the receiver. In the event of the goods being either not as ordered or omitted from the delivery, the delivery man should be informed of the reason and a request for a credit note made and acknowledged by him. Goods should never be signed for without checking them or this being indicated on the delivery note.

Goods Received Books

Large establishments will have their own goods received documentation, either in the form of notes or books specifically designed to meet their own needs. The information contained on such documents needs to include the following details:

(i) Date of delivery.
(ii) Name of supplier.
(iii) Order number.
(iv) Delivery note number.
(v) Space for comments as to any variances in quantity and quality of the goods delivered if they are different from those ordered.
(vi) Signature of the receiver.

Figure 1.12 shows how this information can be laid out on a Goods Received Book. These forms may be more complex than the sample shown, to include prices of deliveries or an analysis of different commodity groups or materials.

HAYMARKET STEAK HOUSE
Goods Received Book   DATE: 25 Nov 8__

Order No	Supplier	Delivery Note No.	Comments	Received By
1432	Samson Fruiters	74	1 Case Apples Substandard	A. Sweet
1433	Kealey & Tonge	11362		A. Sweet
1436	Bailey & Co	1777		A. Sweet
1434	Adams Frozen Foods	2326		A. Sweet
1431	Bass Brewery	A7621	1 Litre bottle Bells Whisky broken	J. Brindley

Fig. 1.12   *Goods Received Book for a medium size catering operation*

These forms may also have a dual purpose, in the control function perhaps, to spread the work load in analysing purchases, or as a second method of checking purchases and departmental expenditure.

Returning goods to suppliers

From time to time it may be necessary to return goods to suppliers for the reasons we have previously mentioned. When this situation arises it is necessary to have a set procedure to avoid any misunderstandings. We have mentioned this on signing delivery notes and indicating the request for credit to deliverymen. Some suppliers give authorisation to deliverymen to issue credit notes. When dealing with suppliers who do not give this authority to deliverymen a formal request for a credit note should be made; this should be done either by letter or on a standard form as illustrated in figure 1.13. This form should contain the details relating to the order and delivery, the goods returned and the reason for return being signed by the receiving officer and deliveryman. The form should then be sent with the goods, back to the supplier and a duplicate copy retained for control purposes and for them to follow up if necessary.

At this stage in the stores control procedure goods should now be accepted into the store, having received the goods ordered to our specifications. Any variance having been accounted for both with the suppliers and the establishments control procedures.

CREDIT NOTE REQUEST			No. 36
From: **HAYMARKET STEAKHOUSE** _47 Haymarket, London WC1_ To: **SAMSON FRUITERERS** _Pinching Lane, London SW2_			Date: 25 Nov 8_
Our Order No: 1432 Your Delivery No: 74			
Items Returned	Reason		Price
1 Case Apples	Substandard		£14.60
Goods Returned By: A. Sweet		Goods Accepted for Return By: S. Couch	

Fig. 1.13 _Example of a Credit Note Request Form_

Student Activity No. 1.12
Draw up a standard set of forms for an establishment of your own choice to control the ordering, receiving and returns procedures.

Suppliers Documents
We have so far covered documents used by establishments in the specification, ordering, receiving and return of goods. In doing so we have mentioned suppliers' documents sent to us for their own control and accounting purposes as well as our own.

Different establishments have documents to meet their own needs, suppliers' documents will vary according to their respective needs. These documents however, do have a standard function and purpose and whilst some suppliers may use a delivery note doubled up as an invoice or vice-versa we will look at them separately. The process will go from acknowledging orders right through to receipts for accounts paid.

Advice Notes
Advice notes are sent from the supplier to the purchaser, informing him that goods ordered have been despatched, giving the date of despatch and method of carriage used eg. post, rail etc. This procedure is not

used by most suppliers on a regular basis, the most common use would be for equipment or deliveries of high value.

Delivery Notes

Delivery notes are sent by the supplier to the purchaser accompanying the goods ordered. We have discussed their use and the procedure for receiving goods earlier in this section, in so much as the goods must be checked against the delivery note and then signed for. In figure 1.14 the illustration shows the essential details required on a delivery note, ie. purchaser's and supplier's names and addresses, reference to the order number, details of the goods delivered outlining quantity and unit cost and the date of delivery. Space should be allowed for the receivers signature, some suppliers will add other information relevant to the delivery. The delivery note should be in duplicate, one copy for the purchaser and another for the supplier.

WILLS WHOLESALE SUPPLIERS LTD   DELIVERY NOTE
233 Ridgeway, Exeter   No: 173
Tel: (0392) 44555   Date: 29 Nov 8__
To: **Armada Way Hotel**   Round No. 4
    Armada Way, Plymouth
Order No. 28

Quantity	Unit	Description	Unit Cost	Checked
2	12 no	Cos Lettuce	4.20	
1	20 no	Avocado Pears	8.00	
2	12 lb	Guernsey Tomatoes	3.60	
6	1	Cucumber	35	
		Goods Received by:		

Fig. 1.14 *Example of Delivery Note*

Invoices

An invoice is sent by the supplier to the purchaser usually a few days after the delivery has been made and accepted, giving financial details of the transaction, ie. the 'bill'. Some smaller suppliers will incorporate the invoice with the delivery note to minimise their paper work. A disadvantage of this system is the complications that may be created when goods are returned involving the issue of credit notes. The financial details included are a breakdown of the total purchase price, discounts given and VAT charges where they apply. Figure 1.15 shows an example of the invoice that would be sent relating to the delivery note in Figure 1.14. It should be noted that each item has been separately priced and that the discount has been deducted from the total of the whole order. VAT has not been charged on this order because almost all foods are exempt from the tax, if it was charged it would be added to the total cost after any discounts have been deducted. The layout of an invoice will vary according to the suppliers and their particular system, a copy is retained by the supplier for accounting purposes.

33

WILLS WHOLESALE SUPPLIERS LTD 233 Ridgeway, Exeter Tel: (0392) 44555 VAT No. 71 56 05				**Invoice** No. 5177 Date: 02 Dec 8__		

Order No: 28	Delivery No: 173		Round No: 4		Trade Discount 10%	
Description	Unit	Quantity	Unit Cost	Total Cost £	Total Cost p	VAT Rate
Cos Lettuce	12 no	2	4.20	8	40	—
Avocado Pears	20 no	1	8.00	8	00	—
Guernsey Tomatoes	12 lb	2	3.60	7	20	—
Cucumber	1	6	35	2	10	—
To: **Armada Way Hotel** *Armada Way, Plymouth*		Total		25	70	
		Less Discount		2	57	
		Sub Total		23	13	
		VAT		—	—	
Account No. 88		Total Due		23	13	

Fig. 1.15 *Example of an Invoice*

Credit Notes

Credit notes are sent from the supplier to the purchaser when an adjustment on an invoice has to be made, rather than altering the invoice which could cause confusion and be open to dishonesty. Credit notes are issued usually for returned goods or errors made on invoices. In short, the credit note is sent when a deduction has to be made on the purchaser's account. In figure 1.16 the credit note illustrated assumes that some of the goods supplied have been returned because they were of poor quality. It should be noted that the credit note is of the same layout as that of an invoice, to avoid any confusion they are usually printed in red to indicate credit. A duplicate is retained by the supplier for their accounting purposes.

WILLS WHOLESALE SUPPLIERS LTD 233 Ridgeway, Exeter Tel: (0392) 44555 VAT No. 71 56 05				**CREDIT NOTE** No. 55 Date: Dec 8__		

Order No: 28	Delivery No: 173		Round No: 4		Trade Discount 10%	
Description	Unit	Quantity	Unit Cost	Total Cost £	Total Cost p	VAT Rate
Guernsey Tomatoes	12 lb	1	3.60	3	60	—
To: **Armada Way Hotel** *Armada Way, Plymouth*		Total		3	60	
		Less Discount			36	
		Sub Total		3	24	
		VAT		—	—	
Account No. 88		Total Credit		3	24	

Fig. 1.16 *Example of a Credit Note*

Statements

Statements are sent from the supplier to the purchaser at regular intervals, usually monthly, showing a list of all the transactions that have taken place between them and sets out details for payment and any incentives for early payment. The statement is set out in date order, giving details of the amount owing at the beginning of the accounting period, then listing all invoices issued during the period, any credit notes issued, payments received and discounts given. The balance outstanding after each transaction is shown in the final column; the purchaser is expected to pay the final amount in this column. The illustrated statement in figure 1.17 shows details of the Invoice and Credit Note shown in figures 1.15 and 1.16 respectively and how they affect the balance owing.

WILLS WHOLESALE SUPPLIERS LTD   STATEMENT

233 Ridgeway, Exeter
Tel: (0392) 44555   Date: 31 Dec 8__
VAT No. 71 56 05   Monthly

To: **Armada Way Hotel**   Note: 2½ % Discount for Accounts
      Armada Way, Plymouth   settled by 10 Jan 8__
Account No. 88

Date	Details	Debit	Credit	Balance Outstanding
01 Dec 8__	Balance			170.35
02 Dec 8__	Invoice No. 5177	23.13		193.48
08 Dec 8__	Payment		166.10	27.38
08 Dec 8__	Discount		4.25	23.13
09 Dec 8__	Invoice No. 6240	71.35		94.48
10 Dec 8__	Credit No. 55		3.24	91.24
17 Dec 8__	Invoice No. 7503	43.80		135.04
24 Dec 8__	Invoice No. 8766	60.62		195.66
30 Dec 8__	Invoice No. 9914	25.10		220.76

Fig. 1.17   *Example of a Statement*

Receipts

Receipts are sometimes issued to acknowledge payment, however most suppliers do not do this unless cash payment is made on delivery of goods. It is generally accepted that either the following statement acknowledges payment, or the purchaser has paid by cheque, which is a receipt in its own right when cashed by the bank. When receipts are issued they should include details of the amount paid, the date of payment, what the payment relates to and be signed by the recipient of the money.

The supplier's documents shown in this section relate to the whole series of transactions between supplier and purchaser. The supplier needs them for his own accounting and control purposes. The same must be said for the purchaser who needs to record details of all his transactions in order to maintain control.

Stores Procedures and Records

We have so far examined stores control in this section taking into consideration the receiving of goods into the store and the related use of suppliers documents. It is necessary to record details of goods entering the stores, as well as details of goods being issued out of the stores to the different departments in an establishment. There are a variety of systems used by different establishments, each one tailored to the individual requirements of that particular organisation. The basic principle of any system is that departments send an order for materials to the store, this is known as a requisition (see figure 1.20). On receipt of a requisition the storeman will issue the materials required. The storeman will have his own records to keep as he is responsible for all stock held in the store. These records have four basic purposes:

(i) To record goods received into the store.
(ii) To record goods issued from the store.
(iii) To inform the storeman of stock levels for re-ordering purposes in order to maintain a continuity of supply without being over stocked.
(iv) To calculate the value of stocks held in the store.

The records most commonly used for this purpose are Bin Cards and Stores Ledger Cards although the latter are called Stock Record Cards by some establishments.

Bin Cards

A bin card is kept for every commodity in the store, they are either attached to the shelf on which the commodity is stored or kept in a small box file or loose leaf file. Each bin should have a number and this is entered on the card together with details of the commodity, the size, (to avoid confusion if more than one size is stocked) and the maximum and minimum stock holding of that commodity. Details are recorded on the card of all receipts and issues of that commodity as and when it happens, the balance of stock remaining is recorded for checking purposes. The storekeeper who receives or issues the stock and makes the entry should initial the card in case of later queries. When the storekeeper sees the stock is approaching its minimum level he informs the

Bin No: *105*		Commodity: *Canned Peach ½s*		
		Unit Size: *A10*		
Maximum Stock: *18*		Minimum Stock: *4*		
Date	Received	Issued	Balance	Initials
25 Mar 8__	12		12	RSC
28 Mar 8__		2	10	RSC
01 Apr 8__		3	7	RSC
05 Apr 8__		2	5	JM
07 Apr 8__	12		17	RSC
09 Apr 8__		2	15	RSC
13 Apr 8__		2	13	JM

Fig. 1.18 *Example of a Bin Card*

purchasing officer of the fact and the amount required to bring the stock up to its maximum level.

Stores Ledger Cards
A stores ledger card can be regarded as an extension of the bin card and is kept in a loose leaf file, the card keeps a record of the value of commodities received, issued and the balance remaining. Other details included on the cards are the names of the suppliers of that commodity. Figure 1.19 shows a completed stores ledger card which has been recorded for the bin card in figure 1.18 showing how the value of stock has changed with each receipt and issue. Details of the invoice number and requisition number is recorded for cross checking purposes in control.

When this system of stock control is used it is possible to check the ledger card with the bin card and a physical count of the commodity for stock taking or other purposes. Medium sized establishments may well use a stores ledger card as its only method of stock control, thus doing away with a bin card.

Stores Requisitions
All issues from the stores must be made in exchange for a requisition for the materials. Each department in the establishment is issued with a numbered requisition book; to differentiate between departments they are often either colour or number coded. Each order from the stores must be made on a requisition form, whether it is for one or many items and a duplicate copy kept for control purposes. The goods required should be entered in quantity, size and description and the requisition signed by the head of department eg. Chef, Housekeeper.

HIGH PEAK HOTEL

Buxton
Department: *Housekeeping*

STORES REQUISITION
No: *29*
Date: *16 Oct 8__*

Quantity	Unit	Description	Stores Use Only				
			Quantity Issued	Unit Cost	Total Cost £	p	Bin No
2	100	Guests Soap	2	2.90	5	80	203
1	24	Toilet Rolls	1	3.60	3	60	42
6	1	Vim	6	36	2	16	81
1	5 Ltr	Bleach	1	80		80	201
4	10	Black Bags	4	46	1	84	170
Ordered by:				Total	14	20	

Authorised by:
Issued by: Received by:

Fig. 1.20 *Example of a Stores Requisition*

Bin No: 105 Commodity: *Canned Peach ½s* Unit Size: *A10*
Maximum Stock: *18* Minimum Stock: *4*
Supplier 1. **Sutch & Sutch**
Supplier 2. **Wills Wholesale Suppliers**

Date	Invoice/ Requisition Number	Unit Price	Received			Issued			Balance			Initials
			No	£	p	No	£	p	No	£	p	
25.3.8__	73126	1.60	12	19	20				12	19	20	RSC
28.3.8__	735	1.60				2	3	20	10	16	00	RSC
01.4.8__	771	1.60				3	4	80	7	11	20	RSC
05.4.8__	799	1.60				2	3	20	5	8	00	JM
07.4.8__	74550	1.60	12	19	20				17	27	20	RSC
10.4.8__	887	1.60				2	3	20	15	24	60	JM

Fig. 1.19 *Example of a Stores Ledger Card*

Student Activity No. 1.13

Complete the Stores Ledger Card shown below by calculating the unit stock balance and the values of receipts, issues and stock balance after each movement of stores.

Bin No: **88**
Maximum Stock: *45kg*
Supplier 1. **Sutch & Sutch**
Supplier 2. **Wills Wholesale Suppliers**

Commodity: *Spaghetti*
Minimum Stock: *10kg*

Unit Size: *1kg*

Date	Invoice Requisition Number	Unit Price	Received			Issued			Balance			Initials
			No	£	p	No	£	p	No	£	p	
20.4.8_	22514	55p	40									
23.4.8_	125	55p				8						
29.4.8_	149	55p				5						
10.5.8_	178	55p				12						
13.5.8_	24110	55p	40									
16.5.8_	199	55p				6						
21.5.8_	230	55p				10						
25.5.8_	261	55p				7						
01.6.8_	294	55p				8						

39

After issuing the stores the storeman will then cost the order and make the appropriate entry onto the Stores Ledger Card, before sending it on to control who will 'marry' it up with the duplicate at a later stage in the control procedure. The example in figure 1.20 shows a Stores Requisition which is designed for this purpose, establishments will design a requisition form to meet their own needs.

Student Activity No. 1.14

Design a Stores Requisition form suitable for your college stores and complete the requisition with an order for your next kitchen practical session.

Issues Procedures

We have already shown in this section the documents necessary and how they are completed for stores to be issued. Whilst procedures will be similar in all establishments there will be some variations. It is important to establish an issues system which gives the stores adequate time to prepare orders, although consideration must be given for emergency requirements. Requisitions for regular orders should be handed into the store the day before they are required, unusual requirements should be given earlier or discussed with the head of department concerned. Most establishments will have small stores within each department for materials in daily use and use the central stores to maintain stocks within them as well as other issues. This will eliminate materials in constant use being returned to the store; there should be regular checks to make sure that levels of stocks are not too high in departmental stores.

Returns Procedures

It is important to establish a returns procedure for unused materials, for three main reasons:
(i)   To prevent the deterioration of materials.
(ii) To eliminate the risk of unused materials going astray.
(iii) To calculate the true cost of materials consumed.
All returns should be credited to the department concerned and stores records adjusted accordingly. Departmental returns forms should be completed by the storeman in duplicate, one copy for the stores record and the other for the department returning goods. The layout of these forms would be the same as a stores requisition, only indicating returns. They may also be colour coded by being a different colour from requisitions.

Liquor Returns

The most regular use of returns procedures will be in establishments which issue liquor stocks to portable bars, either for guests' rooms or small functions. The storeman will issue a liquor stock according to the customers' requirements, recording the details of the issue on a bar consumption sheet as shown in figure 1.21. When the bar is closed the stock will be returned to the store, details of all returns will be recorded on the bar consumption sheet and the amount of liquor consumed is calculated by subtracting the returns from the issues and priced at cost price and at selling price. The reason for two prices is that the cellar stock is valued at cost price and that the customer must be charged for the liquor consumed at selling price. The unit used for recording issues, returns and consumption will vary for different types of drink depending on how they are sold. In the example sherry is issued by the bottle which contains 15 measures, the issue of 150 measures shows that 10 bottles were issued. When returns are made the liquor storeman (steward in some establishments) will count the number of bottles and any part bottles will be checked to see how many measures it contains. The example for Bristol Cream shows that 5 bottles and 5 measures were returned. Where whole bottles are the normal method of sale eg. wine or bottled beer and fruit juices, then this would be the unit of sale. Where liquor returns are concerned accuracy is of great importance in order to ascertain correct consumption figures and stock levels.

Liquor Consumption Sheet: No. 255 **WINDERMERE HOTEL** Date: 14 Jan 8__ Location: Lake View Room Customers Name: Appletree Wedding Account No. 86												
Commodity	Bin No	Unit	Issues	Retns	Liquor Used	Unit Cost Price	Total Cost Used		Unit Selling Price	Total Selling Price	
Tiopepe Sherry	76	Msr	150	60	90	30	27	00	70	63	00
Cream Sherry	78	Msr	150	80	70	30	21	00	70	49	00
Piesporter	12	Bot	36	16	20	2.40	48	00	5.20	104	00
Macon	9	Bot	36	17	19	2.90	55	10	6.40	121	60
Moet & Chandon	28	Bot	18	4	14	8.30	116	20	18.50	259	00
Britvic Orange	61	Bot	48	18	30	19	5	70	50	9	50
Stock Issued by: Returns Received by:						Total	273	00		606	10

Fig. 1.21 *Example of a Liquor Consumption Sheet*

Stock Taking

Stocks should be checked as regularly as practically possible, either weekly or fortnightly and the occasional spot check should be carried out. A full stock take should take place during each accounting period of a business organisation. The purpose of a stock take is to check the actual stock held against stores records, ie. bin cards and stock ledger cards. The procedure to be followed in taking stock is to count stock units held. In the case of loose commodities stored in bins such as flour, the contents of the bin would be weighed. Where liquor is concerned part bottles should be measured in tenths for closer accuracy, beer barrels or kegs can be weighed to calculate their contents. A stock list should be completed similar to the example shown in figure

1.22. For each bin number the stock is counted and the value calculated, any variance from the stores ledger should be recorded and a space is left for any comments, either on the variance or condition of the stock. This report is sent to management for them to take appropriate action in the event of any variances.

Student Activity No. 1.15

(i) Complete the Liquor Consumption Sheet shown below by:
- (a) Calculating the stock consumed.
- (b) Calculating the cost of the stock consumed.
- (c) Calculating the selling price of the stock consumed.

LIQUOR CONSUMPTION SHEET Customers Name: Alton Fabrics Ltd												**BUTCHERS BISTRO** 42 Argyle Street, Newcastle Date:

Commodity	Bin No	Unit	Issues	Rtns	Liquor Used	Unit Cost Price	Total Cost Used	Unit Selling Price	Total Selling Price		
Bells Whisky	54	Bot	6	$2^4/30$		7.80		19.50			
Gordons Gin	57	Bot	6	$1^{20}/30$		8.10		20.25			
House Wine	22	Bot	12	$3^1/6$		1.56		3.47			
Lager	81	½ pt	48	37		26		55			
Ginger Ale	71	Bot	120	21		18		35			
Tonic Water	72	Bot	120	16		18		35			

Stock Issued by:	Total						
Returns Received by:							

NB: Whisky and Gin are calculated at 30 measures per bottle.
Wine is calculated at 6 glasses per bottle.

(ii) Prepare an invoice from the Butchers Bistro to the customer. For this exercise we will assume all prices include VAT. The customer is not allowed any discount.

ELECTRO MANUFACTURERS plc

Catering Dept.
STOCK LIST

Stores:
Date:
Stock Taker:

Bin No	Description	Unit	Stock Held	Cost Price	Stock Value	Variance	Comments

Fig. 1.22 *Example of a Stock List*

Student Activity No. 1.16

(i) Draw up a stock list as shown in figure 1.22 listing all items held in your department's restaurant bar.

(ii) Take a physical count of these items counting part bottles in tenths.

(iii) Calculate the value of the stock from the current price list of the supplier or suppliers of liquor stock.

Inventories

An inventory is a list of large and small equipment or fittings which are contained in an establishment. They are usually prepared for different areas or rooms of a department, it is usual for a head of department to be an inventory holder, meaning that he or she is responsible for the equipment and fittings. Inventories are checked on a regular basis, usually every 3 or 6 months, all new equipment is added to the inventory when purchased and any equipment which is removed from the area or room is deleted. In the event of equipment being transferred from one area to another, details are removed from the relevant inventory and added to the other. For equipment of high value the serial number of that piece would be included on the inventory for security purposes. An example of how an inventory is laid out is shown in figure 1.23, note that columns can be added to record details on each occasion the inventory is checked. Inventories are held by senior management in any business organisation and responsibility for them is agreed with heads of department in their conditions of employment.

BRUNEL HALL OF RESIDENCE — INVENTORY

Bristol University
Location: *Refectory*
Date Prepared: *26 May 1985*   Prepared by: Number: *17*

Equipment Details	Serial No if Applicable	Quantity	Date of Additions or Removal

Fig. 1.23   *An example of an Inventory*

Student Activity No. 1.17

Prepare an Inventory for either:

(i) A practical area where you are taught, eg. stillroom, classroom *or*

(ii) The bedroom in your department's accommodation unit.

Controlling Empty Bottles and Containers

An important aspect of receiving liquor stocks is the value of bottles, crates and other containers. These items are the property of the supplier and establishments are charged for them when delivered. When containers are returned to the supplier the establishment is then credited with their value. It is necessary to control all containers received and returned, because of their value. Most suppliers include their value on a separate part of the delivery note and invoice, issuing a credit note when containers are returned or separate documentation is used for the same purpose. It is therefore important that where stores records are concerned an internal record is kept. Figure 1.24 shows an example of the stores records kept to control all containers received and returned, it is completed for each delivery and collection by the supplier. Both the storeman and the deliveryman sign the form once it has been checked, before it is passed to control who make sure the correct charges and adjustments have been made. The difference between those containers received and returned will be the number of containers held on the premises. In public houses where off sales often occur customers are charged for containers and a refund is made when they are returned. When customers fail to return containers this deposit is used to pay the supplier for the container not returned to him.

Computers in Storekeeping

The systems we have examined for the purposes of stores control can easily be adapted for use on a computer. There are several good systems on the market which will provide the stores and management with immediate information regarding purchases, goods received, goods issued and stock in hand, both in unit total and financial value. Programmes for computers are written to meet the specifications of the computer and the needs of the user. It is possible to programme the computer to give a daily printout of goods to be ordered to maintain stock levels, as well as departmental expenditure and other control information. These programmes will be linked to other aspects of the hotel's financial and control operation. The storekeeping staff will key in the information from the usual sources, ie. Goods Received Documents and Stores Requisitions, either by physically keying them in or using data processed documentation. The computer will then store the information to process the data when required. Storekeeping staff will then only have to check actual stock levels of goods against results processed by the computer. Since the development of computer systems the cost of installation has been substantially reduced, making it economically feasible for smaller establishments to consider introducing computerised systems.

TAVERN IN THE TOWN
Norwich

CONTAINERS RECEIVED & RETURNED

Date	Supplier	Received				Returned				Store Man Signature	Delivery Man Signature
		Split Bottles	Large Bottles	Crates	Casks	Split Bottles	Large Bottles	Crates	Casks		
06 Oct 8_	Greene King	144	36	9	8	168	48	11	7		
	Total										

Fig. 1.24   *An example of a Containers Received and Returned Form*

45

Student Activity No. 1.18

Investigate the stores control capabilities of either:

(i) The computer system available in your department or college *or*

(ii) A system which is available on the open market. (Sources of information for this activity would be HCIMA Year Book or advertisements in the Trade Press).

It may be seen from the contents of this section that storage and stores procedures play an important role in food and liquor control. Whilst the systems, procedures and records we have discussed may apply to large organisations, they can easily be adapted for smaller establishments. Proprietors of small catering establishments who control their own stores may find no need for any stores records, because it would not be necessary to exercise control over themselves. However, they must consider some procedures when dealing with external organisations, such as suppliers. Procedures such as checking deliveries against delivery notes and invoices against delivery notes and statements must still exist. The purpose of all stores control is to make an operation more efficient and cost effective by eliminating unecessary stocks, wastage, pilfering, overcharging by suppliers and lack of supplies.

Further Reading

Storage of Commodities and Storekeeping — Theory of Catering
    Ceserani and Kinton   Chapters 8 and 10

Kitchen Records and Control — Professional Kitchen Management
    Fuller Chapter 17

Receiving Storing and Issuing — Food and Beverage Control
    Kotas Chapters 6 and 7

ASSESSMENT QUESTIONS

1. List the considerations that must be made for effective storage conditions.

2. Explain the best storage conditions for:
   (a) meats
   (b) fish
   (c) fresh fruit and vegetables
   (d) dairy produce
   (e) frozen foods
   (f) dry goods
   (g) cleaning materials.

3. Explain the different storage conditions that are necessary in the liquor store or cellar of a public house.

4. Explain the principles to be followed when considering the layout of stores areas.

5. Explain the legal constraints on the storage of:
   (a) meats
   (b) milk
   (c) prepared foods
   (d) spirit for duplicating machines.
6. Describe the security considerations to be made when:
   (a) planning stores areas
   (b) setting up stores procedures.
7. Describe a procedure suitable for receiving goods into the store.
8. Explain briefly the documents of a business transaction sent by the supplier.
9. Explain the purpose of a bin card, a stores ledger card and a departmental requisition.
10. Describe a procedure suitable for the issuing of goods from a store.
11. Draw up a stores ledger card suitable for 4 kilo bags of Carolina Rice costing £2.20 in a hospital stores, the maximum stock holding being 28 units and minimum 6 units. Enter the following receipts and issues on the card calculating the value at each stage.

01 June	Purchased	24 Units
04 June	Issued	3 Units
06 June	Issued	3 Units
10 June	Issued	4 Units
14 June	Issued	4 Units
16 June	Issued	3 Units
18 June	Purchased	20 Units
20 June	Issued	4 Units
24 June	Issued	3 Units

12. Explain the procedure to be followed and any documentation necessary to carry out a stock take in a small store.
13. Prepare a liquor consumption sheet for a small function and enter the following issues and returns on the sheet before calculating the cost and selling price of that function.

Commodity	Bin No	Unit	Cost Price	Selling Price	Issues	Returns
Chablis	8	Bottle	2.80	6.30	18	7
Claret	14	Bottle	3.20	7.10	18	5
Bristol Milk Sherry	46	$1/15$ Bottle	36	75	60	12
VSOP Brandy	87	$1/30$th Bottle	48	1.20	60	17
Britvic Orange	91	Bottle	20	45.	24	15

14. Prepare an Inventory suitable for hotel bedrooms.
15. Describe the procedure for recording empty bottles and containers.
16. Explain how a computer can be used for compiling stores records.

Basic Costing, Pricing and Control Procedures

We have so far examined Purchasing and Stores Control Procedures to the extent of materials being issued from the stores to the departments within a hotel and catering operation. In this section we will examine basic dish and menu costing techniques with the intention of fixing a selling price to the customer, whilst understanding the important aspect of portion control. We will also take into account the influences of service charges and the effects of Value Added Tax on the prices we charge. Whilst we have studied material costs and their control at some length, it is apparent that there are other costs involved in the sale of food and drink, those costs being the payment of wages and business expenses. It is important that these costs are controlled and analysed as they contribute to the efficiency and profitability of an establishment when there is more than one area of sale, as in hotels which sell rooms, food and drink all at different levels of profit. A final element of control is that of cash, all business organisations have systems to make sure that the customer is charged the correct amount and that this money reaches its intended destination. We must therefore examine methods of cash control both in payments made by a business and payments received by a business.

COSTING STANDARD RECIPES

Standard recipes aid food costing and portion control by giving an accurate list of ingredients used in the preparation of dishes. By listing the ingredients and methods in a readily understood layout, the results will be uniform every time, thus minimising any losses through wastage. If a series of prices columns are introduced to a standard recipe then costings can be made regularly to check for any changes that may occur. This may be of great importance if an organisation wishes to maintain a menu price for a long period of time, the recipe card will indicate when the price charged becomes uneconomic. Figure 1.25 shows an example of a standard recipe adapted as a costing sheet for the same dish; it is not necessary to show the method of preparation but it does make preparation staff aware of costs if they are able to see them as well.

STANDARD RECIPE *No. 38*								
CHICKEN PIE			4 Portions					
Ingredients	Quantity	Cost 04 Feb 8__		Cost		Cost		Cost
		£	p	£	p	£	p	£ p
1 Chicken	1125 gms (2lb 8oz)	1	45.0					
Button Mushrooms	125 gms		30.0					
Onion	90 gms		1.3					
Chicken Stock	¼ ltr		9.0					
Streaky Bacon	125 gms (4oz)		17.5					
Egg	1 (size 2)		7.5					
Salt Pepper & Parsley	to taste		2.0					
Puff Pastry	225 gms		13.5					
	Total	2	25.8					
	Cost Per Portion (÷4)		56.4					

Method 1. Bone out chicken and cut into pieces 3 × 2cm.
2. Wrap each piece in bacon and place in pie dish.
3. Slice the mushrooms and chop onion.
4. Add all ingredients and cover with stock;
5. Cover pie with puff paste.
6. Cook for 10 mins in a hot oven to set paste and for 1 hour more in moderate oven.

Fig. 1.25   *Example of a Costed Standard Recipe*

Costing a standard recipe is carried out by calculating the cost of the ingredients used; up to date prices which must be used are available from the purchasing officer. Food items are priced either by the unit of purchase or in bulk and to add to the problem both metric and imperial quantities are used. Bulk prices are used for most vegetables whereas meats are quoted by the pound. It is best to treat each ingredient individually when it comes to metric or imperial price quotes as conversion to one or the other can lead to mistakes being made.

Ingredient Cost Calculation
In the example the following prices have been quoted:
  (i)   Chicken   58p per lb.
 (ii)   Mushrooms   £2.40 per kilo.
(iii)   Onions   £3.80 per 25 kilo sack.
 (iv)   Streaky Bacon   70p per lb.
  (v)   Eggs   90p per dozen.
 (vi)   Chicken Stock   36p per litre.
(vii)   Puff Paste   60p per kilo.
Each ingredient must be costed separately because of the variations in quantity, price and type of quotation as shown below:
  (i)   Chicken 2½ lbs @ 58p per lb
       58p × 2.5 = £1.45
 (ii)   Mushrooms 125 gms @ £2.40 per kilogram
       £2.40 × 125 ÷ 1000 = 30p

49

(iii) Onions 90 gms @ £3.80 per 25 kilogram
£3.80 × 90 ÷ 2500 = 13.5p
(iv) Streaky Bacon 4 oz @ 70p per lb
70p × 4 ÷ 16 = 17.5p
(v) Eggs 1 @ 90p per dozen
90p × 1 ÷ 12 = 7.5p
(vi) Chicken Stock ¼ ltr @ 36p per litre
36p × 1 ÷ 4 = 9p
(vii) Puff Paste 22.5 gms @ 60p per kilogram
60 × 22.5 ÷ 1000 = 13.5p

Note: Seasoning is costed at 2p as it is not defineable. The total cost of the ingredients are ascertained on the costing sheet and divided by the number of portions that the standard recipe has been prepared for, to give the cost per portion. This may be expressed by the formula:

Total dish cost ÷ number of portions

In the example this would be calculated as shown below:

Total dish cost ÷ number of portions = 225.8p ÷ 4 = 56.4 per portion

Student Activity No. 1.19
(i) Prepare costed standard recipes for either:
(a) your next practical session *or*
(b) two dishes from your establishment's menu.
(ii) Calculate the cost per portion in either case.

Pricing

The purpose of pricing is to fix the selling price of a product to cover the material costs, labour costs, overhead costs (business expenses) and to produce a profit sufficient to make the owner's investment worthwhile. The other important purpose of pricing is to fix a price which is competitive with similar products or services available. Fixing the correct price which satisfies all these purposes requires a great deal of skill and in some cases an element of luck. We will be considering the labour and overhead costs later in this study and students who study at a higher level will learn to appreciate the cost and profit requirements of different types of business organisations. Fixing the wrong price can lead to a business making losses which could involve its eventual bankruptcy or closure. If the price is too low a business may not be able to cover its expenses or it may fail to make sufficient profit. Prices which are too high will not attract customers; this would have the same effect. It is therefore crucial that a business organisation has the correct pricing policy.

The system of pricing used by most hotel and catering operations is known as 'profit margin', this is better explained by all costs being expressed as a percentage of the sales which are always 100%. Other industries use a system known as 'mark-up' where the cost is expressed as 100%. Both methods of pricing are shown in the example illustrated in figure 1.26. Where the same food cost, gross profit and selling price are shown both the percentages are different according to the method used.

Profit Margin Pricing			Mark Up Pricing		
Food Cost	60p	40%	Food Cost	60p	100%
Gross Profit	90p	60%	Gross Profit	90p	150%
Selling Price	£1.50	100%	Selling Price	£1.50	250%

Fig. 1.26 *Example of Pricing Methods*

Gross Profit
The gross profit is the difference between the material cost of a dish and the selling price. It must be sufficient to cover the expenses involved in running a business and leave a profit for the owner, this profit is known as net profit. Gross profit is sometimes called 'kitchen profit' but as far as this study is concerned it will always be referred to as gross profit because we also have to consider liquor profits and other accounting terms at a later stage.

A hotel and catering operation will fix its gross profit percentage to cover all expenses and its desired net profit, the gross profit will vary according to the type of establishment and the market to which it aims to sell. At this stage we will assume that a gross profit margin has been set for the sale of food. Using the profit margin method this would be further explained as:
- Gross Profit of 65% + Food cost of 35%
- Gross Profit of 60% + Food cost of 40%
- Gross Profit of 50% + Food cost of 50%
- Gross Profit of 45% + Food cost of 55%

Note: That the selling price is always 100%.

Student Activity No. 1.20
Complete the following chart using the profit margin method:

Food Cost %	Gross Profit %	Selling Price %
40%	60%	100%
34%	66%	100%
30%	70%	100%
60%	40%	100%
25%	75%	100%
42%	58%	100%
34%	66%	100%

51

Selling Price Calculation

When the gross profit margin has been set we are able to calculate the selling price. Firstly, the cost percentage must be calculated. This we carried out in Student Activity no. 1.20 by subtracting the gross profit % from the selling price % (always 100%).

Example:

Selling Price %	—	Gross Profit %	=	Food Cost %
100%	—	65%	=	35%

The selling price is now calculated by the following formula:

Cost price × 100 ÷ food cost percentage

Example:

The food cost of a dish is 57p. Calculate the selling price of the dish to achieve a gross profit of 60%.

Selling price = 57p × 100 ÷ 40 = £1.42½p

therefore the selling price would be £1.43.

To illustrate the variations that exist when fixing selling prices let us assume that for the same dish a gross profit of 70% is required.

Selling price = 57p × 100 ÷ 30 = £1.66

The difference between the two profit margins of 10% shows a price difference of 23p, indicating the variation in price of the same dish between two establishments.

Student Activity   No. 1.21

Calculate the selling prices per portion for the dishes you prepared standard recipes for in Activity No. 1.19 to show a gross profit of:

(i)   45%
(ii)   55%
(iii)   65%.

Gross Profit Calculation

Gross profit is expressed as a percentage of the selling price as we have already considered in this section. It may be necessary on occasions to calculate the gross profit of a dish which has a fixed selling price. This is calculated by the following formula

Selling price × Gross profit % ÷ 100

Example

A dish on an à la carte menu is priced at £4.60 per portion, the establishment works on a gross profit margin of 60%. Calculate the gross profit and the food cost:

£4.60 × 60 ÷ 100 = £2.76 Gross profit

The food cost would be calculated by deducting the gross profit from the selling price:

£4.60 − £2.76 = £1.84 Food cost

This may also be expressed by using the following formula:

Selling price × Food Cost % ÷ 100

eg. £4.60 × 40 ÷ 100 = £1.84

We have now come to the full circle; we have calculated the cost price of a dish, its selling price to achieve a certain level of profit and the food cost and gross profit when given the selling price per portion.

Student Activity   No. 1.22
Complete the following table by calculating the selling prices of the listed dishes from the food cost given to achieve the required gross profit percentage.

Dish	Food Cost (per portion)	Gross Profit Required	Selling Price (per portion)
Minestrone	18p	70%	
Veal Escalope	£1.20	60%	
Vegetables	43p	65%	
Cream Caramel	24p	65%	

Student Activity   No. 1.23
Complete the following table by calculating the food cost and gross profit of the listed dishes from the selling prices given, to achieve the required gross profit percentage.

Dish	Selling Price (per portion)	Gross Profit Required	Food Cost (per portion)	Gross Profit (per portion)
Egg Mayonnaise	£1.10	65%		
Chicken Chasseur	£3.80	55%		
Duchesse Potatoes	65p	60%		
Carrots Vichy	55p	60%		
Gateau Mocha	£1.30	70%		
Coffee	50p	75%		

Costing Table D'Hote Menus
A table d'hote menu is a set menu forming a complete meal at a set price. To cost a table d'hote menu it is necessary to cost each dish separately and add these individual costs together to make the total cost of the meal, as shown in the example below. It is important to cost accompaniments into the menu to achieve an accurate figure.

Some establishments offer a limited choice of dishes for each course on their table d'hote menus. It is important that they select dishes which have a similar cost for each course and that the average price of the dishes is used when the menu is costed. For example, if the choice on the menu is:

Pork Chop Normande @ 82p food cost,
or Navarin of Lamb   @ 78p food cost,
or Filet of Plaice à l'orly   @ 88p food cost,
then the average cost of 83p would be used.

53

Recipe Number	Dish	Cost *per portion*
14	Cream of Tomato Soup	14p
28	Filet of Plaice	94p
30	Sauce Tartar	4p
59	French Fried Potatoes	12p
67	Garden Peas	10p
90	Banana Flan	18p
104	Cream	8p
2	Coffee	13p
	Total Cost	£1.73
	Gross Profit %	60
Date: 24 Oct 8__	Selling Price	£4.33

Fig. 1.27　*Example of Table 'D'Hote Menu Costing*

Calculation of Menu Selling Prices

The same method of price calculation is used for menus as that used for individual dishes. The gross profit percentage will be used for the total food cost of all the dishes, as shown in figure 1.27.

Establishments which have à la carte menus may vary the gross profit margin for expensive dishes or for main courses. The reason for this is that the average gross profit required may make dishes too expensive, or, in some cases, to make the price more attractive. If an establishment wishes to achieve a gross profit of 60% overall they may price starting and dessert courses at a gross profit of 65-70% and main courses at 50-55%. Most starting and dessert dishes have a much lower food cost than main course dishes; by using this method it will give a better balance to the menu prices. Customers, when reading menus, tend to judge the price of the main course when selecing a restaurant; careful pricing can therefore stimulate customer choice. This method is sometimes used by industrial catering operations where much lower gross profit margins, ranging from 5 to 20%, are used.

Student Activity   No. 1.24

(i)　Select two three course table d'hote menus from the following selection of dishes.

Dish	Food Cost	Dish	Food Cost
Melon Frappe	24p	Chicken Maryland	80p
Ravioli	19p	All Potato Dishes	11p
Chilled Fruit Juice	12p	Sliced Green Beans	14p
French Onion Soup	14p	Carrots à la Creme	16p
Steak & Kidney Pie	78p	Meringue Glacé	28p
Grilled Gammon	92p	Bakewell Tart	24p
Omelette Fines Herbs	32p	Sherry Trifle	21p
Cod Mornay	70p	Apple Flan	19p

(ii)　Calculate the total food cost for each menu and fix a selling price to show a gross profit of 65%.

(iii)　Using the same menus, fix a selling price to show a gross profit of 55%.

(iv) Arrange the dishes in the form of an à la carte menu, calculating the prices for starting and dessert courses to make a gross profit of 65% and main courses to show a gross profit of 55%.

(v) Select a shortened à la carte menu suitable for an industrial catering operation, with each course having an alternative choice. Price each dish to show a gross profit of 15%.

Student Activity No. 1.25

(i) Prepare standard recipes and food costs for an English Breakfast that would be suitable for a small hotel and a motorway services restaurant.

(ii) Price the menu to show the following gross profits:

(a) Small Hotel at 50%.

(b) Motorway Services at 60%.

(c) Factory Canteen at 20%.

PORTION CONTROL

Portion control may be defined as the amount or size of a portion of food which is served to a customer. The purpose is to satisfy customer demand and to control food costs within set down specifications. If the portion is too small then the customer feels cheated at not getting value for money and will not return to the establishment again. If the portion is too big, against the size set down in the standard recipe, then the food cost will be greater than the planned price thus affecting profits. Planning the size of portions to be served will be influenced by the following factors:

(i) Type of customer eg: in industrial catering, portions will vary considerably, as office workers and manual workers will be catered for.

(ii) Type of establishment and menu eg: portions will be smaller for table d'hote menus than for à la carte menus. On a table d'hote menu portions for vegetables will vary in size according to the number of different types offered and main course portions will be smaller if there is a fish course.

(iii) Prices charged eg: in a first class hotel or restaurant where customers are prepared to pay more, larger portions are available, if so required, whereas in cheaper establishments cost will dictate the portion size.

When menus and portion sizes have been decided it will have an obvious influence on the purchase specifications, as we discussed in the first section of this book. Portion control will have an obvious effect on the cost of the food served. Fast food operations practice portion control very carefully, the effect on the food cost of frozen chips is illustrated in figure 1.28 by showing the cost of different portion sizes used in these establishments. If we assume a gross profit of 60% for fast food operations, a variation in portion size of 1oz, will result in a

Frozen Chips × 24p per lb	
Portion Size	Cost
3oz	4½p
4oz	6 p
5oz	7½p
6oz	9 p
7oz	10½p
8oz	12 p

Fig. 1.28 *Example of Food Cost Variations caused by Portion size*

loss of almost 4p per portion. This may seem very little but if you consider 300 portions each day for a year it results in an £8000 loss of sales. This alone justifies the need for portion control.

Student Activity   No. 1.26
Find out the sizes of portions used for main courses and vegetables in either your college teaching restaurant or where you work.

Portion Control Aids
There are a variety of portion control aids available to the caterer in the form of equipment, pre-portioned foods and visual aids. Once the portion size has been determined then the appropriate aid should be used and selected. For further study on portion sizes a list of portion sizes for different dishes is included in the Purchasing chapter of The Theory of Catering by Ceserani and Kinton.

Portion Control Equipment
Equipment used for portion control maybe put into two categories; equipment used for the preparation and cooking of food and equipment used for the service of food, some of these will have a dual purpose.

Food preparation and cooking equipment available to aid portion control is listed below:

Scales	Pudding Sleeves
Measures	Dariole Moulds
Electric Slicing Machines	Pie Dishes
Tea & Coffee Dispensers	Baking Tins
Milk Dispensers	Moulds
Butter Pat Machines	Serving Spoons & Scoops

Serving Equipment available to aid portion control is listed below:

Ladles	Vegetable Dishes
Glasses	Tureens
Coupes	Sauce Boats
Soufflé Cases	Entrée Dishes
Cocottes	Casseroles
Soup Bowls	Bar Optics & Measures

56

Pre-Portioned Foods

Many convenience food products available to the caterer are packaged individually, such as: butter pats, jams, breakfast cereals etc. If a caterer has prepared purchase specifications for certain meat and fish products, such as steaks, chops, whole fish etc, these are themselves pre-portioned foods. Many desserts which are purchased outside the establishment are pre-portioned, the portions are often indicated by rosettes of cream or artistic designs. Beverages may be purchased pre-portioned, in the form of tea bags, individual coffee filters or cream and milk sachets. It is now possible for the caterer to use solely pre-portioned foods if he so wishes, this gives each customer a standard product and allows the caterer rigid portion and cost control.

Visual Aids to Portion Control

Many hotel and catering companies prepare illustrated charts or manuals of dishes to make their staff familiar with the portions required and their presentation. The cycle of operations in the preparation of the dish is shown and precise details of garnishing to make each dish identical is also given.

Whilst we have explained aspects of portion control in detail and its importance in helping to control food costs, we must also consider training staff to carry it out effectively. Portion control will not be successful unless staff are aware of what a portion is and how it is achieved. All food preparation and service staff must be trained in recognising portion sizes and the use of correct equipment and utensils. Training such as this can be achieved by the use of visual aids such as illustrations or demonstrated to them prior to service. Caterers often forget that an important aspect of portion control is the staff who have to serve the customer, without them it would be ineffective.

Student Activity   No. 1.27

(i) List the portion control equipment that is used in either your department's main restaurant kitchen or in the kitchen where you work.

(ii) List the pre-portioned foods used in either:
   (a) your department's restaurant   *or*
   (b) your college refectory   *or*
   (c) the establishment where you work.

ANALYSING SALES AND COSTS

We have so far considered costs and selling prices on a unit basis, the unit being the dish or meal. For a caterer to assess his success or failure it is necessary for him to analyse his sales, cost and profits in total. He will then be able to make any adjustments to his operation with the purpose of making it more efficient and profitable.

Sales Analysis

Most hotel and catering operations sell more than one product; a hotel will sell rooms, food, drink and ancilliary goods or services, a restaurant will sell food, drink and tobacco and so on. Where there is more than one area of sale then it is necessary to break these areas down departmentally. It is also worthwhile to calculate daily or monthly sales of each department and follow their patterns and trends, as well as the average spending per customer in hotels and restaurants. The purpose of such an analysis is to help the caterer to plan his business and its development well in advance and to take advantage of any trends he has observed.

Sales Mix

A sales mix is a breakdown of departmental sales in relation to the total sales and expressed as a percentage.

Formula

Departmental Sales ÷ Total Sales × 100

Example

A hotel has total sales of £132,800 for the year, a breakdown of these sales show Rooms Sales were £82,700, Food Sales were £27,450 and Liquor Sales were £22,650. The sales mix would show:

Room Sales = 82,700 ÷ 132,800 × 100 = 62.27%
Food Sales = 27,450 ÷ 132,800 × 100 = 20.67%
Liquor Sales = 22,650 ÷ 132,800 × 100 = 17.06%

Expressing this as a percentage enables the caterer to compare the results of his business from day to day, month to month or year to year and to see the affect of any changes he has tried to make. The information obtained can be plotted on a graph, this will show results in a more visual form which in addition helps in the observation of trends. A sales graph for a restaurant selling food and liquor can be plotted from the daily, weekly or monthly sales figures, as shown in figure 1.29. In this example of a seasonal restaurant the monthly sales from April to September are as follows:

Month	Food Sales	Liquor Sales
April	£1680	£ 820
May	£2260	£1040
June	£2740	£1100
July	£3380	£1300
August	£3900	£1950
September	£2660	£1340

Drawing a graph to show the above figures is carried out in the following stages:

(i)   The horizontal axis shows the passing of time (ie months April to September).

(ii) The vertical axis show the amount of sales from 0 to the maximum possible (ie £0-£4000).

(iii)   Each month's sales figures are plotted on to the graph for both food and drink.

(iv)   Each figure plotted is connected by using a different colour for each, eg. black for food and red for liquor.

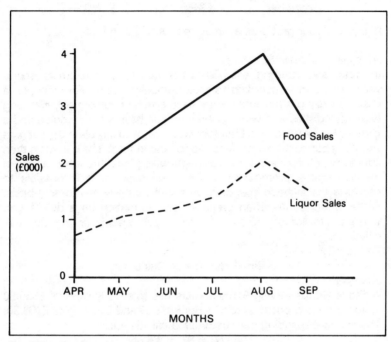

Fig. 1.29 *Graph Analysing Departmental Sales*

The example shows that liquor sales have not been increasing in proportion to food sales for May and June; the restauranteur was able to take corrective action in July to increase liquor sales, bringing them into line with his food sales.

Student Activity   No. 1.28

Prepare a Sales Mix and a departmental sales graph for the 'El Sombrero Restaurant' from the information given below.

Month	Food Sales	Liquor Sales
January	£1400	£ 600
February	£1350	£ 450
March	£1500	£ 500
April	£1750	£ 850
May	£2200	£1100

59

June	£2600	£1250
July	£3550	£1750
August	£3950	£2000
September	£3450	£2300
October	£2700	£1350
November	£2250	£1100
December	£3450	£ 750

Discuss in your group what there results might indicate.

Average Customer Spending
In hotel and catering establishments guests or customers spend varying amounts according to their particular needs. For example, a customer using a restaurant may have a three course meal, selecting expensive dishes and wine, or he may just have a main course and a glass of house wine. It is therefore worthwhile to calculate the average spending per customer on food, liquor and in total. The caterer is then able to watch for variations that might take place through changes in menus, special promotions or for other reasons. It is possible to calculate the average spending on a daily, weekly or monthly basis. Large organisations often prepare this information on a daily basis, whereas smaller organisations tend to use weekly or monthly calculations.

Formula

$$\text{Sales} \div \text{Number of Customers}$$

Example
A Steak House serving 91 customers has total daily sales of £550.80 which is broken down as food sales £382.50 and liquor sales £168.30. The average spending per customer is calculated:

$$£550.80 \div 91 = £6.05$$

The average spending per customer on food is calculated:

$$£382.50 \div 91 = £4.20$$

The average spending per customer on liquor is calculated:

$$£168.30 \div 91 = £1.85$$

Student Activity No. 1.29
Calculate the average spending per customer on food, liquor and in total for each day of last week in either,
 (i) your teaching restaurant, *or*
 (ii) the restaurant where you work.

Cost Analysis
The elements of cost in hotel and catering operations are material costs, labour costs, overhead costs and profits. We have already examined material costs in some detail; labour and overhead costs are explained in greater detail in the third level of study. Profits are also regarded as a cost because a profit target is set for a business and con-

sidered when monitoring efficiency. Total costs are expressed as a percentage of sales and at this stage it is necessary to be able to calculate these costs. The information regarding elements of cost is taken from the accounts of a business; it is expressed as a percentage because sales and cost figures vary from month to month or year to year whereas a percentage is always out of a hundred. The use of percentages means that it is easy to compare between one accounting period and another.

Calculating Elements of Cost as a Portion of Sales
Formula

Element of Cost ÷ Sales × 100

Example
The accounts of Macimpy Fried Chicken Restaurant for the month of May 198_ show:

Sales	£14,500
Food Cost	£ 6,525
Labour Cost	£ 2,320
Overhead Cost	£ 2,900
Net Profit	£ 2,755

To express these costs as a percentage of sales the calculations and results show:

Food Cost %	= 6,525 ÷ 14,500 × 100	= 45%
Labour Cost %	= 2,320 ÷ 14,500 × 100	= 16%
Overhead Cost %	= 2,900 ÷ 14,500 × 100	= 20%
Net Profit %	= 2,755 ÷ 14,500 × 100	= 19%

The gross profit for this operation is calculated by:

Sales − Food Cost = Gross Profit
In value = £14,500−£6,525 = £7,975
As a percentage 100−45 = 55%

Elements of Costs and Profit in Different Types of Operation
Figure 1.30 shows examples of different types of hotel and catering establishments and variations in percentage costs between them. Although there will be variations in each type of establishment due to their individual characteristics, such as: location of type of service offered etc. These figures are a guideline only. We should note that the proportions of labour and overhead costs increase in the more luxurious types of establishment; profits in hotel food operations are less because the provision of food is also regarded as a service to residents. Industrial catering does not make a profit and their proportions of costs may vary according to the companies' policies towards their staff catering. The greatest variation in cost is shown in food costs, hence the policy adopted for pricing by most establishments explained in the previous section. Further consideration will be given to these costs at a later stage in these studies.

Type of Establishment	Elements of Cost %			
	Food	Labour	Overheads	Net Profit
1st Class Restaurant	30	25	27	18
Hotel Restaurant	40	24	24	12
Popular Catering	40	20	22	18
Snack Bar	50	18	16	16
Industrial Catering	70	15	15	—

Fig. 1.30 *Comparison of Costs and Profits in Hotel & Catering Operations*

Presentation of Sales and Costs Information

The analysis and comparison of sales and costs information is often better presented by using visual and pictorial techniques such as graphs, pie charts and histograms. The use of graphs has been shown in figure 1.29 as a means of analysing the sales trends of an operation. We will now examine these other methods of presenting management information.

Pie Charts

A Pie Chart is a circle divided into sections (like slices of a cake or pie), each section is in proportion to the size of the figure being represented. A pie chart is constructed by drawing a circle and calculating the angles to be represented at the centre of the circle. These angles are drawn from the centre point to the inner edge of the circle. The example in figure 1.31 is drawn to show the proportions of departmental sales for a hotel with total sales of £200,000 per year. The sales are broken down departmentally as: Rooms £110,000, Food £55,000 and Liquor £35,000. To calculate the angles from these figure the method is as follows:

Proportion of Sales ÷ Total Sales × 360°
(the total number of degrees at centre of circle)

Room Sales   = 110,000 ÷ 200,000 × 360° = 198°
Food Sales   = 55,000 ÷ 200,000 × 360° = 99°
Liquor Sales = 35,000 ÷ 200,000 × 360° = 63°

The pie chart may now be drawn using the angles calculated, details of the departmental sale being entered into each section.

A pie chart may also be used to illustrate the elements of cost in an operation as shown in figure 1.32. In this example an outdoor catering company has sales of £275,000, the elements of cost being: Food £96,250 (35%), Labour £71,500 (26%) and Overheads £49,500 (18%), the Net Profit being £57,750 (21%). The proportions of the pie chart are calculated using the following method:

Element of Cost/Profit % ÷ 100 × 360°

giving the results of:

Food Cost	$35 \div 100 \times 360 = 126°$
Labour Cost	$26 \div 100 \times 360 = 93.6°$
Overhead Cost	$18 \div 100 \times 360 = 64.8°$
Net Profit	$21 \div 100 \times 360 = 75.6°$

NB: The element of cost proportion can be calculated either by using percentages or volume of costs and sales.

Fig. 1.31 *Example of a Pie Chart showing proportions of Total Sales*

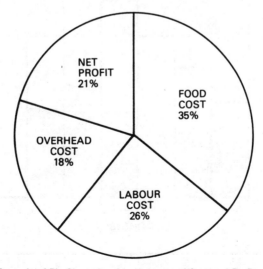

Fig. 1.32 *Example of Pie Chart showing elements of Cost and Profit*

Student Activity   No. 1.30
A hotel has sales of £23,000 for the month of May, these sales are made up of: Rooms £13,500, Food £6,300 and Liquor £3,200. The hotel's costs are: Materials £4,700, Labour £5,800 and Overheads £6,400.
(i)   Draw up a pie chart showing the sales mix.
(ii)   Draw up a pie chart showing the proportions of costs and profit.

Histograms
A histogram is a graph of a frequency distribution and is mostly used to display sales over a period of time, although other information can be included, if so required, eg. material costs. The sales graph shown in figure 1.29 may be better displayed in this manner, as shown in figure 1.33. The same method of drawing the axis is used for this purpose, the difference is that instead of points on the graph being drawn, each period of time is represented by a block on the histogram. Different areas of sales may be represented by either colours or shading. Figure

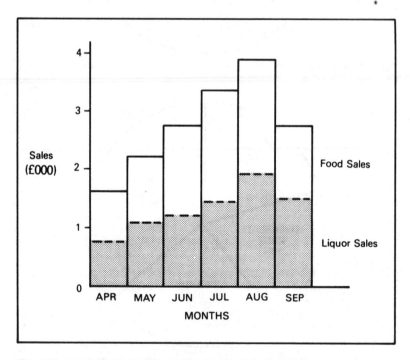

Fig. 1.33 *Example of a Histogram showing Departmental Sales*

1.34 shows a histogram drawn for sales and liquor costs in a Public House over a period of 6 months from July to September. A breakdown of the information is shown below:

Month	Sales	Costs
July	£13,500	£8,100
August	£14,750	£9,150
September	£13,250	£7,550
October	£11,250	£6,300
November	£11,000	£5,900
December	£14,750	£7,650

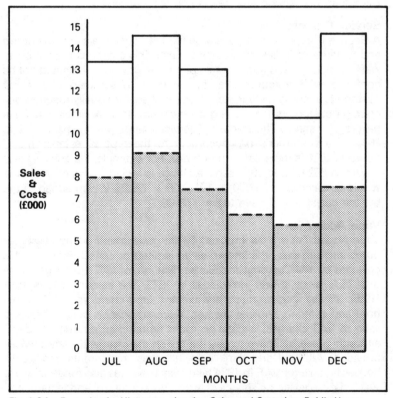

Fig. 1.34 *Example of a Histogram showing Sales and Costs in a Public House*

It should be noted that there are some variations in the proportion of costs to sales, this will probably indicate that more people drink beer or lager in summer months which makes less gross profit than wines and spirits.

Student Activity No. 1.31

From the following information prepare a histogram showing the food and liquor sales for the 'Walrus and Carpenter Bistro' over the six months, May to October.

Month	Food Sales	Liquor Sales
May	£4,100	£1,250
June	£4,700	£1,450
July	£5,600	£1,800
August	£5,950	£1,950
September	£5,400	£1,850
October	£4,500	£1,600

Discuss in your group any trends you have observed.

Service Charges

A Service Charge is an extra charge made to customers in some hotels and restaurants in lieu of gratuities (tips). This charge is passed on to staff as either an addition to, or as part of, their wages. It should not be confused with a 'cover charge', which is a standard charge for customers in some restaurants. A cover charge is usually made to dis-courage customers from using a restaurant at peak times just for a beverage or snack. The amount of service charge will vary from 10% to 20% of a customer's bill, according to the type of establishment, however 10% is the most common rate. For example, if a guest's bill in a hotel is £52.80 and 10% service charge is levied, the service charge would be calculated £52.80 × 10 ÷ 100 = £5.28. When added to the bill, the guest would have to pay £58.08.

Value Added Tax

Value Added Tax is a tax imposed by the government on non essential goods and services, it is known as an indirect or consumer tax and is collected by HM Customs and Excise. The rate of VAT has ranged from 8 to 15% since it was introduced in 1973, the current rate is 15% (1985). Whilst food products are exempt (zero rated) from VAT most hotel and catering services are not. Accommodation sold in hotels is liable to VAT charges, except on room rental charges after 28 days, although guests still have to pay the tax on the charge for any services provided. All food and drink sold in hotels, restaurants and public houses is liable for VAT. In 1984 takeaway food was also made liable for VAT. It is also levied on service charges made in hotels and restaurants. Institutional catering is exempt from the tax because it is regarded as non-profit making and an essential service, eg. hospitals and school meals.

Calculation of VAT Charges

Some establishments add VAT to their customer's accounts whilst others charge prices that are inclusive of the tax. We will consider two

examples which show the two methods of VAT calculation:
Example 1.
The bill for a hotel guest is £66.00. Service Charge at 10% and VAT at 15% are to be added.

Guests Bill	£66.00
+ Service Charge @ 10%	
£66.00 × 10 ÷ 100 =	£ 6.60
	£72.60
+ VAT @ 15%	
£72.60 × 15 ÷ 100 =	£10.89
Total Guest Bill =	£83.49

Example 2
The price of a night's bed and breakfast, inclusive of VAT is £25.00. To calculate the price excluding VAT:

Price charged × 100 ÷ (100 + VAT Rate)
= £25.00 × 100 ÷ 115 = £21.74

Therefore VAT paid £25.00−£21.74 = £3.26.

The second example can also be adapted to calculate the VAT collected from customers when they pay inclusive prices in, for example, a public house. In this case if the till reading for an evening is £336.40, the VAT paid can be calculated as follows:

£336.40 × 15 ÷ 115 = £43.88

using the formula:

Total Takings × VAT Rate ÷ (100 + VAT Rate)

Student Activity   No. 1.32

(i)   A customer's bill in a restaurant amounts to £26.30, exclusive of VAT. Calculate his total bill, including VAT at 15%.

(ii)   A hotel guest's account amounts to £138.40 before service charge of 12½% and VAT at the current rate is added. Calculate the total amount to be paid by the guest.

(iii)   A doner kebab takeaway records the following sales for a week, inclusive of VAT. Calculate the VAT collected at the current rate and complete the Sales Analysis Form.

Day	Sales (including VAT)	VAT	Sales (excluding VAT)
Monday	£136.40		
Tuesday	£141.80		
Wednesday	£150.40		
Thursday	£168.20		
Friday	£270.40		
Saturday	£290.60		
Sunday	£100.20		
TOTAL			

CASH CONTROL

An important element of any hotel and catering operation is the control of cash receipts (cash coming into a business) and cash expenditure (cash going out of a business). So far, we have examined methods of stock control relating to stores coming into and going out of a business. We have emphasised the importance of control because of the attraction of food and liquor commodities to pilfering. We should also stress that the control of cash is equally important. In this section we will examine methods of security for cash, procedures for checking cash in an establishment and operations to control cash receipts and expenditure.

Security of Cash

A problem of handling cash in a hotel and catering operation is that monies are collected by the various departments up to twenty-four hours a day. In these cases an operation must establish a secure system, enabling staff to pay in cash taken to a central point as and when is necessary. The cashier's office in such operations is only open during normal working hours and access should be limited to those times, except in the case of senior management requirements. It is usual for the hotel safe to be located in the cashier's office, which will be subject to maximum security. In order to facilitate staff payments of money when the cashier's office is closed, a night safe similar to the type used by banks is sometimes provided. Staff are then able to pay in their takings in a special wallet or bag designed for the purpose, including details of the amount paid in as illustrated in figure 1.35. The duty manager or controller will read the till at each change of shift or cashier, the till rolls will then be collected and taken to the cashier's office, usually on two separate occasions each day. Staff should not have access to till rolls except for reading purposes, control staff only should be allowed to renew or remove them. Tills should be checked regularly for change requirements and emergency stocks of change be kept in a secure place to cope with any needs outside normal hours. It is important that procedures are established and strictly followed.

The transportation of cash from the establishment to the bank needs careful consideration by all types of operation. Security companies provide an excellent service and are used by bigger operations who handle large sums of cash, they are however expensive and cannot be considered by smaller organisations. When cash has to be taken to the bank by these organisations consideration must be given as to who takes it and when. Only trusted members of staff should have this responsibility or the proprietor himself; 'cash in transit' insurance should be taken out in the event of any mishap. Cash should not be transported at the same time each day or week and ideally not always by the same person, it is also advisable for the person carrying the cash to be accompanied and not make it obvious as to what is being carried.

Procedures for Checking Cash Balances

An important aspect of cash control is that of establishing a procedure for the many sales points that receive cash in a hotel and catering operation. In the previous section we looked at the physical aspect of paying cash in to a central point. We will now consider a procedure that could be adapted for use in any type of operation that handles cash. All establishments should use tills that record all transactions and have a control function that enables totals to be read and reset. The till should be read at the beginning of each shift or reset where practical, details of the reading should be entered on the cashiers control form illustrated in fugure 1.35. This form can be printed onto the paying in envelope and issued to staff at the start of their shift. The cashier should then check that the 'float' in the till is correct. A 'float' is the cash in a till used for the purpose of giving change to customers, it should consist of a sufficient amount of change in different denominations sufficient to meet the needs of the transactions that take place during the shift.

At the end of the shift, or when the department closes, the cashier should take a closing till reading and calculate the amount of cash taken, by deducting the opening reading from the closing reading, as shown in the example. The cashier should then count the cash in the till and replace the float in the smallest possible denominations of cash. The remaining cash is entered onto the paying in form in its different denominations and totalled, the cash is then paid into the chief cashier together with the completed form.

The cash paid in and the cashier's control form are checked with each other at a later stage in control and differences noted. Control must also check that the float is intact as often as is practically possible and should remove the till roll to check that everything is in order between readings of different shifts and cashiers and also that it agrees with the cash paid in. Cash should never be left in the till when a department is closed, till drawers should be removed and taken to the chief cashier's office for safe keeping.

A similar procedure to that shown in the example should be used in all establishments regardless of their size. Smaller operations may have a less formal procedure but one must exist even if it is for the proprietor to check himself. Any differences that occur must be investigated, the reason for the difference explained by the person responsible and the appropriate action taken.

Student Activity   No. 1.33

List the departments that receive cash in a large luxury type of hotel.

Cashiers Paying in Control No. 146	Cash Paid In		
		£ 00	p 00
DATE: *16 Jan 8__* TIME: *11.20pm*	£50	00	00
DEPARTMENT: *Cocktail Bar* FLOAT: *£50*	£20	60	00
NAME: *K Porter*	£10	70	00
SHIFT: Start: *5.30pm* Finish: *11.15pm*	£ 5	95	00
TILL READ (closing): £246.55	£ 1	10	00
TOTAL READ (opening): £ 0.00	Silver	11	40
TOTAL CASH RECORDED: £246.55	Bronze		15
SIGNATURE: *K Porter*	Total	246	55
CHECKED BY:	CHECKED BY:		
CASH DIFFERENCE:			

Fig 1.35 *Cashier's Control Form*

Recording Cash Received

We have examined methods of security and controlling cash in operations which receive cash in different sales areas, we will now look at the function of the cashier's office with regard to receiving cash. Once the individual cash deposits have been checked they must be recorded in a 'Cash Received' book before being paid into the bank. 'Cash Received' books will vary in layout according to the individual needs and size of an operation.

Large operations with several different sales outlets will use an analysis type of cash received book similar to the example shown in figure 1.36. A separate page is recorded for each day, the departmental payments being recorded when they have been checked by the cashiers office. At the end of each day, or, according to the establishment's organisation, every morning, the cash book is balanced and the total is paid into the bank. The bank paying in form is then used as proof that the day's receipts have been banked, which in itself is part of the cash control procedure.

Small operations will use a similar procedure, except that it will be used on a monthly basis, although cash will be paid into the bank more regularly, probably twice weekly to avoid holding large sums of money. The example shown in figure 1.37 is a specimen of the type of cash received book used for a public house or small restaurant. The cash taken each day is recorded, separating the food and liquor sales for their own accounting purposes and any appropriate notes made for irregular cash receipts. At the end of each month the 'total cash received' column should equal the 'cash banked' column, the bank

HILCESTER HOTEL, *PARK LANE, LONDON W1*

CASH-RECEIVED BOOK   DATE:_____

Time	£	p	£	p	£	p	£	p	£	p	£	p	Daily Total £	p	£	p
Reception/Cashier																
Restaurant																
Coffee Shop																
Lounge Service																
Cocktail Bar																
Hyde Park Bar																
Banqueting — Food																
Banqueting — Bar																
Other																
Deposits																
Ledger A/Cs																
Total																
Received By																

Fig. 1.36 *Example of a Cash Received Book used in a large hotel operation*

paying in book again forming a part of the cash control procedure. The till rolls are normally retained as a check against any differences and for stock control calculation purposes. The main function of this stage in cash control is to complete the overall control system, from cash being paid by the customer to details of all cash received being recorded on the bank statement.

BREAKWATER INN   MONTH:

Date	Liquor		Food		Other		Daily Total		Cash Banked		Notes
1	150	68	38	20			188	88			
2	194	36	51	70	22	60	268	66			22.60
3	187	40	50	10			237	50			Fruit Machine
4	162	91	46	20			209	11	904	15	
5	177	70	49	30			227	00			
31	155	83	42	50			198	33			
TOTAL											

Fig. 1.37 *Example of Cash Received Book for a small hotel and catering operation*

Student Activity 1.34

(i) Draw up a Cash Received Book suitable for a large hotel with the following cash taking departments:
Front Office Cashier, Buttery, Cocktail Bar, Restaurant, Ballroom Bar and Lounge Service,

(ii) Record the following payments made by staff responsible for cash at the end of their shift:

8.00am	Night Lounge Waiter	£ 68.42
11.00am	Front Office Cashier	£2,788.30
11.30am	Buttery Cashier	£205.65
3.00pm	Restaurant	£196.70
3.15pm	Cocktail Bar	£105.46
4.00pm	Lounge Waiter	£ 36.65
7.00pm	Front Office Cashier	£583.82
10.00pm	Lounge Waiter	£ 47.20
10.30pm	Buttery Cashier	£462.35
11.30pm	Restaurant	£742.94
11.30pm	Cocktail Bar	£321.80
1.10am	Ball Room Bar	£428.30

(iii) Balance the Cash Received Book and record the amount to be paid into the bank the following day.

Recording Cash Expenditure

Most business transactions that take place in hotel and catering operations are on account (ie. credit) with regular suppliers, however, some small, irregular or emergency payments are made by cash. Such transactions are usually made for emergency food items, postage, payments made on behalf of guests (VPOs), travelling expenses and small miscellaneous items of equipment or services. It is therefore as necessary to control this expenditure as it is to control cash received. The most common method of recording this type of expenditure is by setting up a petty cash system. A person in the cashier's office would be given as part of their duties that of petty cashier, or, in small operations, this would be the responsibility of the manager or someone in a similar position.

A method of petty cash control is the 'imprest' system, the petty cashier is given a float of say £80 at the beginning of the week, note how this is entered in figure 1.39. When it is necessary he will pay money out for goods or services, asking the recipient to sign a voucher recording the details of the transaction as shown in figure 1.38. Vouchers are numbered for control purposes and authorisation for expenditure is made by the appropriate head of department or other senior member of staff before the cash is issued. The receipt for goods or service obtained is stapled to the back of the voucher. The cashier will then make the appropriate entry into his petty cash book as shown in figure 1.39, (note the entry for voucher no. 3 shown in figure 1.38).

72

Some operations have a separate VAT column where the VAT paid is entered. In the example, the corkscrew cost £2.53 which included 33p VAT, the application of this will be explained at a later stage.

PETTY CASH VOUCHER	No. 3
Details	Amount
3 Bunches Watercress	£1.35

Date: 8—	Authorised by: *A Chef*
Received by: *K Porter*	Petty Cashier: *D. Imprest*

Fig. 1.38 *Example of a Petty Cash Voucher*

At the end of the week the petty cashier will balance his account by totalling all the analysis columns, he should have vouchers representing this amount and the remainder of his initial £80 in cash. The example shows expenditure of £51.74, therefore the cash remaining is £28.26. He will then draw from the head cashier £51.74 to make his cash balance back up to £80 to start the next week. The cash analysis sheet and vouchers are retained by the cashier and sent to the main accounts office.

There are other methods of cash expenditure control but they are based on a system which is similar to the petty cash 'imprest'. It must be emphasised that for complete cash control records of cash expenditure should be kept separately from those of cash receipts.

Student Activity No. 1.35
(i) Draw up a petty cash 'imprest' system with the following analysis headings. Food, Postage, Travelling expenses, Wages, VPO, Miscellaneous items.
(ii) Record the following transactions on to your petty cash book.
Sept 1. Received £100 cash
Sept 2. Purchased parsley costing £1.10
Sept 2. Paid casual wages £22.00
Sept 3. Paid for chef's taxi £2.90
Sept 3. Purchased postage stamps £11.30
Sept 4. Purchased bags for cleaning machine £3.20
Sept 5. Purchased 4 lemons 56p
Sept 5. Paid for recorded delivery letter £1.05
Sept 5. Paid for theatre tickets (Room 17) £9.00
Sept 6. Purchased typewriter ribbon £3.60
Sept 6. Purchased gherkins £1.30
Sept 7. Paid casual wages £12.00
Sept 7. Purchased candles £3.60
(iii) Balance off your petty cash book.

Debit	Date	Details	Voucher Number	Total	Food	Postage	Travelling Expenses	VPO	Misc	VAT
80 00	1 Aug	Imprest								
	2 Aug	Postage Stamps	1	9 50		9 50				
	2 Aug	Guests Flowers — Room 120	2	6 60				6 60		
	3 Aug	Watercress — Kitchen	3	1 35	1 35					
	4 Aug	Window Cleaning	4	12 50					12 50	
	4 Aug	Corkscrew	5	2 53					2 20	33
	4 Aug	Tabasco Sce — Kitchen	6	1 40	1 40					
	5 Aug	Registered Letter	7	2 36		2 36				
	7 Aug	Managers Taxi	8	4 50			4 50			
	7 Aug	Lobster — Kitchen	9	11 00	11 00					
				51 74	13 75	11 86	4 50	6 60	14 70	33
				28 26						
80 00	7 Aug	Balance		80 00						
28 26	8 Aug	Balance								
51 74	8 Aug	Cash Received								

Fig. 1.39 *Example of a Petty Cash 'Imprest' System*

74

Further Reading
Catering Costs and Control   Chapters 1-4 *Grace Paige* (Paige)
Food and Beverage Control   Chapters 2 and 9 *Kotas/Davis*

ASSESSMENT QUESTIONS

1. (i) Transfer the following recipe for Steamed Sponge Pudding to a standard recipe sheet:
       100gms (4oz) Castor Sugar
       2 Eggs
       10gm (½oz) Baking Powder
       100gm (4oz) Margarine
       150gm (6oz) Flour
       few drops of milk
    (ii) Calculate the cost of each ingredient required by the standard recipe using the following price list:
       Castor Sugar 32p per kg
       Eggs 80p per doz
       Baking Powder 48p per 100 gm
       Milk 24p per pint
       Flour 30p per kg
       Margarine 70p per kg
    (iii) Calculate the total dish cost for the recipe.
    (iv) Calculate the cost per portion for the recipe.
    (v) Calculate the selling price per portion to achieve a gross profit of (a) 65%; (b) 60%; (c) 45%.

2. (i) From the following list of costed dishes calculate the cost price of the menu for one cover:
       4 portions Asparagus soup — 48p
       8 portions Saddle of Lamb — £5.80
       Selection of vegetables are costed at 60p per portion
       6 portions Soufflé Pudding 78p
    (ii) Calculate the selling price in order to achieve a gross profit of (a) 65%; (b) 55%; (c) 40%.

3. Explain the role Portion Control plays in accurate costing.

4. List the various items of Portion Control equipment that may be used in a hotel and catering operation.

5. Explain how Portion Control equipment and visual aids may be used together.

6. A restaurant has total sales of £64,380 of which Food sales are £41,770 and Liquor sales are £22,610. Express these sales as a percentage of the total sales.

7. Calculate the avarage spending per customer from the following information: Total sales £7,445 from 2926 customers.

8. (i) Express the following costs as a percentage of total sales of £18,920; Food cost £7,230; Labour cost £4,660; Overhead cost £3,380
   (ii) Calculate the gross and net profits.
   (iii) Express these profits as a percentage of sales.
9. (i) Define Value Added Tax
   (ii) Define Service Charge and state the rates you expect to find.
   (iii) Express the current rate of VAT as it applies to hotel and catering sales.
10. A guest's bill in a hotel amounts to £47.30. How much will he have to pay after Service Charge of 10% and the current rate of VAT has been added to the account.
11. The daily takings of a public house are £471.85 inclusive of VAT. How much VAT has been collected.
12. A hotel has sales of £96,784 for the month of October, these sales are made up of Rooms £55,140; Food £29,060 and Liquor £12,584.
   The hotel costs are Materials £15,880; Labour £28,770 and Overheads £25,990.
   (i) Show the hotel's sales mix by using a Pie Chart.
   (ii) Show the proportions of costs and profit by using a Pie Chart.
13. Mr Barret's Restaurant has the following sales for the months January to June 198__

	Food	Liquor
January	£3,486	£1,235
February	£3,242	£1,204
March	£3,570	£1,220
April	£3,988	£1,346
May	£4,260	£1,620
June	£4,990	£1,980

Compare the sales of food and liquor by using a method of visual presentation suitable for this.
14. Describe the procedure for recording cash received.
15. State the principles and practice for cash security.
16. Outline the procedure to be followed when checking cash tills.
17. Draw up a cash received book suitable for a large hotel operation.
18. Explain the principle of a Petty Cash 'Imprest' system.
19. List the types of transaction that would be recorded in a Petty Cash system.
   (i) Design a Petty Cash book to show expenditure under the headings of Provisions, Postage and Stationery, VPO, Travelling Expenses and Sundry Expenses.

21. (ii) Post the following transactions to your Petty Cash book and balance it as at 16 June 8___

June		
9	Balance from Central Cashier	£40.00
9	Bought Postage Stamps	5.54
10	Purchased Envelopes	1.12
10	Paid for flowers for Room 27	4.50
11	Paid Chefs Fares	1.60
11	Bought Lemons	0.70
12	Bought Drawing Pins	0.60
12	Bought Cleaning Materials	3.20
12	Taxi for Room 80	3.00
13	Paid Taxi for evening Waitress	2.60
13	Paid for Recorded Delivery Letter	0.80
14	Bought Typewriter Cassette	2.85
15	Bought Candles	1.56
15	Bought Kiwi Fruit	1.60

Purchasing Costing and Control

STUDY BOOK TWO

Principles of Purchasing

In the first study book we examined the principles of purchasing and the contribution they make in effective business management. We have identified how the sources of supply are selected and the correct procedures to be used for ordering in different types of hotel and catering operations. For effective purchasing procedures to be able to take place it is necessary to know the legal requirements that apply to the purchasing of commodities and equipment.

LEGAL REQUIREMENTS RELEVANT TO PURCHASING

When an agreement is made between a purchaser and a seller that goods will be supplied at a certain price, both have certain obligations to each other. In this section we will examine these legal obligations, from the contents of valid contracts and the exclusion of liability to the law of agency between the purchaser and seller. We will also study the legal aspects of purchasing documents and any implications they may have.

Valid Contract
A contract may be defined as a legally binding agreement made between two or more persons by which certain rights are acquired by one party on the part of the other party. The parties to a contract of purchasing would be the purchaser and the seller; 'legally binding' means that the agreement is enforceable in a court of law. The laws of contract may be very complex and in the majority of hotel and catering establishments they are not used in their formal sense, except in the case of contract purchasing, which is used by institutional organisations eg. local authorities and hospitals, or by large hotel and catering companies. However a contract does exist between purchaser and seller even if it is not formalised in writing, that is to say a contract may be verbal. A valid contract will exist on the principle of offer and acceptance, that is an offer made by one party and the aceptance of that offer by the other party. We will examine this more closely in the purchasing situation by use of the following example.

A hotelier wishing to purchase some crockery for his restaurant will make enquiries to suppliers as to his requirements. The different suppliers will make offers to the hotelier giving details of the crockery, availability, price and any other conditions relevant; this is the first stage of the contract. When the hotelier accepts the offer made by one of the suppliers then the contract has been made between them. It is important to note that the enquiry by the hotelier is not a part of the contract, unless a formal order is made by the hotelier in the first place. In which case the hotelier is making the offer to supply crockery and the supplier accepts that offer.

It is important, therefore, that the offer must be clear, complete and final to avoid any misunderstanding. The acceptance of an offer must correspond exactly with the terms set out in the offer, again to avoid any misunderstanding.

In the event of either party failing to comply with the details contained in the contract then that party would be in 'breach of contract', that is they have broken the agreement. Examples of this in the case of a purchasing contract would, on the part of the seller, be the failure to supply the commodities or equipment to the specification ordered at the right time and price. Similarly, in the case of the purchaser, would be the failure to accept the goods if they arrive as ordered and are delivered at the correct time or there is a failure to pay. In either case the offended party would be able to sue the other party through the civil courts for breach of contract. The compensation payable to the offended party would be judged as a sufficient amount to compensate for the inconvenience and to put the offended party in the same financial position as if the agreement had been carried out.

Student Activity No. 2.1
List the points that you would wish to discuss with a prospective supplier when drawing up a contract for him to supply you with fresh meat and poultry.

Exclusion of Liability
An exclusion or exemption clause is a term in a contract intended to exclude or restrict the liability of one of the parties to the contract, usually the seller. The 'Unfair Contract Terms Act' 1977 places restrictions on excusion clauses that are designed to excuse any breaches of contract. Where a purchaser deals with a seller on the seller's written standard terms of business exclusion clauses, they are valid only if they are deemed reasonable. Therefore an exclusion clause will be regarded by the courts as reasonable if it 'shall have been a fair and reasonable one to be included having regard to the circumstances which were, or ought reasonably to have been, known to or in the contemplation of the parties when the contract was made'.

The Sale of Goods Act 1893, by implication, inserts into sale of goods contracts the following broad terms:
(i)   The seller has the right to sell or transfer title.
(ii)   The goods are of merchantable quality.
(iii) The goods are equal to sample or as displayed.
(iv)   The goods comply with their description.
The Supply of Goods (Implied Terms) Act 1973 made important

changes in the rules prohibiting and restricting from contracting out of these implied terms.

This legislation therefore affects the seller by prohibiting him from presenting or including unreasonable terms into sales agreements. It is therefore protecting the purchaser from such unreasonable actions which may be contained in the small print of sales agreements.

Legal Points of Purchasing Documents

In the first study book we dealt with the information that should be contained in all documents related to the purchasing of materials. The important legal points that should be contained in these documents relate to the charging or payment of Value Added Tax. Suppliers must include on invoices the following details:

(i)   VAT Registration Number.

(ii) The VAT payable.

(iii) The amount inclusive of VAT.

(iv) The Date of the Transaction.

Other documentation that must be kept is a record of all purchases made, again for VAT purposes. These records must show the value of goods and services supplied by other firms, the tax that these firms have charged, the name of the supplier and the date of the transaction. These records are known as 'Input Records', an example of which is shown below.

Date	Supplier	Total (excluding VAT)	VAT	Total
15 Jan 8_	Whitbread Brewery	110.60	16.59	127.19
15 Jan 8_	Zoppas	346.00	51.90	397.90
16 Jan 8_	Sacombe Speed	43.40	6.51	49.91

Fig. 2.1   *Example of Records for VAT Input Tax*

Law of Agency in Purchasing

The law of agency as it affects purchasing comes into being when another party is engaged in the contract of sale. An agent is a person who acts on behalf of the seller. For example, if a wholesaler sells goods to a retailer, who in turn sells them to a restauranteur and the goods are defective or not delievered, the restauranteur can, if necessary, sue the retailer, as it is the retailer from whom the goods are purchased. Sometimes, however, the supplier acts as the wholesaler's agent in selling goods to the restauranteur, in which case the restauranteur buys from the wholesaler through his agent the supplier; it is with the wholesaler that he made his contract of sale and he can sue him for breach. The answer to the question of who sold the goods to the restauranteur depends on whether the retailer/supplier was a buyer and re-seller or was he an agent for the wholesaler. Therefore when purchasing goods through an agent it is important to ascertain the nature of his contract with his supplier. If he buys and re-sells it is possible to take re-course against him, if not re-course is taken against the agent's supplier.

ASSESSMENT QUESTIONS

1. Describe the essential stages that must take place for a contract of sale to be agreed.
2. Describe examples of situations that may be regarded as 'breach of contract' in the purchasing situation.
3. Describe the effect that exclusion clauses may have in a contract of sale when made by a seller to a purchaser.
4. Explain the legal requirements necessary when designing an Invoice.
5. Explain the records that a purchasing officer must keep to satisfy legal requirements.
6. Explain the law of agency as it affects purchasing.

Storage and Stores Procedures

In the first study book we examined the requirements for safe and sound storage of commodities, materials and equipment; we also studied the principles of stores operation and methods of stores control. To expand on storage and stores procedures, we will study in this section further legal requirements relevant to the storage of materials used in the industry and the methods of storage used to comply with these requirements. We will also examine methods of stock valuation and accounting systems used in the stores for effective stock control.

LEGAL REQUIREMENTS RELEVANT TO STORAGE

We have already studied the legal constraints on storage of food as required by The Food Hygiene Regulations (1970), as well as liquor and other dangerous materials as required by The Fire Precautions Act (1971) and The Health and Safety at Work Act (1974). Whilst this legislation covers the physical aspect of the storage of food, liquor and other materials there is other legislation which applies to stores records concerning the receiving and selling of spirits on licensed premises. The Customs and Excise Act 1952 states that a record of all deliveries of spirits must be kept on licensed premises. If the quantity received by a person exceeds one gallon of a type of spirit (eg. whisky, gin, rum and vodka), at any one time a consignment note must be sent either with the spirits or despatched on the same day, a copy must also be retained by the consignor (supplier) for 12 months. The licensee must file his copy of the consignment notes in date order for 12 months and produce them if required for inspection by a Customs and Excise Officer. This legislation also states that no excisable liquor may be despatched from licensed premises unless it has been previously ordered and details concerning the quantity, description of liquor, price and the name and address of the person supplied is entered in a Day Book. The liquor must be accompanied by a Delivery Note or Invoice containing the same details as the day book.

STORES ACCOUNTING AND STOCK TAKING PROCEDURES

We have examined procedures for receiving goods into an establishment and the records used within the store, in the previous study book. In this section we will take store keeping and the records involved a stage further, by looking at procedures for the different types of stock involved and methods of calculating its value. It is essential for any stores control procedure that the system of organisation, accounting and recording is so designed that no individual person is in a position to handle or deal with any transaction involving stock or money without being supervised by at least one other person, making fraud difficult unless collusion is involved. Stocks in stores and cellars should be checked at irregular intervals with the stores records by persons other than those responsible for the stores itself; this should be done in addition to independent stock taking. Another consideration of store control systems is that they should not be over elaborate, because of the cost involved in employing control clerks, computer staff and the like. This may cost more than the savings they are designed to make by eliminating pilfering or other fraud. When selecting stores staff this should be an important consideration when checking references and assessing their integrity.

Receiving Goods into the Store

The procedure to be followed when receiving goods into the store will, in most cases, vary according to the type and value of the commodity and the size, layout and systems of the operation. The first stage of any procedure will be to check the goods delivered against those ordered and the details recorded on the delivery note. This is the responsibility of the goods received clerk as we have previously mentioned; it should, however, also be carried out when the goods enter the store. These checks should be for quantity, either by count or weight, and for quality, against the purchase specification and also that goods are fresh. Once goods have been checked the procedure will be different according to the type of stock involved.

Receiving Perishable Foods

Perishable goods such as meat, poultry, fish, vegetables and dairy produce are transferred directly to the kitchen in most cases. The store-keeper will enter details onto the appropriate stores ledger card or stores issue sheet. Issues such as this would be known as a direct issue, the value of the goods would be the purchase price of the commodites. A stores issue sheet would take the same form as a stores requisition, as shown in study book one figure 1.20.

Receiving Non-Perishable Foods

Non-perishable foods such as dry goods, canned and frozen foods etc. will be taken into the store and the details recorded onto the appropriate stores ledger card. The price entered onto the stores ledger card would be the purchase price of the commodity.

Receiving of Expensive Stock

Expensive items of stock such as smoked salmon and sides of meat should receive appropriate consideration as to their value and control. Once accepted the item should be tagged with a label showing details of its description, value and the supplier. Each tag should be dated and have a control number, this may then be used as a reference for yield testing and as an additional form of control.

Receiving of Liquor
Liquor is usually delivered directly to the cellar and it is the cellarman who has the responsibility for checking its quantity and quality with the relevant documents. He is also responsible for entering the details into the stores ledger, the value entered being the purchase price.

Pricing of Stores Issues
In the previous study book we examined methods of stores issue and the fact that issues should not be made without properly completed and signed requisitions. The pricing of stores issues is one of the most important aspects involved in costing dishes or fixing liquor selling prices. The pricing of issues will depend on the type of food. Perishable foods transferred directly to the kitchen will be priced at the purchase price. Non-perishable foods may well have been held in the store for sometime, during which the price has changed, or there may be stock held in the same bin at two or more different purchase prices. This may often be the case with food items which are liable to market price fluctuations.

There are a variety of methods of fixing the price of stores issues, which we will examine in this section. These methods are also used when calculating the value of stock for stock-taking purposes, as we will examine later in this section.

First In First Out (FIFO)
This method is used for items of stock which are subject to price fluctuation. Issues are made from items which came into the stores first and priced at their value when received.

Last In First Out (LIFO)
This method is again used for items of stock which are subject to price fluctuations. Although items are issued in a normal stock rotation system (ie. the stock which has been in the store longest will be issued first) the pricing of the issues will always be at the current market price.

Simple Average Price
This method is also used for items of stock which are subject to price fluctuations. The average price is calculated for the stock after each purchase, if the price has changed. For example, if purchases are made for a stock item costing £1.20 each and the following month purchases are made costing £1.40 each, then the value should be calculated as:
$$£1.20 + £1.40 \div 2 = £1.30$$

All issues would be changed at £1.30 until there was another price change.

Weighted Average Price

This method of pricing stock is a more accurate form of average pricing which is used for stock items which are subject to price fluctuations. Price changes are considered against the volume purchased at each price. For example, an industrial catering company may purchase 6 × 1 kilo tins of instant coffee at £7.40 each, and the following week 10 × 1 kilo tins may be purchased at £7.80 each. The weighted average price would be calculated as:

6 × 1 kilo at £7.40	=	44.40
10 × 1 kilo at £7.80	=	78.00
		£122.40

$$\frac{\text{Total cost}}{\text{Volume Purchased}} = \frac{£122.40}{16} = £7.65$$

Therefore, all issues made would be priced at £7.65, this price will take into consideration both purchase prices and the fact that different quantities were purchased at each price.

Standard Price

This method is also used for items of stock which are subject to price fluctuations. A standard price for the stock item is set by the establishment for a period of time, after considering any changes that are likely to occur during that period. Favourable and adverse price changes from the standard are recorded when they occur and the effect they may have is taken into consideration against the costs of the department concerned.

Whilst it is difficult to consider which method of pricing stock issued is the most suitable for a given operation, it remains an important part of the control function. Many department heads will blame the rise in purchase price of materials for falls in their gross profit percentages. The use of such systems of stock pricing gives an accurate reflection of stock values and price changes and, supported by adequate communication, will make all concerned aware of these values and fluctuations.

Student Activity No. 2.2

Calculate the price for the following stock issues using the FIFO, LIFO, simple and weighted average methods of price calcuation.

Bin No. 27: Granulated Sugar
Unit: 1 kilo
Goods Received: 12 Jan 20 kilo @ 48p per kilo
19 Jan 40 kilo @ 50p per kilo
26 Jan 20 kilo @ 51p per kilo

Bin No. 34: Butter (Anchor)
Unit: 250 gms
Goods Received: 12 Jan 20 × 250 gms @ 56p
19 Jan 60 × 250 gms @ 50p
26 Jan 20 × 250 gms @ 54p

Test Yields

When calculating the value of meats, certain types of fish and other commodites which have either a high value or a high degree of wastage, it is necessary to carry out a test yield. A test yield is defined as the calculation of the value of the usable or edible amount of a commodity after preparation and cooking. The purpose of carrying out a test yield is to establish the average or standard yield for a commodity when standard purchase specification, standard recipes and portion control are used. We are aware that weight loss occurs during the preparation, cooking and portioning of certain goods, creating a difference between the raw weight purchased and the amount which is actually served to customers. This is shown in the following example:·

1 Oven Ready Duckling	1.58kg	(3½lbs)
Actual Weight Purchased	1.6kg	(3lb 9oz)
Giblets	0.12kg	(3 ½ oz)
Weight (after cooking)	1.25kg	(2lb 12oz)
(cooled)	1.18kg	(2lb 10oz)
Sliced Weight (off Bone)	0.62kg	(1lb 6oz)
Weight Loss	0.98kg	(2lb 3oz)

Fig. 2.2 *Example of Weight Loss in the Preparation and Serving of Duckling*

The example shows a weight loss of 0.98kg (2lb 3oz) from the raw weight 1.6kg (3lb 9oz), therefore the yield may be calculated as 0.62kg (1lb 6oz). To express this yield as a percentage, we use the following formula:

Usable Weight of Cooked Meat ÷ Raw Weight of Meat × 100
= 0.62kg ÷ 1.60kg × 100
= 38.75% Yield
Therefore the Weight Loss = 61.25%

To calculate the price per kg of usable meat, when given the raw weight price per kg, we use the following formula:

Raw Meat Weight × Raw Meat Price per kg ÷ Usable Meat Weight

Therefore, if the price of duckling used in the example is £1.84 per kilo the cost of the usable meat per kilo would be:

1.6kg × £1.84 ÷ 0.62kg = £4.75 per kg

When using percentage yields to calculate the usable meat price per kg, the following formula can be used:

Raw Meat Price per kg × 100 ÷ Yield Percentage

Therefore, in the example used, the usable price per kilo is calculated as follows:

$$£1.84 \times 100 \div 38.75 = £4.75 \text{ per kg}$$

In most cases it is necessary to calculate the cost per portion the raw weight would yield. If, for example, the duckling used in the example yields 5 portions the following formula can be used:

Raw Weight × Raw Price per kg ÷ no of Portions

Therefore, the cost per portion is calculated:

$$1.6\text{kg} \times £1.84 \div 5 = 59\text{p}$$

Some establishments may wish to serve a specific weight of cooked meat per portion according to their portion control policy. For example, if the establishment wished to serve a portion of 115gms (4oz) of duckling, the number of portions would be calculated using the following formula:

Usable Meat Weight ÷ Portion Size

The number of portions yielded from the duckling is calculated:

$$0.62\text{kg} \div 0.115\text{kg} = 5.4 \text{ portions}$$

Therefore, the cost per portion in the example would be calculated:

$$1.6\text{kg} \times £1.84 \div 5.4 = 55\text{p per portion}$$

An alternative method of calculating the price per portion using the usable meat price per kg may also be used. Firstly, we must calculate the number of portions per kg. If, for example, we wished to serve 115gm portions, the number of portions is calculated:

$$1000\text{gms} \div 115\text{gms} = 8.7 \text{ portions}$$

The price per portion, if the price of usable meat per kilo is £4.75, is calculated:

$$£4.75 \div 8.7 = 55\text{p per portion}$$

We will now examine a Yield Test set out on the Yield Test Card as shown in figure 2.3. In this case the raw meat is prepared, cooked and carved, the costs of raw and usable meat are calculated and expressed at a cost per portion, using the formulas we have considered in this section.

The advantages of preparing test yields to establish the standard yield of food products may be listed as follows:

(i)   Establishing a standard food cost for dishes and menus.
(ii) Assisting in dish and menu pricing.
(iii) Establishing the number of portions obtained from different types or cuts of meat and fish.
(iv) Comparison of different methods of preparation and cooking by the yield produced.
(v)   Assisting in the preparation of purchase specifications.
(vi) Assisting in the preparation of orders for raw materials.
(vii) Measuring efficiency of food production.

```
YIELD TEST: Leg of Lamb (New Zealand)        No: 1762
Purchase Specification No: 38        Weight: 3.4kg
```

Raw Weight	3.36kg		100 %
Trimming	0.12kg		3.5%
Cooked Weight	2.41kg		72 %
Cooked Weight (cold)	2.30kg		68.4%
Sliced Weight	2.14kg		63.7%
Weight Loss	1.22kg		36.3%
Cost per kg (raw)	£ 3.55		
Total cost	£ 3.55	× 3.4	= £12.07
Cost per kg (usable)	£12.07		
	2.14		= £5.64
Portion Size:	100gms	Cooked Meat	
No. of Portions Yield:	2.14		= 21.4
	0.1		
Cost Per Portion:	£12.07		
	21.4		= 56p
Yield Test Carried Out By:	A. Bromley		
Yield Test Date: 22 Jan 8__			

Fig. 2.3   *Example of a Yield Test Card for a Leg of Lamb*

Important aspects of yield testing are that once a method of preparation and cooking has been established, tested and found to be satisfactory this method is maintained and recorded in standard recipes. Secondly, any deviation that may occur in either the size or cut of meat will almost certainly produce a different yield, which will affect raw weight or portion costs.

Student Activity   No. 2.3

(i) Draw up a list of meats and fish which would necessitate a yield test.

(ii) Carry out research in your Catering Theory text books or those in your library to find the weight loss that may be expected to occur in the preparation and cooking of the foods you have listed in part (i).

(iii) Using current market prices for raw weights, calculate the usable weight price per kg (lb) for the foods listed in parts (i) and (ii).

Student Activity   No. 2.4

Either in your next practical class, *or* at your place of work, *or* at home, carry out a yield test on the meat you are cooking and prepare a yield test card showing the following:

(i) The raw weight and price per kg (lb)

(ii) The cooked weight and price per kg (lb)

(iii) The percentage yield.

(iv) The percentage weight loss.

(v) The cost per portion.

(vi) The number of portions per kg (lb) cooked weight.

(vii) The number of portions per kg (lb) raw weight.

Student Activity No. 2.5

A fore-rib of Beef weighs 8kg costing £2.30 per kg. After preparation, cooking and carving it produces 48 × 100gm portions. Calculate the following:

(i) The total raw meat cost.

(ii) The yield percentage.

(iii) The weight loss percentage.

(iv) The usable meat cost per kg.

(v) The cost per portion.

(vi) The selling price per portion to achieve a 60% gross profit margin.

(vii) The gross profit made from the beef in £ p.

Stock Taking and Stock Records

In the previous section of this study book we examined methods of pricing stock for issuing purposes, which may also be used for calculating the value of stock when stocktaking. We must now examine the types of records that may be used to control issues and those that are used for stocktaking purposes. The records we have studied so far have been as follows: Bin Cards figure 1.18, Stores Ledger Card figure 1.19, Stores Requisitions figure 1.20, Liquor Consumption Sheets figure 1.21 and Stock Lists figure 1.22. The purposes of these records are to control the flow of food and beverage stock items in and out of the store and to facilitate the calculation of the value of stock held when stocktaking.

Whilst the objective of stocktaking is to check that the stock items held in the store agree with the difference between goods purchased and goods issued, there are other purposes in calculating the value of stock and controlling the volume held. The cost of holding stock represents money invested in the business lying idle (ie. Capital). Investors expect to see a return for their investment by way of profit, dividends or interest and it would be natural for them to expect a greater return when investing in a hotel and catering business than in a building society, because with the former they are taking a greater risk than with a safe investment offered by a building society or similar organisation. The cost of holding high levels of stock may therefore be expensive, when the cost of capital, storage space, deterioration of stock and insurance costs are considered. Accountants state this cost is between 15-20% of the actual value of the average stock. For example, the cost of holding stock valued at £2,000 throughout the year would be £300-£400. It is therefore important that stock is turned over as quickly as is practically possible. In Study Book 3 we will study methods of setting and calculating stock levels and ordering to maintain them.

Stock Turnover
It is important therefore to control stock turnover, which means the number of times the average stock is used; this may be expressed as the number of times each year, or the number of days it takes.

The formula to calculate the stock turnover in a year is:

Annual Cost of Sales (stock consumed) ÷ Average Stock Held

For example, if a restaurant consumed £38,000 worth of stock during a year to achieve its sales, and held an average stock of £1,000 throughout the year, the stock would be calculated:

38,000 ÷ 1,000 = 38 times per annum

This may be expressed in days by dividing the number of times per annum into the number of days open during the year. For example, if the operation was open 360 days a year, the stock would be turned over every ($360/38$) 9.4 days. In a seasonal operation open 200 days the stock would be turned over every ($200/38$) 5.2 days.

Different types of hotel and catering operation would have varying stock turnover periods. Fast food operations selling fresh foods may well turn their stock over 150 times a year (every 2 days) whereas, a first class hotel restaurant would have a stock turnover of 25-30 times a year (every two weeks) and be equally satisfied. It is important to treat food and liquor separately as the stocks behave in a different way. Food is more perishable than liquor and if an establishment relies mainly on fresh foods the stock will be turned over quickly; wines and spirits do not deteoriate with keeping and a wider range of products are kept. It would be reasonable for a liquor stock to be turned over every 4-8 weeks depending on the type of establishment. A pub selling real ale would expect to turn its stock over every 4 weeks because 40-50% of its stock would deteoriate quickly. Whereas a hotel cocktail bar not selling draught or keg beers would have a stock turnover of 8 weeks because it would have a far greater range of products.

When deciding the stock turnover necessary for an establishment to operate efficiently, the caterer must consider the following:
(i)   Location and the frequency of deliveries.
(ii)   Cost restrictions of stock and capital available.
(iii)   Range of products necessary ie. menu and liquor sold.
(iv)   Deterioration of materials to be used.
(v)   Storage facilities available.

Student Acvitity   No. 2.6
(i)   Calculate the stock turnover in times per annum and in days for the following establishments:
(a) A Seasonal Hotel open 190 days a year
        Cost of Sales   £ 76,540
        Ave. Stock Held   £   3,220

(b) An Industrial Canteen open 300 days a year
   Cost of Sales   £106,200
   Ave. Stock Held   £   1,610
(c) A School Meals Canteen open 200 days a year
   Cost of Sales   £ 30,000
   Ave. Stock Held   £   4,950

(ii) A Sandwich Bar with sales of £53,700 operating at a gross profit margin of 55% wishes to turn its stock over every 3 days. Calculate the value of stock necessary to achieve this if it is open 310 days a year.

Stock Valuation
When valuing stock it is important that a method of valuation is decided upon and the policy is not changed, as this would lead to inaccuracies and variances in the value of stocks held. An example of stock pricing, using the LIFO and FIFO methods, which shows the difference in results that these methods would produce.

During a 3 month accounting period the purchases and issues of large size packets of Cornflakes were as follows:

	Purchases	*Issues*
January	36 @ 62p = £22.32	30
February	30 @ 64p = £19.20	26
March	24 @ 65p = £15.60	25
	£57.12	

LIFO Method of Stock Valuation and Pricing:

	Issues	*Stock Remaining*
January	30 @ 62p = £18.60	6 @ 62p
February	26 @ 64p = £16.64	6 @ 62p
		4 @ 64p
March	24 @ 65p = £15.60	6 @ 62p = 3.72
	1 @ 64p = £ 0.64	3 @ 64p = 1.92
Total	£51.48	£5.64
Cost of Issues	£51.48	
Value of Stock	£ 5.64	
	£57.12	

93

FIFO Method of Stock Valuation and Pricing:

	Issues	*Stock Remaining*
January	30 @ 62p = £18.60	6 @ 62p
February	6 @ 62p = £ 3.72	
	20 @ 64p = £12.80	10 @ 64p
March	10 @ 64p = £ 6.40	
	15 @ 65p = £ 9.75	9 @ 65p = 5.85
Total	£51.27	
Cost of Issues	£51.27	
Value of Stock	£ 5.85	
	£57.12	

From this example it can be seen that the cost of issues varies between the two methods used by 21p and there is a similar variation in the value of the stock remaining.

Using a Stores Ledger Card similar to the example used in figure 1.19 the purchases, issues and stock remaining for each month, using the FIFO method of stock valuation and pricing, would be as shown below, in figure 2.4, using the information from our previous example.

Stock Records
Other records which record the value of issues and stocks will be designed to meet the particular needs of an establishment. They will have a variety of titles but basically they will record the following information from similiar sources:

Information	*Source*
Bin No. and Description	
Unit.Size	Delivery Note or Invoice
Unit Cost	Delivery Note or Invoice
Opening Stock	Last Week/Month Stocktake
Purchases Received	Delivery Note or Invoice
Issues	Stores Requisitions
Goods Returned	Credit Notes
Stock Remaining	Calculated
Stock Remaining	Physical Stocktake
Value of Issues	Calculated
Value of Stock	Calculated

Notes:
(i) The Stock remaining is calculated by Opening Stock + Purchases — Issues — Purchases Returns.
(ii) The Stock remaining should be the same for the calculated and the physical stocktake.
(iii) Value of Issues is calculated by Issues × Unit Cost.

Bin No: 116
Maximum Stock: 36
Supplier 1. **Sutch & Sutch**
Supplier 2. **Wills Wholesale Suppliers**

Commodity: *Cornflakes*
Minimum Stock: *6*

Unit Size: *Large*

Date	Invoice Requisition Number	Unit Price	Received			Issued			Balance			Initials
			No	£	p	No	£	p	No	£	p	
02.1.8__	69425	0.62	36	22	32				36	22	32	
30.1.8__	583	0.62				30	18	60	6	3	72	
03.2.8__	69816	0.64	30	19	20				36	22	92	
27.2.8__	639	0.62				6	3	72	30	19	20	
	639	0.64				20	12	80	10	6	40	
03.3.8__	70588	0.65	24	15	60				34	22	00	
30.3.8__	710	0.64				10	6	40	24	15	60	
	710	0.65				15	9	75	9	5	85	

Fig. 2.4   Example of a completed Stores Ledger Card using FIFO method of pricing

BARBICAN HOTEL LTD

Issues Control Record Dept: *Cellar*   **Week Ending:** *13 Feb 8___*

Bin No.	Description	Unit Size	Cost	Opening Stock	Purchases	Sub Total	Issues S	M	T	W	T	F	S	Total	Returns	Stock In Hand	Stock Take	Issues Value	Stock Value
5	Piesporter	1 Bot	1.90	12	24	36	6	-	2	2	4	6	6	26	-	10	10	49.40	19.00
16	Bells Whisky	Bot	9.30	16	12	28	2	1	1	2	3	3	4	16	-	12	12	148.80	111.60
25	Tia Maria	Bot	7.70	2	—	2	-	-	-	-	-	1	-	1	-	1	1	7.70	7.70

Fig. 2.5   *Weekly Cellar/Stores Issues & Control Record*

(iv)   Value of Stock is calculated by Stock remaining × Unit Cost.
An example of a record showing the information listed is illustrated in figure 2.5 and may be referred to as a weekly Cellar/Stores Issues and Control Record.
The example shows cellar issues to the restaurant and bars for the week and, when totalled, will show the value of all issues and the stock remaining. This form may be used for controlling all food and other stocks held, such as cleaning materials. The information gained by the establishment would be an accurate cost of all materials consumed and their stock valuation at the end of each week. For smaller establishments it would be possible to design a form showing the information for each month.

Student Activity   No. 2.7

(i)   During the 3 months ending 31 Dec 8__ the purchases and issues of Gordons Gin were as follows:

	Purchased	Issued
October	30 @ £7.90 each	22
November	30 @ £8.25 each	26
December	24 @ £8.40 each	30

Calculate the value of issues and stock held using:
(a) The LIFO method of stock pricing.
(b) The FIFO method of stock pricing.

(ii)   Using the FIFO method of pricing transfer the information from part (i) on to a Stores Ledger Card.

Student Activity   No. 2.8

(i)   Using a weekly cellar issues and control record form, enter details of the wines held in your college restaurant.
(ii)   During the week record all purchases and issues made.
(iii)   At the end of the week take stock of the wine remaining in the cellar and calculate its value.

Computer Stock Record Systems

In the previus study book we examined the scope of computers in the store-keeping situation with regard to Stock Control on a unit basis. With regard to calculating stock value, pricing of issues and coping with price changes some of the methods or systems we have examined in this section may seem cumbersome or time consuming. Computerised Stock Record Systems will have built into their programmes facilities to cope with different methods of stock pricing whether it be average, weighted average, FIFO, LIFO or projecting standard prices. All price changes may be keyed into the computer and the value of issues and stocks will be adjusted accordingly. The benefits of such programmes will be the speed and accuracy that price changes can be dealt with and, if linked to Standard Recipes and Portions

Costs, may be calculated as and when price changes occur. Stock values will always be available and will enable purchasing staff to plan future purchases to maximise profits from any price changes impending. The computer will be able to produce a history of the purchases and their cost, to take advantage of seasonal fluctuations in both costs, consumption and sales.

We may summarise this section of the study book by saying that we are able to utilise stores control procedures and records in the preparation of accurate costs of materials consumed, in order to achieve accurate selling prices, in line with the profit policy of the organisation. This is also linked to turning over our stock quickly and efficiently, thus utilising the amount of capital which is tied up in stock effectively. We have also gone a stage further in controlling wastage of resources and attempting to eliminate pilferage and other inefficiencies.

Further Reading
Food and Beverage Control: *Kotas and Davis*   Chapters 7 and 8
Hotel and Catering Costing and Budgets: *Boardman*   Chapter 7
Theory of Catering: *Ceserani and Kinton*

ASSESSMENT QUESTIONS

1. Define the restrictions placed on the storage of liquor by the Customs and Excise Act 1952.
2. Describe the procedure on receiving goods into the store with regard to perishable foods, non perishable foods and valuable stock.
3. Explain the following methods of stock pricing:
    (a) FIFO.
    (b) LIFO.
    (c) Weighted Average.
    (d) Average.
    (e) Standard.
4. Explain how a Test Yield may be taken.
5. Calculate the yield percentage for the following items:
    (a) An Oven Ready Chicken weighing 1.81kg produces 0.96kg of sliced meat.
    (b) A Leg of Pork weighing 4.95kg produces 3.72kg of sliced meat.
    (c) 5kg of Fresh Green Beans produces 42×85gm portions.
6. List the advantages of preparing Test Yields.
7. List the purposes of stock taking.
8. Calculate the stock turnover for the following operations:
    (a) A Creperie with a turnover of £71.200 pa operates at a 65% gross profit margin, the establishment is open 362 days a year and holds an average stock of £410.

(b) A Wine Bar has an annual cost of sales of £42,340 from trading 364 days a year, the average stock held is £5,740.

9. List factors which may influence the level of stocks held.

10. (a) Calculate the stock value using the FIFO method of pricing for the quarter ending 30 Jun 8__.
The purchases and issues for 1 kilo cartons of dish washing machine detergent for that period were:

	Purchases	Issues
April	50 @ 1.16	32
May	40 @ 1.21	35
June	30 @ 1.32	33

(b) Calculate the stock value using the weighted average method of pricing for month ending 28 Feb 8__.
The purchases and issues for boxes of 200 tea bags each week were:

	Purchases	Issues
Wk end 07 Feb	20 @ £2.90	14
Wk end 14 Feb	15 @ £3.00	12
Wk end 21 Feb	25 @ £3.30	16
Wk end 28 Feb	15 @ £3.10	17

11. List the stock records necessary to control purchases, issues and stock value calculation.

12. List the headings you would expect to find on a stores control record sheet.

13. State the benefits of computer based stock record systems.

Costing Concepts

In the first study book we examined basic costing procedures with regard to material costs and the calculation of food costs for standard recipes and menus. This element of cost is regarded as the prime element when calculating selling prices. We have already mentioned that the selling price must be sufficient to cover all elements of cost (ie. food, labour and overheads) as well as make an adequate profit for the caterer. In this section we will examine the various types of costs and how they behave in different types of hotel and catering operation. The hotel and catering industry sells accommodation, food and drink in a whole range of different types of establishments to a variety of markets. Whilst some establishments only sell one of these products others sell all three and it is a known fact that a certain dish or drink will vary in price, although the main element of cost (ie. food and drink) is similar to them all. We must therefore look at methods of expressing the costs and profits made by departments within an overall operation and how these may compare with other operations.

TYPES OF COST

The various types of cost that may be found in hotel and catering operations are described as Fixed Costs, Variable Costs and Semi-Variable Costs. We will look at each of these types of cost in more detail with the use of examples and examine how they behave in different situations.

Fixed Costs

Fixed costs may be defined as costs which remain the same whatever the volume of sales. They are costs which an operation has to pay and which increase with the passing of time. Examples of these costs are Rent, Rates, Insurances, Management Salaries and Depreciation of Property and Equipment.

Variable Costs

Variable costs may be defined as costs which increase directly in proportion to the volume of sales. As sales increase these costs will increase at the same rate. Examples of these costs are food, liquor and tobacco products. These costs are in most cases expressed as a percentage of sales as we have already learnt.

Semi-Variable Costs

Semi-variable (sometimes called semi-fixed) costs may be defined as costs which increase with the volume of sales, but not in direct proportion to them. As the volume of sales increases there will also be an increase in this type of cost but not at the same rate. Examples of these costs are Wages, Fuel Charges, Cleaning, Laundry, Renewals of Equipment and Maintenance. This type of cost may be best explained in that an establishment has to employ staff, pay fuel costs for heating, lighting and cooking whether it has any customers or not. However, as the number of customers increases it may be necessary to employ extra staff and stay open longer, or use more rooms, thus incurring extra fuel costs.

An important feature of these types of cost is that they are within the relevant range of the operation concerned. If, for example, a restaurant calculates the proportions of fixed, semi-variable and variable costs according to a range of 1,000-1,500 covers, over a specific period of time, then this would be known as the relevant range. When changes occur, for example, the restaurant extends its opening hours or provides facilities for more covers to be served, then the relevant range would change. Any change in the business capacity will cause changes in the nature of costs, this particularly affects fixed and semi fixed costs and in many cases will also effect variable costs if they include elements of labour costs.

The behaviour of these different types of cost is shown in the example of a simple operating statement in figure 2.6. The statement shows the sales, costs and profit for two consecutive months; in July there has been a 50% increase in business over June. Fixed costs have remained the same for each month but it should be noted that the cost percentage in relation to sales has decreased by 5.9%, from 17.5% to 11.6%. Variable costs have increased by £4,000 (50%) in proportion to the sales volume and their cost percentage has remained at 40%. Semi-variable costs have increased by £2,000 between the two months, from £6,500 to £8,500, representing a 30% increase, although sales have increased by 50%, because of the nature of this cost being part fixed and part variable the cost percentage has dropped 4.1% from 32.5% to 28.4%.

	June	July
No. of Covers	2,000	3,000
Average Spending	£10	£10
Sales	£20,000	£30,000
Fixed Costs	£ 3,500 (17.5%)	£ 3,500 (11.6%)
Variable Costs	£ 8,000　(40%)	£12,000　(40%)
Semi-Variable Costs	£ 6,500 (32.5%)	£ 8,500 (28.4%)
Total Costs	£18,000　(90%)	£24,000　(80%)
Net Profit	£ 2,000　(10%)	£ 6,000　(20%)

Fig. 2.6 *Operating Statement for a Small Restaurant Showing Cost Behaviour*

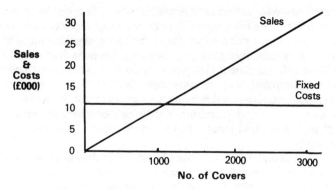

Fig. 2.7   *Fixed Costs*

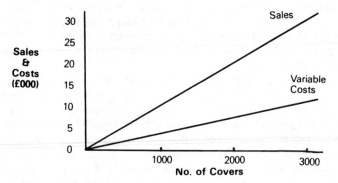

Fig. 2.8   *Variable Costs*

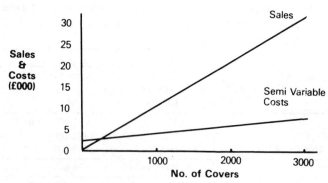

Fig. 2.9   *Semi-Variable Costs*

The types of costs are illustrated graphically to further show their behaviour against changes in sales volume. Figure 2.7 shows that whatever the number of covers sold or volume of sales, the fixed costs remain constant. However, variable costs increase in proportion with sales as shown in figure 2.8. Semi-variable costs are illustrated in figure 2.9. This shows the increase in these costs between 2,000 and 3,000 covers from the operating statement shown in figure 2.6. It is therefore possible to read from the chart the fixed element of these costs by reading where the semi-variable cost line crosses the vertical axis showing that no covers have been sold. This is shown in figure 2.9 as £2,500; it is now possible to calculate the variable element of this cost by subtracting £2,500 from the total semi-variable cost for the different sales volumes.

For 2,000 covers:

Semi-Variable Cost — Fixed Element = Variable Costs
£6,500 — £2,500 = £4,000

∴ Variable Cost per Cover
= Variable Costs ÷ No of Covers
= 4,000 ÷ 2,000 = £2 per cover

For 3,000 covers:
£8,500 — £2,500 = £6,000
∴ Variable Cost per Cover
= £6,000 ÷ 3,000 = £2

We are now able to establish the total fixed costs and the total variable cost per cover:
Total Fixed Costs = £3,500 + £2,500 = £6,000

Total Variable Cost per cover:
= £10 × 40 ÷ 100 + £2
= £4 + £2
= £6 per cover

Expressed as a percentage of the Selling Price of £10 by:
Variable Costs ÷ Selling Price × 100
= £6 ÷ 10 = 60% Variable Cost

Once the actual fixed and variable costs have been established we are able to use this information to calculate at what sales volume the operation starts to make a profit. This may be established by preparing either a contribution chart or a break-even chart.

Contribution
Contribution may be defined as the amount each unit of sale (eg. room or cover) contributes to the total fixed costs of an operation. It is calculated by:
Selling Price — Variable Cost = Contribution

In the example shown in figure 2.6 the contribution is £10 – £6 = £4. We are therefore able by using the contribution to calculate the Break Even point (ie. the number of covers that must be sold to cover all costs). The formula to calculate the break even point is expressed by:

Fixed Costs ÷ Contribution = Break Even Point

In the example shown in figure 2.6 the break even point is calculated as:

£3,500 ÷ 4 = 875 covers

The contribution may also be used to calculate the number of covers necessary to achieve a certain profit target. If, for example, the profit target for the restaurant shown is £1,500 per month, this amount is added to the fixed costs and divided by the contribution per cover, it calculates how many covers would be needed to achieve this target.

£3,500 + 1500 ÷ 4 = £5,000 ÷ 4 = 1250 covers

It is necessary to use the principle adopted by contribution calculation when preparing contribution tables and charts.

Contribution Tables and Charts

Contribution tables and charts will show the profit or loss made per cover at different sales volumes. However, when we examine the unit cost per cover, we will notice that the fixed and variable costs take on a different form of behaviour. Fixed costs, we have learnt, are constant and do not alter when there is a change in turnover. When we consider unit sales however, as the number of units sold increases, so the fixed cost per cover decreases as shown in figure 2.10. We have established that variable costs increase parallel to the volume of sales, but when considered as a unit cost per cover they remain constant, again as shown in figure·2.10.

In the example of a contribution table shown in figure 2.10 we have used the fixed costs of £3,500 for the restaurant used in our previous example. To calculate the fixed cost per cover we have used the formula:

Fixed Costs ÷ No of Covers Sold
(ie.) £3,500 ÷ 1,500 = £2.33 per cover

	Number of Covers Sold Per Month					
	500	1000	1500	2000	2500	3000
Average Spend Per Cover	£ 10.00	£ 10.00	£ 10.00	£ 10.00	£ 10.00	£ 10.00
Fixed Cost Per Cover	7.00	3.50	2.33	1.75	1.40	1.15
Variable Cost Per Cover	6.00	6.00	6.00	6.00	6.00	6.00
Total Cost Per Cover	13.00	9.50	8.33	7.75	7.40	7.15
Net Profit/Loss Per Cover	– 3.00	+ 50	+ 1.67	+ 2.25	2.60	2.85

Fig. 2.10 *Example of a Contribution Table*

104

This information may also be expressed graphically on a Contribution Chart. The chart is prepared by drawing a vertical axis for the average spend and costs per customer, using the mid point as the average spend. The horizontal axis is drawn to represent the number of covers sold on a scale from 0 to the maximum relevent sales for the establishment. The average spend is drawn on to the chart and the total cost per cover at the different sales levels are plotted. These costs are linked by a continuous line; the point where the average cost per customer crosses the average spend line is known as the break-even point.

The broken line on the chart shows the number of covers at which this point occurs (ie. 875 covers). It is then possible to read how much profit or contribution to total profit is made per cover at different sales levels.

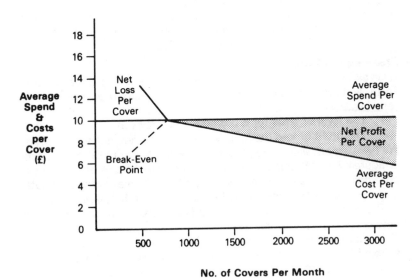

No. of Covers Per Month

Fig. 2.11   *Example of a Contribution Chart*

Student Activity   No. 2.9
A pizzeria has fixed costs of £4,600 per month which covers Rent, Rates, Insurance, Depreciation and the fixed elements of labour and fuel charges. All other costs are regarded as variable, variable costs are calculated as 65% of sales. The average spend per cover is £2.80.
  (i) Calculate how many covers must be sold each month for the establishment to break-even, using the contribution method.

(ii) Calculate how many covers must be sold each month for the establishment to make a profit of
   (a) £1,200
   (b) £1,900

(iii) Prepare a contribution table to show the profit or loss per cover for the establishment at sales volumes of 3,000, 4,000, 5,000, 6,000 and 7,000 covers.

Student Activity No. 2.10

A medium sized hotel in the centre of a large town has fixed costs of £2,940 per week. The variable cost per guest per night is calculated at 30% of sales. The average spend per guest per night is £21.00.

(i) Calculate how many guests must stay in the hotel each night for the establishment to:
   (a) Break-even
   (b) Make a profit of £630 per week

(ii) Prepare a contribution chart to show the profit or loss per guest for the hotel with the following number of guests staying each week — 100, 150, 200, 250, 300 & 350.

Break-Even Charts

A break-even chart shows the relationship between Total Sales, Total Fixed and Variable Costs and Profit. The chart may be used to ascertain:

(i) The level of sales for a business to breakeven.

(ii) The profit or loss made by a business at different levels of sales.

We have already illustrated graphically the behaviour of sales and costs in figures 2.7, 2.8 and 2.9. A break-even chart shows all these cost behaviours on one chart and the point at which sales exceed the total of fixed and variable costs may be said to be the break-even point.

The example shown in figure 2.12 is prepared from the restaurant figures we have previously used:

• Average spend per customer £10.00 per cover.
• Fixed Costs of £6,000 per month. • Variable Costs 60%.
• Range of number of covers 0-3500.

To prepare a break-even chart from this information the following procedure may be followed:

(i) Draw the vertical axis showing total sales and costs within the range of 0 (minimum sales volume) to £35,000 (maximum sales volume). This is calculated by Average Spend × maximum possible covers (£10 × 3500).

(ii) Draw the horizontal axis showing the range of Number of Covers 0-3500.

(iii) Plot the Fixed Cost line at £6000.

(iv) Plot the Sales line at each point for the Range of Covers, calculated by Average Spend × No of Covers eg. £10 × 1,500 = £15,000.

(v) Calculate the Variable Cost at each point for the Range of Covers
and add to the Fixed Costs as shown below:

(£6.00 ×   500) + £6,000 = £ 9,000
(£6.00 × 1,000) + £6,000 = £12,000
→
(£6.00 × 3,500) + £6,000 = £27,000

(vi) Plot the Fixed and Variable Cost line as calculated.
(vii) Plot the Break-Even point at the position where Sales equal
Costs.

The broken line indicates the break-even point at 1,500 covers per
month which confirms the calculation made using the contribution
method in the previous section. We are now able to read the level of
profit or loss made by the restaurant at different sales volume, by
calculating the difference between Total Sales and Total Costs. For
example, the profit made for 2,500 covers may be read from the chart
as: Sales £25,000 less costs of £21,000 giving a net profit of £4,000.
Similarly, it is possible to read from the chart the number of covers
necessary to achieve a certain profit, by using the depth of the net
profit to show the amount required, and taking a line down to read off
the number of covers. For example, to show how many covers that
need to be sold to achieve a profit of £2,000, when the difference
between sales and total costs shows £2,000, the reading can be taken
off the horizontal axis as 2,000 covers.

It is important to note that when using break-even charts they must
be drawn accurately with the largest possible scale, in order to achieve
precise results.

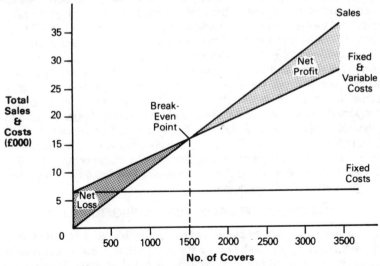

Fig. 2.12 *Example of a Break Even Chart*

107

Student Activity No. 2.11

A first class restaurant has fixed costs of £1,900 per week, serving a maximum of 200 covers per week. The average spend per cover is £28.00, variable costs are calculated at 35% of sales.

(i) Prepare a Break-Even chart showing the break-even point.

(ii) How many covers must be sold to achieve a profit of £750 per week?

Student Activity No. 2.12

A hotel has fixed costs of £16,000 per month. The average spending per guest is £18.00 per night with a variable cost of £5.00 per guest per night. The hotel has accommodation for 60 guests, assume the average month has 30 nights.

(i) Prepare a Break-Even chart showing the number of guests that have to stay in the hotel each month in order for it to break-even.

(ii) How many guests have to stay in the hotel to achieve a profit of £3,000 per month?

(iii) How much profit or loss is made if 1,000 guests stay at the hotel during one particular month?

Fixed and Variable Cost Considerations

It is important to consider at this stage the proportion of Fixed to Variable Costs that different types of hotel and catering operations may have. No two businesses are the same where their costing policies are concerned, thus making it impractical to be specific regarding these proportions. However, in general terms hotels and first class restaurants are regarded as having a greater reliance on fixed, rather than variable costs, either because of their location, greater space occupied by customer in area and time or in some cases both. These establishments also offer a higher degree of service to their customer, thus incurring higher fixed labour costs. Small restaurants, cafés, fast food operations and outdoor catering companies generally have less fixed costs and will therefore have a greater proportion of variable costs. It must be emphasised that there are exceptions to the proportions discussed. In the ideal world it would be better to have all costs as variable which would mean that it would be impossible for a business to make a loss. Therefore, the conclusion that can be drawn from this is that, the greater the proportion of variable costs the better, because a business would then have to sell less units (ie. meals and rooms) before it can break-even.

THE EFFECT OF SALES MIX ON PROFITABILITY

In the previous study book we defined Sales Mix as a breakdown of departmental sales in relation to the total sales, these departmental sales being expressed as a percentage of the total sales. The reasons for preparing a sales mix are two fold. The first reason, as we have previously learnt, is that it is for the purpose of comparing sales from period to period (usually monthly). The second reason is that the individual departments in a hotel and catering operation work on different profit margins. It is therefore necessary to breakdown total sales and calculate separate gross profits for each department. A hotel may decide that accommodation must make a 100% gross profit, food sales must make 65% gross profit and liquor sales 55% gross profit. The calculation of the total gross profit would therefore tell us nothing about the efficiency of the operation, as we do not know the proportion of the total sales for each department. Therefore an accommodation based operation would show a higher gross profit than an operation that relies on food and liquor as its main area of sale, yet both could be operating efficiently or, needless to say, inefficiently.

For example, a hotel has total sales of £51,620 for July, the sales mix shows the following breakdown of sales:

Acommodation Sales	52.1%
Food Sales	33.2%
Liquor Sales	14.7%

The Actual Sales for each department are calculated:

Accommodation	£51,620 × 52.1 ÷ 100 = £26,894
Food	£51,620 × 33.2 ÷ 100 = £17,138
Liquor	£51,620 × 14.7 ÷ 100 = £ 7,588

The Gross Profit for each department may be calculated assuming that accommodation makes 100%, food 65% and liquor 55%:

Accommodation		= £26,894
Food	£17,138 × 65 ÷ 100	= £11,140
Liquor	£ 7,588 × 55 ÷ 100	= £ 4.173
Total Gross Profit		= £42,207

A change in Sales Mix will affect the proportions of Sales and Gross Profit. If, for example, the hotel has sales of £51,750 for August and the sales mix is calculated as:

Acommodation Sales	55.1%
Food Sales	30.0%
Liquor Sales	14.9%

The Actual Sales for each department are calculated:

Accommodation	£51,750 × 55.1 ÷ 100 = £28,514
Food	£51,750 × 30.0 ÷ 100 = £15,525
Liquor	£51,750 × 14.9 ÷ 100 = £ 7,711

Assuming the Gross Profit % required is the same as in the previous month it may be calculated as follows:

Accommodation		= £28,514
Food	£15,525 × 65 ÷ 100	= £10,091
Liquor	£ 7,711 × 55 ÷ 100	= £ 4,241
Total Gross Profit		= £42,846

The difference in total gross profit between July and August is £639 and yet the difference in total sales is only £130. The reason for this may be attributed to a 3% increase in Accommodation Sales, causing a similar drop in Food Sales. Accommodation makes a greater contribution to total gross profit than food and the consequent affect is shown in the results. Naturally, a change in sales mix to food and liquor sales would have the affect of reducing the gross profit. The importance therefore of breaking down sales and gross profits by department must be emphasised if an operation wishes to make use of results to improve efficiency and productivity.

Student Activity No. 2.13

(i) The policy of The Bella Napoli Restaurant is to achieve a food gross profit of 60% and a liquor gross profit of 55%. The Sales Mix for October was: Food Sales 72.5%; Liquor Sales 27.5% on Total Sales of £9,140. Calculate:
   (a) The actual Liquor Sales and Gross Profit.
   (b) The Total Gross Profit.

(ii) The restaurant's owners are concerned about the low proportion of Liquor Sales and have decided on a sales drive to improve matters. The results for November were as follows: Sales Total £9,460; Sales Mix Food 63.5%; Liquor 36.5%. Calculate:
   (a) The Actual Food Sales and Gross Profit.
   (b) The Actual Liquor Sales and Gross Profit.
   (c) The Total Gross Profit.

(iii) Explain the reasons for the change in Total Gross Profit in relation to the change in Sales.

Student Actitity No. 2.14

The Accounts for the Metropole Hotel set out below show an analysis of the Trading results for 3 months ending 31 Dec 8__.
(i) Calculate the following:
   (a) Sales Mix.
   (b) Departmental Gross Profit.
   (c) Total Gross Profit.
   (d) Total Gross Profit %.

	Rooms	Food	Liquor	Total
Sales	91,460	37,120	19,240	147,820
— Cost of Sales	—	11,940	9,710	21,650
Gross Profit	91,460	25,180	9,530	126,170

(ii) Food and Liquor sales and costs increased proportionately by 10% during the next 3 months. Draw up a new set of trading results and calculate new sales mix and gross profit results.

(iv) Explain the change that has taken place in the Total Gross Profit %.

OPERATING STATEMENTS

An Operating Statement sets out all departmental sales, costs and profit and compares them with the forecasted results in both £ p and by percentage of sales or a period of trading, which is usually monthly. The statement shows the cost for the period in considerable detail as well as the accumulated figures since the start of the financial year. The forecasted figures are taken from the operations budget which is usually planned a year in advance, we will study the preparation of the different types of budget in Study Book 3. The actual figures are taken from the accounts of the operation, which we will study in the final section of this book. The forecasted and actual figures are compared for each period to check the efficiency of the operation; the accumulated figures are also checked to make sure that the operation is achieving its overall target. Any variances which are found between the actual and forecasted figures are thoroughly investigated; if the variance is outside the control of the management eg. rates or fuel price increases, then the forecast is adjusted accordingly. Variances that are within the control of the management eg. over staffing or wastage, causing costs to rise, are acted upon immediately to bring these costs into line with the budgeted figures.

It is important that figures entered on to the operating statement relate to the period in question and reflect their true value. In a detailed monthly operating statement certain fixed costs, such as Insurance for example, may be recorded as £90, normally insurance is paid annually. In order to reflect the fact that it is accrued over the whole year, the annual charge for insurance is divided by 12 and that amount is recorded on the statement for each month. This treatment is given to all fixed costs which are allocated annually, or half yearly, such as rates, depreciation of assets, advertising and other fees. Adjustments are made to other costs either to make them more accurate or when expenses are incurred in one cost area which relate to another. A good example of this is the treatment of Staff Meal costs.

Staff Meal Adjustments
The provision of meals for staff whilst they are on duty is regarded as part of their wages, the cost should therefore be included in the labour cost of an operation. However, the cost of the food consumed for this purpose is in most cases included in the food purchases for the operation. This will obviously have an adverse effect on the gross profit made by the kitchen because it is supposed to reflect the difference between food sales and the cost of those sales. Food used for other purposes will therefore have to be taken into consideration. It is therefore, necessary to calculate the cost of staff meals, deduct it from the food cost and add it to the labour cost. The effect of this adjustment is illustrated in figure 2.13 which shows the before and after

111

effect on the gross profit. Before staff meals were considered the gross profit was 64.7%, however, when the adjustment of £3,000 is made the gross profit is increased to 66.7%. The £3,000 cost of staff meals is added to the labour cost of the operation which will give a more accurate figure for that element of cost. The cost of staff meals may be calculated by one of two methods. Some operations calculate an average cost per employee, either per day, or per week, whereas others make an allowance of say 50p per meal and the kitchen is credited, according to the number of staff meals it serves. Very large organisations sometimes have a separate department for staff catering which is autonomous, that is, different food is purchased and prepared in its own kitchen by staff cooks, and consequently all the costs involved are also separate and appropriately dealt with.

Sales	£150,000	100%
— Food Consumed	£ 53,000	35.3%
Gross Profit	£ 97,000	64.7%
Adjustment for Staff Meal Cost of £3000		
Sales	£150,000	100%
— Food Consumed 53,000		
— Staff Meal Cost 3000	£ 50,000	33.3%
Gross Profit	£100,000	66.7%

Fig. 2.13 *Effect of Staff Meals on Gross Profit*

Student Activity No. 2.15
The Food and Beverage Department of the Ship Hotel has sales of £41,230 for the 4 week period ending 28 Feb 8__. The food consumed during that period was £17,110.
- (i) Calculate the % gross profit for the period. The hotel allows the chef 40p for each staff meal served, the organisation of staff employed by the hotel each day means that 25 staff take 2 meals every day and 13 take one meal per day.
- (ii) Calculate the cost of staff meals for the period.
- (iii) Calculate the true cost of food sales and express the new gross profit %.
- (iv) Calculate the change in gross profit % caused by the staff meals adjustment.

We have considered the adjustments that have to be made when calculating information for an operating statement, we will now look at an example. Figure 2.14 shows a simplified form of an operating statement for the food and beverage department of a medium size hotel. The sales have been taken from restaurant and banquet sales and the costs calculated from the relevant purchases and the appropriate adjustments made. Labour costs are calculated from the wages book to include the gross wages paid (ie. staff wages before tax and insurance deductions), the employer's national insurance contribution, holiday pay, pension and sickness contributions, if they are paid, and staff meals and accommodation allowances for all personnel working in that department. Consideration must also be given to wages and salaries paid to staff who are not directly working in the Food and Beverage department but supply some service to that department eg. management, maintenance and laundry staff. The meaning and method of calculation of these Indirect Labour Costs are explained more fully in the next study book along with indirect overheads. The overheads are calculated as those expenses incurred directly in the preparation and service of food eg. fuel, cleaning, administration and other expenses. Again there are expenses which are shared with the whole operation such as rates, rents, insurances etc, the food and beverage department will have to contribute a share of these costs. The net margin is regarded as the difference between the materials plus labour cost and the sales, it is often used in service industries where labour costs are high and need to be controlled.

GREEN LAWNS HOTEL Dept. Food & Beverage   Month: March
LLANDUDNO   Year End: June 8__

	Actual for Month		Budget for Month		Actual to Date		Budget to Date		Budget for Year	
	£	%	£	%	£	%	£	%	£	%
Sales	6,700	100	6,500	100	60,500	100	58,500	100	78,000	100
— Cost of Sales	2,479	37	2,275	35	21,780	36	20,475	36	27,300	35
Gross Profit	4,221	63	4,225	65	38,720	64	38,025	65	50,700	65
— Labour Costs	1,943	29	1,820	28	17,545	29	16,380	28	21,840	28
Net Margin	2,278	34	2,405	37	21,175	35	21,645	37	28,860	37
— Overhead Costs	1,474	22	1,430	22	13,915	23	12,870	22	17,160	22
Net Profit	804	12	975	15	7,260	12	8,775	15	11,700	15

Fig. 2.14   *Food and Beverage Dept. Operating Statement*

The example shown in figure 2.14 is for an operation which has an all year round trade which means that sales and costs should accrue evenly. It should be noted that there are some variances between the actual and budgeted figures; it is the responsibility of management and the departmental heads to investigate these variances and take appropriate action wherever necessary. Gross profit on sales is below target for the month by 2% but 1% on the figures to date may be attributed to higher food costs during this time of the year, which will adjust themselves by the end of the financial year in June, in which case the budgeted figures should be adjusted. Labour Costs are 1% higher than budgeted for. This may be due to over-staffing in some areas and will therefore need investigating more thoroughly. Alternatively, the increase may be due to increases in national insurance contributions by the government, necessitating a change in the budget.

Overhead costs are on target for the month concerned but are 1% above the budget for the year to date; this may be due to increased fuel consumption because of a hard winter or unforeseen price rises. Once again, appropriate action should be taken. Another reason for the increase in costs generally, could be attributed to the increase in sales affecting the variable cost behaviour. The overall effect of these cost increases is reflected in the net profit being 3% lower than the target figure. Whilst the budgeted net profit of 15% is on the low side for a hotel and catering operation, it must be realised that food sales are only a part of the total sales and that room sales contribute more to the total net profit than other areas of sales. In hotels, food sales, whilst being profitable in their own right, are also regarded as a service to the hotel guest, as we have previously mentioned.

An operating statement for a hotel is illustrated in figure 2.15 as it is set out in the 'Standard System of Hotel Accounting' published by the Economic Development Committee in 1969. This system of operating statement sets out six basic control levels to evaluate the difference between the actual and budgeted figures. These six levels are explained below in relation to the example in figure 2.15.

(i) Sales of the operated departments (ie. Rooms, Food, Liquor/Tobacco) are listed totalled and the Departmental Gross Profit is calculated by:
   Sales — Cost of Sales.

(ii) The Departmental Operating Profit is calculated by:
   Gross Profit — Labour Costs.

(iii) The Departmental Operating Profit is calculated by:
   Net Margin — Allocated Expenses.
   (Allocated expenses are those Overheads that can be directly attributed to a department).

(iv) The Operating Income of the hotel is calculated by:
   Departmental Profits + Other Income.
   (Other income is income gained from sales of newspapers etc, rents received from garages, sales, showcases etc.).

(v) The Operating Profit of the hotel is calculated by:
   Operating Income — Service Departments and General Expenditure.

(vi) The Net Operating Profit is calculated by:
   Hotel Operating Profit — Property Expenses.
   (Property expenses are depreciation, repairs and maintenance).

Student Activity No. 2.16
Prepare a Departmental Operating Statement similar to the illustration in figure 2.14 for the Food and Beverage Department of the Castle

114

This Period				Account	Year to Date			
Budget		Actual			Actual		Budget	
£	%	£	%	Detail	£	%	£	%
				OPERATED DEPARTMENTS				
				Net Sales				
5,000	35.7			Rooms				
6,000	42.9			Food				
3,000	21.4			Liquor & tobacco				
14,000	100.0			TOTAL NET SALES				
				Gross Profit				
5,000				Rooms				
4,010	66.8			Food				
1,140	38.0			Liquor & tobacco				
10,150	72.5			TOTAL GROSS PROFIT				
				Wages & staff costs				
1,300	26.0			Rooms				
1,800	30.0			Food				
460	15.3			Liquor & tobacco				
3,560	25.4			TOTAL WAGES & STAFF COSTS				
				Net margin				
3,700	74.0			Rooms				
2,210	36.8			Food				
680	22.6			Liquor & tobacco				
6,590	47.0			TOTAL NET MARGIN				
				Department operating profit				
3,400	68.0			Rooms				
1,810	30.1			Food				
530	17.7			Liquor & tobacco				
5,740	41.0			TOTAL DEPARTMENT OPERATING PROFIT				
500				OTHER INCOME				
6,240	44.5			HOTEL OPERATING INCOME				
				Service departments & general expenditure				
1,250	8.9			Administration				
550	3.9			Sales advertising & promotion				
520	3.7			Heat, light & power				
1,150	8.2			General expenditure				
(550)	(3.9)			Staff accommodation adjustment				
2,920	20.9			TOTAL SERVICE DEPARTMENTS & GENERAL EXPENDITURE				
3,320	23.7			HOTEL OPERATING PROFIT				
400	2.8			Repairs & maintenance				
450	3.2			Plant & machinery				
450	3.2			Property				
1,300	9.2							
2,020	14.5			HOTEL NET OPERATING PROFIT				
(60)				Non-operating income & expenditure				
1,960	14.0			NET PROFIT, before TAX				

Fig. 2.15 *Operating Statement set out as for Standard System of Accounts*

115

Point Hotel for the month of February from the information shown below:

	Budget for Year	Actual to Date	Budget to Date	Actual for Month	Budget For Month
Sales	£52,000	£12,210	£13,000	£4,050	£4,333
Cost of Sales	32%	£ 4,030	32%	£1,377	32%
Labour Cost	27%	£ 3,540	27%	£1,134	27%
Overhead Costs	20%	£ 2,500	20%	£ 850	20%

Further Reading

Food and Beverage Control: *Kotas and Davis* Chapter 3
Hotel and Catering Costing and Budgets: *Boardman* Chapters 19-20
Standard System of Hotel Accounting: *HMSO*

ASSESSMENT QUESTIONS

1. Explain the types of Costs involved in hotel and catering operations.
2. Give examples of the different types of Cost that may be found in hotel and catering operations.
3. Explain the importance of the 'Relevant Range' when considering Cost Behaviour.
4. Explain the difference between Total Costs and Unit Costs.
5. Define 'Contribution' and explain how it is calculated.
6. A fast food operation has £1,900 fixed costs per week. The average spending by each customer is £1.40, the establishment calculates its Variable Costs as 55% of Sales.
   Calculate:
   (a) The number of covers for the establishment to Break Even each week.
   (b) The number of covers to be served each week for the establishment to make a profit of £26,000 per year.
7. Prepare a Contribution Table from the information below:
   The Cromwellian serves 500-800 meals per week. The average spending per customer is £4.50. Variable costs account for 35% of sales and Fixed Costs are £1,750 per week. The table should cover a range of 500-800 customers at 50 customer intervals.
8. Mark's Seafood Bar has fixed expenses of £1,130 per week. The average spending per customer is anticipated to be £6.00. 55% of sales cover all Variable and Semi-Variable Costs. The restaurant's maximum capacity would be 120 covers per day (open 6 days per week).
   (a) Prepare a Break Even chart on a weekly basis from the information given.
   (b) Prepare a Contribution Chart from the information given on a weekly basis.

9. Define Sales Mix.
10. A hotel has sales of £870,400 per annum with a Sales Mix of Rooms 61%, Food 23% and Liquor 16%. The Gross Profit for each department is Rooms 100%, Food 55% and Liquor 60%. Calculate:
    (a) The Actual Sales per department.
    (b) The Gross Profit per deparment.
    (c) The Total Gross Profit.
11. Explain how staff meals are considered when calculating:
    (a) The Cost of Sales.
    (b) The Labour Cost.
12. Prepare a Departmental Operating Statement including percentages for the Avon Gorge Restaurant for the month of October from the following information:

	Budgeted Results	Actual Results
Sales	£10,500	£12,000
Food Costs	40%	£ 5,400
Labour Costs	20%	£ 2,400
Fixed Expenses	£ 1,200	£ 1,200
Variable Expenses	15%	£ 1,800
Net Profit	14%	£ 1,200

13. Butchers Bistro serves up to 540 meals per week, the average customer spending is £9.00 per head, with a Sales Mix of 70% Food and 30% Liquor. The Food Gross Profit is 65% and Liquor Gross Profit is 55%, other variable costs are 90p per customer. Fixed Costs (including semi-fixed) are £1,490 per week. Calculate:
    (a) The Break Even point in number of covers and Sales Volume for the bistro.
    (b) How much Profit is made if 350 meals are sold each week.
    (c) The maximum Profit that could be made each week.
    (d) How many covers must be sold to achieve a Net Profit of £300 in a week.

Departmental Costing and Pricing Methods

As we have previously explained and no doubt as you have learnt in other subjects, the hotel and catering industry sells a range of products and services to a variety of markets. These products and services have different proportions of costs in relation to materials consumed, labour involvement and overhead costs. The markets they are sold in have different demands regarding price and whether the product or service be for pleasure or necessity. We must also consider the sector of the industry and the profits required by commercial operations, the cost restrictions of institutional organisations and subsidies by industrial establishments. In this section we examine costing and pricing methods for different commodities, the factors which influence function costing and the pricing methods used in the various sectors of the industry.

FOOD AND BEVERAGE COSTING

The principle of all food and beverage costing is based on the unit of the sale ie. cost per portion or measure of drink, this unit cost is then used to calculate the selling price according to the profit margin required. Food and beverages are either purchased by the unit as in the case of steaks, bottled beers, wines etc. or they are purchased in bulk as in the case of joints of meats and bottles of spirit; it may also be said that most dishes are prepared in batches. Therefore, the first important aspect of food and beverage costing will be to ascertain the unit of sale and the unit price. We must also be aware that in most cases food and beverages cannot be costed per unit by using the same methods, therefore each must be considered separately.

Student Activity   No. 2.17
(i)   List foods items that can be purchased by the unit.
(ii)   List beverages that can be purchased by the unit.
(iii) List beverages that are purchased in bulk and dispensed to the customer by the unit.

Beverage Costing and Pricing
When costing and pricing beverages, both alcoholic and non-alcoholic, we must first establish the unit price as we have already mentioned in this section. All alcoholic beverages are purchased either by the unit or

118

in directly related multiples of units, this therefore makes costing of unit prices much easier. Whilst there is no legal requirement for the size of unit sold, a caterer must display in a prominent position the size of unit sold in his establishment for beers, wines and spirits. He must also use standard methods of dispense ie. optics, glasses or meters, all of which must comply with Weights and Measures regulations. Therefore once he has decided on his unit of sale for liquor he has certain legal requirements with which to comply.

Liquor items that are purchased by the unit are in most cases sold to the caterer at the unit price, the caterer is then easily able to calculate his selling price by adding on his gross profit. For example, if a caterer decides to make 60% gross profit on wines his selling price would be calculated:

Liquor Cost × 100 ÷ Liquor Cost % (ie. 40)

Therefore if he purchases wine at £2.20 per bottle the selling price would be calculated:

£2.20 × 100 ÷ 40 = £5.50

Liquor items that are purchased in multiple units ie. spirits, draught beers and aperitifs must firstly be calculated into a unit cost ie. cost per measure or pint etc. Unit cost for a standard bottle of spirits (75 centilitres — 26⅔ fl ozs) which hold 32 standard ⅙ gill measures would be calculated:

Cost per Bottle ÷ Number of Measures (ie. 32)

Therefore a bottle of whisky costing £8.40 would be costed per measure as:

£8.40 ÷ 32 = 26p

The calculation of the unit cost for draught beers will be considered in the same way. If a publican purchases a firkin of draught bitter (ie. 9 galls) for £32.40, which he wishes to sell by the pint, the cost per unit would be calculated using the same method as for spirits:

£32.40 ÷ 72 = 45p per pint

To fix the selling price of these items we use the same method of price calculation previously learned. ie:

Liquor Cost × 100 ÷ Liquor Cost %

Therefore if the publican wishes to make 65% gross profit on spirits and 45% gross profit on beer the selling prices would be calculated as follows:

Whisky: 26p × 100 ÷ 35 = 74p per measure
Beer: 45p × 100 ÷ 55 = 82p per pint

When caterers and publicans are considering the gross profit percentage for liquor pricing, they do not have an 'across the board' gross profit percentage, as is generally the case with food items. The different types of liquor are considered separately and each type has its own gross profit percentage. An example of this is listed below showing each general category of liquor and the gross profit margin that may be expected:

119

Draught Beer	45%
Bottled Beer	50%
Wines	55%
Spirits, Liqueurs & Aperitifs	65%
Soft Drinks, Mixers	65%

Mixed drinks such as cocktails should be costed by preparing a standard recipe for the drink as they are often not prepared by using standard units of dispense. When the standard recipe is prepared it is then costed and a price fixed using the same method we have shown. Care must also be taken when establishing the cost of bottled drinks such as Coca-Cola or Orange Juices because some companies sell them in different size crates or cases.

Non-alcoholic beverages, such as tea and coffee, need careful consideration when a unit cost and subsequent selling price are being established. Some operations may rely on convenient unit size products like tea bags, milk and sugar sachets which enables the caterer to easily calculate the cost and selling prices. When beverages are prepared in bulk a standard recipe cost should be prepared and according to the yield, the cost per portion or cup calculated as shown below. An important factor to be considered when establishing the unit cost of beverages is standardisation in portion by using specific cup sizes and assuming all customers take sugar and milk when listing ingredients.

Example: The production of a 3 pint brew of coffee with an equal quantity of milk being served in normal size cups (8oz size) with sugar would be costed as follows:

4oz Catering Blend Coffee @ 72p	=	72p
3 pints milk @ 24p per pint	=	72p
4oz Sugar @ 24p per lb	=	06p
Total Cost 6 pints (120fl oz)	=	£1.50

No of portions @ 8fl oz = 120 ÷ 8 = 15 cups

Therefore the cost per cup = £1.50 ÷ 15 = 10p

To establish a gross profit of 70% the selling price per cup is calculated:

10p × 100 ÷ 30 = 33p

Student Activity No. 2.18

Calculate the cost price per unit and the selling price for the following beverages:

(i) Bristol Cream Sherry (16 measures per bottle) @ £3.20 per bottle to achieve a gross profit of 65%.

(ii) A firkin of Best Bitter @ £30.24 to achieve a gross profit of 40%.

(iii) A case of 12 bottles of Cote du Rhone Villages @ £26.40 to achieve a gross profit of 60%.

(iv) Gordons Gin (32 measures per bottle) @ £7.90 per bottle to achieve a gross profit of 65%.

(v) A crate of 24 bottles of Coca-Cola @ £3.48 to achieve a gross profit of 65%.

(vi) 2oz of tea @ £1.60 per lb produces 1 gallon of tea plus 2 pints of milk @ 24p per pint. Tea is sold in 8oz cups and 6oz of sugar is provided @ 24p per lb. Gross profit required 70%.

Liquor Stock Pricing

It is generally regarded that cellar stock is valued at cost price, but for bar stock the value is calculated at selling price, because liquor is sold at different prices in the various bars or other departments of an operation eg. Room Service and Restaurants. We have already studied the costing and pricing of liquor consumed in Study Book 1 and stock valuation in the second section of this study. In this section we will use the bar selling price to establish the value of bar stock, for the purpose of calculating bar consumption in retail selling prices and subsequent comparison with cash receipts, to establish any discrepancies between them for control purposes.

When stock taking has taken place and a stock list has been prepared, as shown in figure 2.16, the value of each stock item is calculated. Bar stock is taken in units of sale therefore the value of each stock item is calculated by:

No. of Units × Selling Price per Unit

It should also be remembered from earlier study that bar requisitions are costed at the selling price to show the value of issues to the bar. The example shown in figure 2.16 may be extended, if required, to include the cost price of stock held and the gross profit made for each stock item if the operation so wishes. This information may then be used to double check with the cellarman's records and control.

RUNNYMEDE HOTEL				STOCK LIST	
BAR:				DATE:	
Bin No.	Item	No. of Measures (Units)	Per Measure		Stock Value at Selling Price
			Size	Selling Price	
72	Bottled Guinness	40	½pt	60p	24.00
79	Schweppes Tonic	60	Baby	32p	19.20
86	Smirnoff Vodka	67	sixth gill	65p	43.55
88	Bacardi Rum	82	sixth gill	70p	57.40
104	Directors Bitter	59	pint	90p	53.10
105	Harp Lager	85	pint	92p	79.05
120	Wine (house)	46	5oz glass	60p	27.60

Fig. 2.16 *Example of Bar Stock List calculated at Retail Selling Value*

Student Activity   No. 2.19

Complete the missing spaces in the stock list below, by calculating either the number of units, selling price per unit or the stock value at selling price:

Item	No. of Units	Selling Price Per Unit	Stock Value At Selling Price
Draught Bass	164	86p	
Carlsberg Lager	94		86.48
Bells Whisky	62	62p	
Lambs Rum	35		21.70
Courvoisier Brandy		70p	38.50
Sweet Martini	31	55p	
Dubonnet	18	60p	
Ginger Ales	105		33.60
House Wine		60p	24.60
Pepsi Cola	39		13.65
Mackeson	19		11.02
Barley Wine	26	58p	

Student Activity   No. 2.20

(i)   From Student Activity No. 2.8 calculate the value of the liquor stock in the college restaurant at retail prices.
 (a) The Opening Stock.
 (b) The Purchases and Issues for the week.
 (c) The Closing Stock.
 (d) The value of wine sold for the week.

(ii)   Check with the actual wine receipts for the week and establish any variance there might be.

Food Costing

In the first study book we examined methods of dish and menu costing by using standard recipes and exercising portion control emphasising their importance and the need for accuracy. We have also examined in this study book the need to carry out test yields on raw meats to establish the edible, and therefore usable, amount when they have been prepared. An important aspect of test yields is to establish the cost per portion of usable meat as shown in figure 2.3.

We are able to calculate the yield in weight of cooked meats and fish from a given weight of the raw commodity by using the following method:

Usable weight of Cooked Meat/Fish ÷ Raw weight of Meat × 100

This calculation will give us the yield percentage which we are able to use in calculating the usable meat price by applying the following method:

Raw Meat price per kg (lb) ÷ Yield Percentage × 100

We are able to calculate the cost per portion from the usable meat price providing the portion size has been established. If, for example, a 100gm portion size is decided upon, thus yielding 10 portions per kilo, the cost per portion may be calculated by using the following method:

Usable Meat price per kg ÷ 10

An alternative method to establish the cost per portion from a test yield would be to count the number of portions yielded from the raw meat and divide them into the total raw cost. This method is satisfactory providing the portion size is constant, the end result also establishes the portion size which may then be used to calculate the portion cost by the first method shown.

Example:

A restaurant purchases a Turbot weighing 3.8kg @ £2.85 per kg. A yield test produced 2.1kg of cooked fish, the required portion size is 100gm.

$$\text{Yield \%} = 2.1\text{kg} \times 100 \div 3.8\text{kg} = 55.2\%$$

$$\text{Usable Cost per kg} = £2.85 \times 100 \div 55.2 = £5.16 \text{ per kg}$$

$$\text{Cost per portion} = £5.16 \div 10 = £0.52 \text{ each}$$

It is important therefore that when calculating food costs yield tests are carried out on all expensive commodities. When a yield percentage has been established it may be applied to calculate the new usable commodity price whenever there is a change in the price of the raw materials. This new price is then used to calculate the change in the cost per portion and the selling price adjusted accordingly. However, it must be emphasised that any change in either the purchase specification or method of preparation will affect the yield percentage and consequently portion costs. Therefore such changes will necessitate a new yield test to ensure the costing policy of an operation is maintained.

Student Activity No. 2.21

A yield test on an oven ready turkey weighing 7.5kg costing £1.22 per kg produced 3.7kg of usable meat.

(i) The establishment decides to serve a 120gm portion per customer. Calculate:

(a) The Yield %.

(b) The usable meat cost per kg.

(c) The cost per portion.

(d) The selling price per portion to achieve a gross profit of 60%.

FUNCTION COSTING AND PRICING

When we consider function costing and pricing for events such as weddings and banquets there are different methods that can be chosen. A function in its most basic form may be costed in the normal manner for a dish or menu, however, this usually applies to small events. With larger functions however it is possible for the caterer to be more accurate in establishing the costs involved rather than estimating them. Whilst it will be necessary to estimate profits and some overheads such as those of a fixed nature, other costs which are directly concerned with the function may be easily calculated. The concept of function costing is therefore to establish the direct costs involved to cover food, extra labour and special costs eg. disco hire, and add on a percentage to cover fixed labour, fixed overheads and profit.

The food costs are established by using a standard recipe cost for each dish involved and the total calculated according to the number of covers being catered for. Wages for such functions will have a dual nature; those attributed to permanent members of staff eg. management and kitchen brigade, and those directly engaged for the function eg. casual waiting and cloakroom staff. Overheads are also of a dual nature; a consideration must be made to cover the fixed and semi-variable costs, as well as directly related overheads such as laundry and stationery. Other costs involved directly with the function are also taken into consideration, these will depend on the type of function being planned, but will include such extras as flowers, wedding cakes, disco and band hire, toast masters and other irregular charges. The costs are then totalled and a percentage profit calculated to fix a selling price for the function. The price quoted to the customer will usually be per head but in some cases the actual total will be used for the quotation. The example shown below uses this method of function costing and pricing to achieve both a totally inclusive price and a price per head.

Example:

A wedding party for 200 guests has selected a sit down wedding breakfast with a food cost of £3.35 per head, they have also requested floral decorations costing £80, printed menus costing £24 and a discotheque costing £65 to follow the wedding breakfast. Drinks are to be quoted separately. It is the policy of the establishment to charge 20p per head to cover laundry costs and to allocate 25% of the selling price to cover fixed labour and overhead charges. They also wish to make a profit of 15% on all functions. The calculation of the selling price would be prepared as follows:

Food Cost:	200 covers @ £3.35	= £670.00
Labour Cost:	20 part-time waiting staff	
	for 4 hrs @ £3.50 per hour	= £280.00
Overhead Costs:	Laundry 200 @ 20p	= £ 40.00
	Stationery (Menus)	= £ 24.00
Other Costs:	Floral Decorations	= £ 80.00
	Discotheque Hire	= £ 65.00
Total known Direct Costs		£1159.00

Allocated Indirect Costs	= 25%
Required Net Profit	= 15%
Total Unknown Costs/Profit	= 40%
Total Known Costs	= 60%
Total Selling Price	= 100%

Selling Price calculated by:

$$\text{Known Costs} \times 100 \div \text{Known Cost \%}$$
$$= £1159 \times 100 \div 60 = £1932$$

Cost per cover calculated by:

$$\text{Total Cost} \div \text{Number of Covers}$$
$$= £1932 \div 200 = £9.66$$

The important aspect of calculating a selling price for functions by using this method is the relationship between known and unknown costs. Known costs by their name alone are easily calculated when all costs which relate directly to the function are ascertained. Unknown costs can only be expressed as a percentage of sales. Sales are regarded as 100% and all costs are expressed as a percentage of them, therefore we are able to calculate the known costs percentage by subtracting the unknown cost percentage from the sales (ie. 100%). In the example the known cost percentage is calculated by Sales (100%) — Unknown Costs (40%) = 60%. This enables us to calculate the selling price for the function and the price per cover by using the methods shown in the example.

An alternative method of function pricing would be to calculate the cost of the wedding breakfast, the extra labour involved and add on the allocated percentage to cover overheads and profit. The extra items involved being separately calculated to cover their costs, overheads and net profit contribution. All prices are then quoted separately to the customer. This method is not generally used in the industry except perhaps when quoting prices for conferences or similar events.

Price Sensitivity
We have examined two methods of costing and pricing functions, it can be said that the industry in most cases prefers to quote a price per head. The reason for this is 'price sensitivity' on the part of the

customer. The customer prefers a cost per head which is fully inclusive, rather than a cost per head for the meal and extra charges added on. Psychologically a fully inclusive price per head will seem less to them, as the cost of all extras are spread over all persons attending the function, which will make them seem less. For instance, a function for 100 people with a meal cost of £4.50 per head and extra costs of £250 to cover bands, discos etc, will seem a lot more than £7.00 per head, fully inclusive. This will help the customer to plan their costs if they have to meet their own budget limitations or fix a price for tickets to a dinner dance or similar function. There is however a danger of a price per head being too high and frightening potential customers off. This may often happen if drinks are included in the price quoted, therefore there is a tendency to quote these prices separately, unless the customer specifically asks for them to be quoted. Where the pricing of drinks for such functions are concerned they are usually sold at the normal retail price, the establishment is able to cover the costs involved and profit required within the normal pricing structure for liquor products. It is sometimes necessary to fix a price which is fully inclusive of an aperitif and wine for some types of function, such as Christmas parties. In these cases the caterer must attempt to balance the cost structure of the meal between food and drink costs, being aware that he may have to cut his profit on either or both in order to increase sales overall. Another consideration when pricing functions may well be to reduce prices at certain times of the year or even days of the week in order to generate sales. For example most functions are held on Thursday, Friday or Saturday nights; there is a banquet or dinner dance season from November to February and people tend to get married in the spring and summer. The caterer therefore may wish to cut back on his profit margin in off season periods in order to stimulate sales.

Where the pricing of functions is concerned the caterer must be aware of the price sensitivity of the customer and approach his pricing methods accordingly. It may be necessary to quote each price on its individual constraints and the type of customer involved.

Student Activity No. 2.22
A banquet is prepared for 60 covers, the customer has selected a menu with a food cost of £2.85 per cover, extra labour charges are 6 waitresses for 4 hours @ £4 per hour, overheads for the function are £55, a profit of 15% is required. Calculate:
(i) The selling price per cover.
(ii) The gross profit per cover.

Student Activity No. 2.23
A sailing club has selected a menu costing £3.45 per cover for a dinner dance for 280 guests. They also request a dance band costing £120, special menus and tickets printed costing £84.

The hotel will staff the event by using casual waiting staff serving 10 covers each and being paid £18 each for the evening's work, 2 cloak room staff at £15 each are also to be provided. Overheads are to be costed at 20% of sales and a net profit of 15% is required.

(i) Calculate the following:
    (a) The Selling Price per customer to include VAT at 15%.
    (b) The Gross Profit % being attained.
    (c) The Net Profit made from the function excluding VAT.
(ii) Prepare an Invoice for the sailing club.

Student Activity   No. 2.23A

Your college student union has asked your department to cater for its Christmas Ball estimating 300 people will attend. You are required to:

(i) Prepare a menu suitable for the function.
(ii) Cost the menu per head.
(iii) Calculate the labour cost, assuming a kitchen brigade of 10 is necessary and waiting staff on a ratio of 1 to 12 guests for a sit down meal or 1 to 25 guests for a buffet.
(iv) Fix a selling price to include the following costs:
    (a) Allow 10% of sales to cover overhead charges.
    (b) The college charges £50 to cover room hire and caretaker costs.
    (c) Disco-hire of £70 is to be included in the quoted price.
    (d) Posters and tickets cost £50 to be printed.
    (e) No profit is required.

INDUSTRIAL CATERING PRICING

Many large factories and companies provide catering for their employees while they are at work in the form of canteen facilities which provide meals and snacks. This facility was first provided during the war to ensure that workers had a nourishing meal in times of food rationing and to boost morale generally. Employers after the war continued the practice and it is now regarded as a major part of any staff welfare policy.

The costs involved in providing these facilities for staff are often large; the purchasing of equipment for kitchens and dining rooms, day to day running costs to cover labour and overheads and the cost of the food provided all need to be considered. In commercial operations all these costs, as well as profit, is charged to the customer in the selling price. This would be impractical in industrial and commercial operations and would probably result in staff not using the facilities and therefore defeating the objectives involved.

Therefore companies subsidise their staff catering facilities, some to a greater degree than others, according to their individual policies. Let us look at methods of subsidies that take place.

(i) A company may have its own independently run catering department, the company providing the necessary equipment, paying all running costs and for the materials used. Employees will pay for their meals, the price charged will either cover the food costs or the food costs and a proportion of the running costs. The remaining costs will be paid by the company as a subsidy in their operating costs.

(ii) A company will provide the facilities and pay overhead costs, they will then engage a contract catering company to manage the operation by providing catering staff and food. The contractors will charge the employees to cover their costs and profit requirement.

(iii) A company will engage a catering contract company to provide the necessary equipment, and pay their own running expenses and food costs. Employees will be charged a set price for their meals, the difference between the price paid and actual costs will be paid to the contractor by the company and be recorded as a subsidy.

A subsidy may therefore be defined as the difference between the actual costs involved in the provision of meals for employees and the amount actually paid by the employee. The calculation of selling prices for industrial catering operations will therefore depend on the amount of subsidy granted by the company. In the first example shown the company is subsidising employees catering to cover all costs except food, which the employee will be expected to pay.

Example 1

The food costs in providing employees meals are budgeted at £1,000 a week for 150 employees working 5 days. Therefore the selling price per meal would be calculated by:

Budgeted Food Cost ÷ Number of Meals Sold

$$= 1000 \div (150 \times 5) = £1.33$$

Another application of this method would be to cost each dish individually and charge the customer accordingly. However this would involve a different price being charged each day, which is often impractical to handle and may also lead to confusion or resentment on the part of the employee. The Catering Manager will work to either a weekly or monthly budget period, the daily food cost will vary according to the menu offered but he will be expected to average this out over the period. Snacks and beverages are usually individually priced.

Example 2

The average cost per meal is calculated at £1.10 from the budgeted food cost per month in a factory. The company policy is that employees must also pay a contribution towards labour and overheads of the canteen amounting to 15% of sales. Therefore the selling price is calculated:

Food Cost × 100 ÷ % Food Cost
= £1.10 × 100 ÷ 85 = £1.29

Some companies may use a 'cost plus' method of pricing to cover a contribution towards other costs. For example, the selling price with a 15% contribution would be calculated using this method by:

Food Cost + 15% of Food Cost = Selling Price
eg. £1.10 + (£1.10 × 15 ÷ 100) = £1.10 + 17p = £1.27

Example 3

An Insurance Company has decided to provide catering facilities for its employees; the estimated demand from the 350 employees would be on average 75% for 5 days a week for 48 weeks a year for lunch only.

The company has researched the costs involved in providing the facilities as:

Operating Overheads	£25,000 per annum
Labour Costs	£52,000 per annum
Food Cost per meal	£1.20

The company has decided to charge employees £1 for lunches taken, the remaining costs will be subsidised by them.

Estimated Sales	350 × 75 ÷ 100 × 5 × 48 × £1.00 =	£ 63,000
Estimated Food Cost	350 × 75 ÷ 100 × 5 × 48 × £1.20 =	75,600
Estimated Labour Cost	=	52,000
Estimated Overhead Cost	=	25,000
Estimated Total Cost		£152,600

Subsidy = £152,600 − £63,000 = £89,600
Subsidy per meal = £89,600 ÷ 63,000 = £1.42
% Subsidy = 89,600 ÷ 152,600 × 100 ÷ 1 = 59%

Fig. 2.17 *Example of Budgeted Operating Statement for Industrial Catering Subsidies*

From the budgeted operating statement expenditure can be calculated to show the amount of subsidy necessary to run a catering facility and the cost per employee assessed. In addition to this the company will also have to pay for the equipment necessary and provide the space for the operation to take place. Against this they will have to evaluate the benefits involved in providing facilities for their employees.

Student Activity No. 2.24

The food costs in providing employees with meals are budgeted at £2,760 a week for 600 employees working 5 days a week. The labour and overhead costs are estimated to be £2,410 per week.

(i)　Calculate the following selling prices per meal for the operation:
　　(a)　To cover food costs.
　　(b)　To cover food costs and 20% expenses.
　　(c)　To cover food costs and a 20% of selling price contribution towards the labour and overhead expenses.
　　(d)　To cover food costs and a cost plus contribution of 20% towards expenses.

129

(ii)   Calculate the subsidy that would be paid by the company using the pricing methods in (a), (b) and (c) in total and per meal.

A LA CARTE MENU COSTING AND PRICING

The principle of á la carte menus, that each dish is individually priced and the customers make their own selection from the choice presented, makes pricing straightforward. In the first study book we examined dish costing and pricing to achieve a desired gross profit. This method is used for á la carte menu costing and pricing.

ie. Food Cost × 100 ÷ Food Cost Percentage

Some dishes served in speciality restaurants such as French, Indian and Chinese will have to be prepared for more than one person eg. Châteaubriand. Therefore the cost and price must be considered accordingly and indicated to the customer.

The gross profit percentage for á la carte menus will vary according to the type of establishment, its financial constraints and the market aimed at.

High Margin Return

A High Margin Return is generally used in first class restaurants which will have high operating expenses due to their location and service offered to customers. Therefore the gross profit made on sales will have to cover these high costs and the operation will be said to have a 'high margin return'. The percentage gross profit will range from 65% to as high as 75 or 80%.

Low Margin Return

A Low Margin Return is used for operations such as Cafés and fast food operations. In these, operating expenses are lower due to a lesser degree of service given to customers, because they are sited in cheaper locations and because less space is necessary. Therefore the gross profit made on sales will have less costs to cover before a profit is made; these operations will be said to have a 'low margin return'. The percentage gross profit will range from as low as 45-50% to 65%.

Margin Variations

Because of price sensitivity some operations will vary their margin return on certain courses or dishes to give a better balance to menu prices. This policy is most often carried out in popular catering operations as it can be said that in first class operations customers are not so discerning about price as those who use the lower end of the market. An example of margin variations is that if an overall gross margin of 60% is required, expensive main course dishes will be priced using a 50% gross profit and cheaper dishes such as starters and desserts will be priced using a 70% gross profit.

Selling Price Calculations

If it is assumed that a standard food cost has been calculated and a gross profit margin established, we are then able to calculate the selling price of menu items. The method of calculation is the same as previously considered:

ie. Food Cost × 100 ÷ Food Cost %

Example

If a restaurant using a high margin return pricing policy of 70% gross profit, costs a dish at £2.70, the selling price is calculated:

£2.70 × 100 ÷ 30 = £9.00

When service charge of 12½% and VAT of 15% are added the selling price is calculated:

£ 9.00 + (9.00 × 12.5 ÷ 100)
= £ 9.00 + £1.12
= £10.12 + (10.12 × 15 ÷ 100)
= £10.12 + £1.52
= £11.64

Therefore the selling price would probably be quoted on the menu at £11.65.

Student Activity No. 2.25

The Dolphin Steak House has a mixed margin approach to its pricing; from the shortened menu, dish costs and required profit margins shown below, price the menu to include service charge at 10% and VAT at 15%.

Dish	Cost Price	Gross Profit %
Egg Mayonnaise	41p	65%
Chilled Honeydew Melon	30p	65%
Cream of Asparagus Soup	20p	70%
Prawn Cocktail	69p	60%
Grilled Rump Steak	£2.68	55%
Grilled Dover Sole	£3.15	55%
Mixed Grill	£2.54	55%
(All main courses include vegetables)		
Banana Split	38p	65%
Dutch Apple Tart	24p	65%
Cheese & Biscuits	36p	65%
Coffee	11p	65%

Cost and Contribution Calculations

When we are given the selling price of a dish and the target gross profit, we are able to calculate the food cost of the dish concerned by using the following calculations:

(i)   Selling Price (100%) — Gross Profit % = Food Cost %
(ii) Selling Price × Food Cost % ÷ 100

131

Example
If the selling price of a dish is £6.20 and the required gross profit is 55%, the dish cost would be calculated:
(i) 100% — 55% = 45%
(ii) £6.20 × 45 ÷ 100 = £2.79
If the selling price included VAT @ 15% and service charge @ 10% we would have to calculate the net selling price by:
£6.20 ÷ 1.15 = £5.39 selling price incl. 10% service charge
£5.39 ÷ 1.10 = £4.90 net selling price
£4.90 × 45 ÷ 100 = £2.20 Food cost
When calculating the customer's contribution to fixed overheads and net profit, we use the method adopted in an earlier section of this book (ie. Selling Price — Variable Cost = Contribution). In some operations the only variable cost may well be the food cost, in which case the gross profit figure per meal or dish will also be the contribution. Other operations may also consider some elements of labour and overheads to be variable, as we have already discovered. In these cases, either a percentage of the selling price is considered variable, or a fixed amount per cover.

Example
The selling price of a dish is £3.50 and the required gross profit is 60% with 10% of sales said to cover variable wages and overheads. The total variable cost would be calculated:
Food Cost (40%) + Other Variable Costs (10%) = 50%
Therefore the variable cost for the dish is calculated:
£3.50 × 50 ÷ 100 = £1.75
The remaining amount of the selling price will be the contribution towards the fixed costs and net profit required.
ie. £3.50 — £1.75 = £1.75

Student Activity   No. 2.26
In activity No. 2.25 The Dolphin Steak House allows 8% of its sales to cover variable elements of wages and overheads. Calculate the contribution each dish makes towards the fixed costs and net profit requirement of the steak house.

ACCOMMODATION COSTING

With food and beverage costing and pricing we have used the cost of materials as the main factor when determining costs, gross profits and selling prices. However, when we consider accommodation costing the use of raw materials directly related to the sale of rooms is minimal. The variable costs involved in the sale of accommodation are laundry, 'give aways' such as stationery and book matches and the variable elements of labour and overheads. Therefore, the principle of accommodation costing is to cover the high fixed costs which are incurred by accommodation based operations. As we have already examined in food and beverage costing, the differences between selling price and variable costs contribute to cover the fixed costs and net profit. We also apply this principle to accommodation costing because the fixed costs are higher, therefore the contribution must be greater per unit (room) of sale. For example, if the selling price of a room for the night is £25 and the variable cost is established at £3 per night to cover laundry and lighting etc., the contribution will be £22. This principle makes the fixing of selling prices more difficult for accommodation than for food and beverages. Whilst accommodation pricing is at a higher level of study the basic principle is that a hotel must establish its fixed costs and the profit required. This amount is then spread over each day of the year and divided by the number of rooms available, to establish the fixed cost per room per night. The main problem is that this calculation assumes that the hotel is full every night and this is most unlikely in any operation. It must be remembered that a room which is empty for the night can not be re-sold unlike food and liquor sales which in most cases can be sold the next day. A consideration is therefore made as to the average occupancy of the hotel ie. rooms occupied, against rooms available. For example, if a hotel with 20 bedrooms which is open all the year round, with an average occupancy of 50% (ie. 10 rooms occupied per night) which has fixed costs of £39,600 and wishes to make £15,000 net profit, the contribution each room must make is calculated as follows:

Fixed Costs + Net Profit ÷ Number of rooms sold per year

(£39,600 + 15,000) ÷ (20 × 365 × 50%)

£54,600 ÷ 3650 = £14.95 (say £15.00)

The contribution is then added to the variable cost of say £3 per room per night to fix a selling price of £18.00. The advantage of using this method is that if sales increase above 50% occupancy then the hotel makes substantially more profits. The danger is that if sales drop then there is a substantial drop in profits. A hotel that wishes to quote inclusive terms (ie. bed and breakfast or full board) will add the selling price of the meals to the room rate. Some hotels may wish to quote a per person rate, in which case the number of guests that the hotel can accommodate is used instead of the number of rooms. An added advantage is that if a hotel wishes to increase its occupancy levels by promoting 'bargain weekends' it only has to cover its variable costs in order to make additional profit. This method is known as marginal costing, which we will examine in closer detail in the next study book.

Student Activity   No. 2.27
The Fistral Beach Hotel has 30 bedrooms and is open 200 days a year with an average occupancy of 60%. The variable cost per room is £3.50 per night and fixed costs to be covered are £21,000 and the net profit required is £15,000.

(i)   Calculate the contribution required per room per night to cover the fixed costs and profit.

(ii)   Calculate the selling price per room per night.

(iii) Calculate the selling price per room per night to include breakfast which is normally priced at £3.20 (assume one person per room for this calculation).

VALUE ADDED TAX

In the first study guide we examined Value Added Tax (VAT) and how it applies to the sale of hotel and catering services. We must now examine the principles and practice of VAT and attempt to understand how they apply to the hotel and catering industry. VAT is an indirect tax levied on non-essential services or luxury goods; what is regarded as non-essential or luxury is open to argument in some cases. The rate of VAT, currently at 15%, is known as the standard rate, goods and services that are not taxed are either known as zero rated or exempt, eg. foods, heating fuels etc.

The principle of VAT is that it is levied at all stages of production or at each stage in a transaction. This principle is illustrated in figure 2.18 Where a hotel guest purchases a bottle of wine for £6.00 plus 90p VAT. The wine has passed through the hands of the producer, shipper and the hotel before being sold to the guest. At each stage the seller has added 15% on to the price to cover VAT, but all purchasers can claim back the VAT they paid when purchasing, that is except the hotel customer. So, for example, the shipper sells the wine to the hotel and collects 45p VAT. However, the shipper paid 15p VAT to the producer, therefore the shipper sends the difference of 30p to the Customs and Excise. We can see from the illustration that the guest's 90p is paid to the Customs and Excise by the producer 15p, the shipper 30p and the hotel 45p. These payments and collections of VAT are known as inputs and outputs. Inputs may be defined as the VAT paid by traders when purchasing goods and services. Outputs may be defined as the VAT collected by traders when selling goods and services. The principle of VAT involves the trader paying to the Customs & Excise the difference between the outputs and the inputs.

The practice of VAT is that traders who supply goods and services on which VAT is chargeable must register with the Customs & Excise if their turnover is in excess of £18,700 (1985). This minimum turnover figure is increased every year, usually in line with inflation. The traders must record all transactions their business makes during the course of trading. The minimum details that must be recorded for VAT purposes are: date of transaction, suppliers name or customer details, amount exclusive of VAT paid or charged and the VAT paid or collected. An example of a purchase record and a sales record are shown in figures

2.19 and 2.20. The traders must then send to the Customs and Excise every three months the balance between their outputs and inputs the totals of which are entered onto a standard form known as the VAT return. Traders may be subjected to periodic inspections from Customs and Excise inspectors who will ask to see all the supporting documentation, ie. Purchases and Sales Records etc and marry them up with the quarterly tax returns made by the trader. Naturally, any falsifying of returns will lead to the prosecution of the trader by the Customs and Excise authorities.

All hotel and catering operations must register for VAT (ie. if their turnover exceeds the minimum level) as almost all hotel and catering services are liable to VAT. The exceptions to this are listed below:

Hotels — Charges for newspapers and visitors paid out (VPO) as the tax has been paid elsewhere. Room rates do not apply to guests who stay longer than 4 weeks but the charges for any services provided are taxed. For example, if a hotel charges £105 per room, per week, which is broken down as £85 rent and £20 for services such as cleaning, TV hire etc, then VAT would be charged on the £20 (ie. £3 VAT.) The guest would also have to pay VAT on all meal charges.

Institutional Catering — The supply of accommodation and meals in hospitals, schools and colleges are exempt from VAT except those which are sold to staff and visitors.

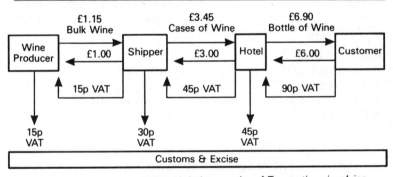

Fig. 2.18 *Example showing VAT paid during a series of Transactions involving the Purchase of a bottle of Wine*

Date	Details	Inv. No.	Net Price	VAT
01 Nov 8__	Youngs Seafood Ltd	17213	126.50	
01 Nov 8__	Fullers Brewery	AK87	310.60	46.59
02 Nov 8__	Sacombe Speed Ltd	4081	108.20	16.23
03 Nov 8__	Cash & Carry	473560	171.83	1.42
04 Nov 8__	Linen Hire Ltd	D774	32.50	4.88
04 Nov 8__	John Chop (Butcher)	46	46.50	

Fig. 2.19 *Example of a VAT Purchases Record*

All Purchases Invoices should be kept for at least 3 years to support entries made above in case of VAT inspection.

Date	Details	Net Price	VAT
02 Nov 8__	Cash Sales — Food	77.20	11.58
	— Liquor	405.60	60.84
03 Nov 8__	Cash Sales — Food	94.60	14.19
	— Liquor	626.30	93.94
03 Nov 8__	J. Arthur Party	75.00	11.25

Fig. 2.20 *Example of a VAT Sales Record*

Sales Invoices, Till Rolls, Banking Recepits etc. should be kept for at least 3 years to support entries made above in case of VAT inspection.

Student Activity   No. 2.28
(i)   Find out the current rate of VAT chargeable to hotel and catering services and list the types of establishment that it applies to.
(ii) Find out the current minimum turnover that operations must exceed before registering with the Customs and Excise.

Student Activity   No. 2.29
A guest stays in a hotel on bed and breakfast terms for 7 weeks at a rate of £140 per week excluding VAT. A breakdown of the rate shows that the hotel allows £5 per day to cover breakfast and services provided. Calculate the amount of VAT the guest will have to pay at the end of the stay.

Further Reading
Hotel Costing and Budgets: Banquets/Meat Costing   *Boardman*
Catering Costing and Control: Industrial Catering/Meat Costing   *Paige*
Food and Beverage Control: Chapter 8   *Kotas and Davis*
HM Customs and Excise Notice No. 709
Innkeeping: Chapter 13

ASSESSMENT QUESTIONS
1.   Calculate the cost price per unit and the selling price for the following beverages:
   (a) A firkin of Best Bitter @ £34.20 to achieve a gross profit of 45%.
   (b) A bottle of Bells Whisky (32 measures) @ £8.20 per bottle to achieve a gross profit of 65%.
   (c) A crate of 24 Pils Lager @ £8.75 to achieve a gross profit of 55%.
   (d) A case of 12 bottles of Niersteiner Domtal costing £17.88 to achieve a gross profit of 60%.

136

2. Calculate the retail selling value of the following bar stock.

Item	No. of Units	Cost per Unit	Gross Profit %
Piesporter Michelberg	14	£1.69	55
Macon	11	£2.46	55
Courvoisier VSOP	64	32p	65
Orange Curacao	30	31p	65
Britvic Orange	36	16p	60

3. A yield test on a Tamar Salmon weighing 6.4 kilos costing £4.60 per kilo produced 5.2 kilos of usable fish. The establishment decides to serve a 60gm portion for fish courses and 100gm portion for main courses. Calculate:
   (a) The yield %.
   (b) The usable fish cost per kilo.
   (c) The cost per portion for fish and main courses.
   (d) The selling price per portion for fish and main courses to achieve a gross profit of 65%.

4. List the costs that are considered when pricing functions.

5. Harrogate Rotary Club has selected a menu costing £4.10 per cover for its Presidents Ball, it is estimated 300 guests will attend. They also request a dance band costing £150 and a master of ceremonies costing £40. The hotel will staff the event by employing 34 casual staff for 4 hours each at £4.25 per hour. Overheads are costed at 22% of sales and a net profit of 16% is required from functions. Calculate the following:
   (a) The selling price per customer to include VAT at 15%
   (b) The net profit made from the function excluding VAT.
   (c) The VAT payable on this function.

6. Define the term 'subsidy' as it is used in industrial catering operations.

7. A light engineering company plans to provide a mid day meal for its 3000 employees. A survey estimates that 70% of employees will use this facility. The company estimates the food costs for serving meals 6 days per week will be £8,000, labour and overhead costs will be £8,200 per week. Calculate the following selling prices per meal that the operation could charge according to the policy it selects:
   (a) Covering food costs only.
   (b) Covering food costs and 20% of expenses.
   (c) Covering food costs and a cost plus contribution of 20% towards expenses.
   (d) Calculate the subsidy the company would make each week for the policies (b) and (c).

8. Define 'High Margin Return' and 'Low Margin Return'.

9. (a) 'Sally Burger' has a mixed margin approach to its pricing. From the abbreviated menu and information shown below, price the dishes listed to include a service charge of 5% and VAT at 15%.

Dish	Cost Price	Gross Profit %
Sally Burger	42p	50%
Sally Cheese Burger	53p	50%
Mixed Salad	18p	60%
French Fries	11p	70%
Apple Pie	13p	65%
Coffee	10p	65%

(b) 'Sally Burger' allows 10% of its sales to cover variable costs. Calculate the contribution each dish makes towards the fixed costs and overheads.

10. Explain the principles of accommodation costing.

11. Explain the principles of charging VAT.

12. Draw up purchases and sales records suitable for recording transactions which include VAT.

13. List catering activities on which VAT is not charged.

14. A guest stays in a hotel on demi-pension terms for 9 weeks at a rate of £165 per week excluding VAT. The hotel allows £10 per day to cover meals and services provided. Calculate the amount of VAT the guest will have to pay at the end of the stay.

Principles and Practice of Preparing Accounts

The purpose of preparing accounts for a business operation may be described in a two-fold way.

(i) To calculate the gross and net profits earned over a period of time in order to ascertain whether or not the operation is achieving its targets.

(ii) To prepare a statement, showing the value of the business at a given time in relation to the money invested (capital) and other debts the operation may have (liabilities), against what the operation has to show for the capital and liabilities by way of premises and equipment (fixed assets) and stock, cash and money owed to the operation (short term assets).

To obtain this information a business will prepare a Trading Account and a Profit and Loss Account to calculate its profits or losses and a Balance Sheet to show its value. However, before we are able to prepare these accounts and statements it is necessary to categorise certain forms of income and expenditure and be able to assemble lists of financial transactions in a logical and organised manner.

INCOME AND EXPENDITURE

It is important, in the first instance, to distinguish between the different types of income and expenditure (receipts and payments) that a business may have. Income may be described as money or value coming into an operation and expenditure as money or value going out of an operation. Both income and expenditure can be categorised into two specific areas known as Capital and Revenue Income or Capital and Revenue Expenditure.

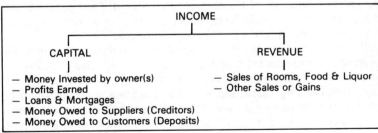

Fig. 2.21 *Difference Between Capital & Revenue Income*

The difference between Capital and Revenue Income is shown in figure 2.21. Capital Income is the money invested in a business, the profits made being re-invested in the business, loans made to the business or the use of credit deposits paid by customers. Revenue income is gained from making sales to customers and receiving rents from such items as kiosks, display cabinets, vending and fruit machines.

Expenditure is also categorised into Capital and Revenue Expenditure and is illustrated in figure 2.22. Capital Expenditure is made to acquire the fixed assets of a business (ie. premises etc.) and pay for stocks of food and liquor held. Revenue Expenditure is payments made which are directly related to sales in the payment for materials purchased, wages and other business expenses.

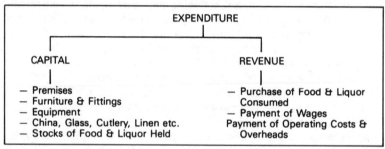

Fig. 2.22 *Difference Between Capital & Revenue Expenditure*

We are therefore able to refer to Capital Income and Expenditure as being complementary as is the case with Revenue Income and Expenditure, this is shown in figure 2.23. The illustration shows the flow of capital income when a business is set up and assets acquired, to the expenditure on operating expenses necessary to generate sales income. The profit made between revenue income and expenditure is calculated in the Trading and Profit and Loss Accounts, then it is transferred to the Balance Sheet as Investment or Capital Income. We are able to see the change in the value of the business from the Balance Sheet after every transaction if we so wish, but this would not be practical because of the accounting involved. Final accounts are therefore prepared periodically, either annually or at more frequent intervals according to the business requirements.

It is important to realise at this stage that whilst the capital invested is used to purchase the fixed assets of a business, it is also necessary to keep some capital aside providing cash to work in the business. This is known as Working Capital and is used to buy stock and keep sufficient cash in hand to pay wages and other expenses before sales are made, or if sales are made on credit to allow the business to operate until payment is received.

140

Student Activity No. 2.30

Make lists of the different types of income and expenditure that you would expect to find in a hotel and catering operation under the following headings: Capital Income, Capital Expenditure, Revenue Income and Revenue Expenditure.

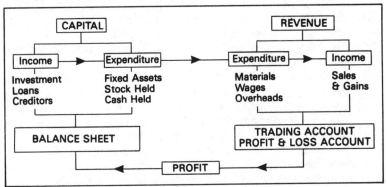

Fig. 2.23   *The relationship between Capital & Revenue Income & Expenditure and how they are accounted for*

RECORDING FINANCIAL TRANSACTIONS

Before we prepare final accounts (ie. Trading, Profit and Loss Accounts and the Balance Sheet) it is necessary to prepare and list the information required. The method used to record financial transactions will vary according to the type of establishment. The factors which influence the method used will be the accounting policy, the size of operation, the types of transactions made and the technology and expertise available. There are many systems available to the caterer, ranging from the traditional double entry system and derivatives thereof, to proprietory systems and computer programmes. The principles of each system are similar, in that the different types of transactions are recorded with the intention of preparing a set of final accounts. In this section we will examine the basis of the systems that may be used to produce a list of totals of the different types of income and expenditure known as a trial balance. The trial balance is the main source of information required to prepare a set of final accounts.

All methods have the same objectives in that they have to record the following different types of business transactions.

(i)   Recording Capital Invested whether it be the share holding in a large hotel group or a small amount of capital invested by a snack bar operator. Capital invested by outside parties, in the form of loans or mortgages, must also be recorded in this grouping.

(ii) Recording expenditure on fixed assets and any adjustments made from time to time by way of improvement, expansion or additions and losses in value due to wear and tear etc. (known as depreciation).

(iii) Recording cash and bank transactions involving money coming in and going out of a business.

(iv) Recording sales and purchases of materials used in the normal running of the operation (ie. food and drink).

(v) Recording wages and overhead payments made during the accounting period.

(vi) Recording the details of any credit given and received by the operation (ie. debtors and creditors), for the purpose of knowing when the transaction was made, when it was paid and how much is owed at any one time. This may be a very sensitive area of accounting as poor control of debtors and creditors is often the cause of financial problems or even bankruptcy.

NB: We studied methods of recording purchases of Stock and Cash Control in the first study book, students should revise these areas before continuing this section.

Double Entry Book keeping

The double entry system of book keeping is the traditonal method of recording transactions and is regarded as old fashioned and cumbersome in the amount of detail that has to be recorded in ledgers, journals and day books etc. This method does however form the basis of all accounting systems including the programmes used in computers.

The principle of the system is that each entry in the books (known as ledgers) has two aspects to it, hence the name double entry book keeping. One entry is to record the receiving of value (debit) and the other to record the giving of value (credit), value may be described as the amount involved in the transaction either in money terms or material terms. Each type of account has its own ledger and the debit or credit entry is made according to how the transaction affects the value of that account, as shown in figure 2.24.

LEDGER ACCOUNT (No.___)	
Date **Debit (DR)** £	**Date** **Credit (CR)** £
Value Received	Value Given
or	or
Value (money or material)	Value (money or material)
Coming In	Going Out

Figure 2.24 *The Meaning of Debit and Credit in Ledger Accounts*

This method is best explained by a series of examples showing the Debit (DR) and Credit (CR) entries made in the appropriate ledgers.
Example 1
A hotel purchased linen worth £78.60 paying by cheque on January 26th.

DR		LINEN A/C			CR
Jan 26	Bank	78.60			

DR		BANK A/C			CR
		Jan 26	Linen	78.60	

The entries show that linen received value (DR) and bank gave value (CR). If, however, the hotel purchased linen for the same value on credit from A.B. Supplies Ltd their entries would show:

DR		A.B. SUPPLIERS LTD A/C			CR
		Jan 26	Linen	78.60	

DR		LINEN A/C			CR
Jan 26	A.B. Supplies	78.60			

The entries show that linen received value (DR) and A.B. Supplies gave value (CR). When the hotel pays A.B. Supplies on February 10th the entries will show:

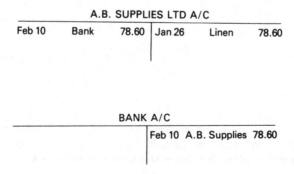

A.B. SUPPLIES LTD A/C

Feb 10	Bank	78.60	Jan 26	Linen	78.60

BANK A/C

			Feb 10	A.B. Supplies	78.60

The entries now show that A.B. Supplies have received value (DR) from Bank who gave value (CR). In effect the ledger records now show that cash gave value to Linen as originally shown, the ledger account for A.B. Supplies originally showed them as a creditor (the hotel owed A.B. Supplies) until they were paid, after which the account is closed off.

Example 2

A hotel pays its staff wages of £1,240 in cash on February 10th:

DR		WAGES A/C		CR
Feb 10	Cash	1240		

DR		CASH A/C		CR
		Feb 10	Wages	1240

The entries show that wages received value (DR) from cash (CR) who gave value. When, a week later, the hotel pays wages again of £1,272 in cash the transactions are recorded in the same ledgers, as shown below:

Dr		Wage A/C		CR
Feb 10	Cash	1240		
Feb 17	Cash	1272		

DR		CASH A/C		CR
		Feb 10	Cash	1240
		Other Cash Transactions given or paid out		
		Feb 17	Cash	1272

It may now be seen that all transactions in specific areas are recorded in the same ledgers, at the end of the accounting period the total value received or given is totalled and transferred to the trial balance.

Example 3

This example shows a series of transactions by a public house with Bass Brewery during the month of March. On the 1st of March the pub owed Bass Brewery £476.60 from supplies received during February (note how this is recorded in the ledger account). The transactions are as followed:

5th March	Liquor Purchases	£151.20
12th March	Liquor Purchases	£128.40
16th March	Return goods to Bass	£ 51.20
19th March	Liquor Purchases	£160.60
24th March	Paid account to end of February	£476.60
26th March	Liquor Purchases	£132.50

These transactions are recorded in the accounts as shown below:

DR			LIQUOR PURCHASES A/C		CR
Mar		£	Mar		£
5	Bass	151.20			
12	Bass	128.40			
19	Bass	160.60			
26	Bass	132.50			

DR			BASS BREWERY A/C		CR
Mar		£	Mar		£
16	Returns	51.20	1	Balance b/d	476.60
24	Bank	476.60	5	Purchases	151.20
			12	Purchases	128.40
			19	Purchases	160.60
31	Balance c/d	521.50	26	Purchases	132.50
		1049.30			1049.30
			Apr		
			1	Balance b/d	521.50

DR		BANK A/C		CR
		Mar		£
		25	Bass	476.60

DR		PURCHASE RETURNS A/C		CR
		Mar		£
		16	Bass	51.20

145

The Ledger Account for Bass Brewery shows all the transactions that have taken place with them. On the Credit side the amount of all value given to us has been recorded and all value received by them in goods returned and cash payment has been recorded. On the Debit side the account has been balanced off by each side being totalled and the side with the lesser amount is made up with the balance to equal the side with the greater amount. This balance is carried down (c/d) to the Credit side showing the amount brought down (b/d) at the beginning of the next month, this balance or difference is the amount owed to them and is the figure recorded in the Trial Balance. This figure will later be used in the Balance Sheet recording Bass Brewery as a Creditor. The Purchases Ledger for liquor has recorded all goods received, this ledger will also contain a list of all liquor purchased from the different suppliers in date order. The Purchases Returns Ledger will list all returns made to suppliers for goods delivered but which were either not up to the standard required or for some other reason. These details are usually entered on receipt of a Credit Note. Some operations will record goods received on the Debit side of the Purchases Ledger and goods returned on the Credit side. The Bank Ledger shows the value given to Bass Brewery when the account was paid. The totals of the Liquor Purchases and Purchases Returns Ledgers together with the balance of the Bank Ledger will be recorded in the Trial Balance.

Example 4

A hotel has cash sales of £900 on April 10th.

DR		CASH A/C		CR
Apr 10	Sales	900		

DR		SALES A/C		CR
		Apr 10	Cash	900

The entries show the hotel received cash (DR) from sales which gave value (CR).

Example 5

A Snack Bar proprietor Mr C. Martin starts his business May 1st with a capital of £10,000 in the bank.

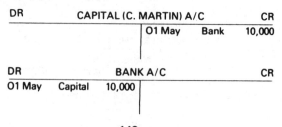

DR		CAPITAL (C. MARTIN) A/C		CR
		01 May	Bank	10,000

DR		BANK A/C		CR
01 May	Capital	10,000		

146

The entries show that the cash account receives value (DR) and the appropriate ledger account is debited. The Capital acount for C. Martin records the fact that he gives capital (CR). This may be difficult to understand, but it must be remembered that we are completing the accounts of the snack bar which has a separate identity to its owner, we must therefore record the fact that the capital is owed.

When using the double entry system of book keeping it is important to keep separate purchases and sales ledgers for food and beverages because they are sold at different profit margins. It is necessary to prepare separate results for them to enable us to analyse and evaluate their respective results. We must also consider the preparation of separate accounts for cash and bank transactions. Most business operations will have a mixture of cash and bank transactions which necessitates separate records being maintained. In the previous study book we examined methods of Cash Control and recording transactions that may be made in cash. However, most transactions are made through a bank and therefore must be recorded separately. The examples we have used so far have only dealt with one type of transaction ie. Cash or Bank. Most business operations will keep a separate record of cash and bank transactions by using a Petty Cash record and a bank ledger or similar record which will in turn marry up with the bank statement. Bank and cash income and expenditure analysis is examined in further detail in the next section.

A Series of Transactions to a Trial Balance
We will now take a series of transactions made when setting up a hotel and catering operation, through to a trial balance, by using the double entry method of book keeping.

Mark Robinson decides to set up 'Marks Seafood Bar' on May 1st with a capital in the bank of £20,000 and a bank loan of £10,000, the transactions for the first period of trading are as follows:
May 1 Purchased Leasehold Premises by Cheque for £14,000
May 2 Purchased Catering Equipment by Cheque for £6,000
May 2 Purchased Furniture by Cheque for £3,500
May 4 Purchased food by Cheque for £1,480
May 5 Paid Insurances by Cheque £360
May 5 Paid Rent by Cheque £1,000
May 6 Purchased Food on Credit from Frozen Foods Ltd £220
May 7 Banked Cash Sales £560
May 7 Paid Wages by Cheque £200
May 8 Purchased additional Equipment by Cheque for £1,200
May 9 Purchased Furniture on Credit from Courts £380
May 10 Purchased Food on Credit from A. Fishmonger £300
May 10 Purchased Food on Credit from Frozen Foods Ltd £400
May 11 Banked Cash Sales £600
May 12 Purchased Cleaning Materials by Cheque £80

May 12 Paid Frozen Foods Ltd by Cheque £220
May 13 Paid Electricity by Cheque £300
May 14 Paid Wages by Cheque £380
May 14 Banked Cash Sales £790
May 14 Sales on Credit to Yeovil Tyre Co £100

A stock take on May 14 showed that the value of Food Stock held was £1,300. The Ledger Accounts for the operation show:

DR	CAPITAL A/C (Robinson)		CR
	MAY		
	1	Bank	20,000

DR			BANK A/C		CR
MAY		£	MAY		£
1	Capital	20,000	1	Premises	14,000
1	Bank Loan	10,000	2	Equipment	6,000
7	Sales	560	2	Furniture	3,500
11	Sales	600	4	Purchases	1,480
14	Sales	790	5	Insurance	360
			5	Rent	1,000
			7	Wages	200
			8	Equipment	1,200
			12	Cleaning Materials	80
			12	Frozen Foods	220
			13	Electricity	300
			14	Wages	380
					28,720
			14	Balance c/d	3,230
		31,950			31,950
14	Balance b/d	3,230			

DR	BANK LOAN A/C		CR
	MAY		
	1	Bank	10,000

DR	PREMISES A/C		CR
1	Bank	14,000	

```
DR                      EQUIPMENT A/C                   CR
MAY
2     Bank              6,100
8     Bank              1,200
                        7,200


DR                      FURNITURE A/C                   CR
MAY
2     Bank              3,500
9     Courts             380
                        3,880


DR                      INSURANCE A/C                   CR
MAY
5     Bank               360


DR                      RENT A/C                        CR
MAY
5     Bank              1,000


DR                PURCHASES (Food) A/C                  CR
MAY
4     Bank              1,480
6     Frozen Foods       220
10    A. Fishmonger      300
10    Frozen Foods       400

                        2,400


DR                      SALES A/C                       CR
                                          MAY
                                          7     Bank           560
                                          11    Bank           600

                                          14    Bank           790
                                          14    Yeovil Tyre Co  100
                                                               2,050


DR              CLEANING MATERIALS A/C                  CR
MAY
12    Bank                80
```

149

```
DR                    FROZEN FOODS LTD                  CR
MAY                             |  MAY
12    Bank             220      |  6     Purchases      220
14    Balance c/d      400      |  10    Purchases      400
                      ____      |                      ____
                       620      |                       620
                                |  14    Balance b/d     400


DR                       WAGES A/C                       CR
MAY                             |
7     Bank             200      |
14    Bank             380      |
                      ____      |
                       580      |


DR                       COURTS A/C                      CR
                                |  MAY
                                |  9     Furniture       380


DR                      ELECTRICITY                      CR
MAY                             |
13    Bank             300      |


DR                   A. FISHMONGER A/C                   CR
                                |  MAY
                                |  10    Purchases       300


DR                    YEOVIL TYRE CO                     CR
MAY                             |
14    Sales           100       |
```

When all the entries are made and the accounts are balanced off or
totalled, as the case may be, it will now be possible to prepare a Trial
Balance. It should be noted that whilst it is possible to balance off each
account, it is only necessary when an account has both debit and
credit entries, as in the case of the Bank and Frozen Foods Ltd.
Accounts with more than one entry are totalled and the accounts with
only a single entry recorded may be left as they are.

The trial balance is the main source of information necessary to
complete the Trading Account, Profit and Loss Account and the
Balance Sheet of the business which we will study as this section
progresses.

MARKS SEAFOOD BAR
TRIAL BALANCE AS AT 14 MAY 198__

LEDGER ACCOUNT	DR	CR
Cash at Bank	3,230	
Capital		20,000
Bank Loan		10,000
Premises	14,000	
Equipment	7,200	
Furniture	3,880	
Rent	1,000	
Purchases (Food)	2,400	
Sales		2,050
Insurance	360	
Frozen Foods Ltd		400
Wages	580	
Courts		380
A. Fishmonger		300
Cleaning Materials	80	
Electricity	300	
Yeovil Tyre Co.	100	
	£33,130	£33,130

NB: Stock Held at 14 May 198__ £1,300

Important points to remember on Double Entry Book keeping are listed as follows:

(i) Every transaction has two entries.

(ii) Every Debit Entry has a Credit Entry and vice versa

(iii) Debit Entries record the account, person or type of expenditure that receives value of some kind.

(iv) Credit Entries record the account, person or type of income that gives value of some kind.

Student Activity No. 2.31

(i) From the following list of transactions make the appropriate entries in ledger accounts. July 1st, D. Gregory sets up business as an Outdoor Caterer with a capital in cash of £15,000 and a bank loan of £5,000. He purchases leasehold premises for £3,000 cash.

July 2nd   Purchases Equipment for £5,760 cash

July 3rd   Purchases Motor Van for £6,500 cash

July 4th   Pays Rent of £550 in cash

July 5th   Purchases Equipment for £3,500 on Credit from Marquee Supplies Ltd.

July 6th   ·Purchases Food for £2,360 cash

July 6th   Purchases Food for £1,200 on Credit from Ginsters Pies Ltd

July 7th   Pays Insurance in Cash £350

July 8th   Makes Cash Sales of £4,210

July 8th   Pays Wages of £740 in cash

July 9th   Pays Ginsters Pies Ltd £1,200

July 10th   Purchases Calor Gas for £230 cash

July 10th Purchases Food for £1,460 cash
July 10th Purchases Food for £1,100 on Credit from Ginsters
          Pies Ltd
July 11th Purchases Calor Gas for £165 cash
July 12th Makes Cash Sales of £4,080
July 12th Pays Wages of £700 in cash
July 12th Pay Marquee Supplies Ltd £1750 in cash

(ii) Balance or total off your ledger accounts and prepare a trial
     balance.

Other Methods of Recording Transactions

Whilst we have examined the traditional double entry method of
keeping a record of business transactions, other methods are also used
which adopt the same principles. These methods are usually designed
to meet the individual needs of different operations. We are now aware
that there are two aspects to every transaction. For example, when an
operation pays wages in cash there is a need to record the amount
spent on wages and a need to record the outflow of cash. Similarly,
when materials (food and drink) are purchased on credit from a
supplier, with the later intention of selling those materials at a profit, the
operation needs to know how much it owes its creditors, the total cost
of materials purchased, how much they were sold for and whether
these sales were for cash or who owes the firm for them and the
amount they owe. There are a variety of systems available which have
been designed to meet the needs of small and medium sized
operations, the most common being 'Simplex' or 'Kalamazoo'. The
principles of these systems are that transactions are recorded on a
weekly basis using a page per week and that accumulative totals are
recorded each week leading to final accounts being prepared from
them in a set format. Whilst the advantage of using them is their
simplicity, their format is not generally suited to hotel and catering
operations where a variety of products and services are sold at different
profit margins.

Many operations design their own method of book keeping, the
system being tailor made to meet their specific accounting requirements. Again the basic principles are followed in that both aspects of
each transaction are recorded, though not necessarily in ledgers. A
method which is often used in small and medium sized operations is an
analysis form of accounting. Income and Expenditure of both a Capital
and Revenue nature are split up into their respective categories (ie.
Revenue Income, Revenue Expenditure etc), each category having its
own analysis sheet with entries being recorded as and when they
occur. A system using these principles, which would be suitable for a
small or medium sized hotel and catering operation is shown in figures
2.25 to 2.34 which explains how each type of income or expenditure
would be recorded.

Capital Income

The Capital Income for small and medium sized operations usually involves investment by the owners and financing by way of a loan or mortgage from an external organisation such as a bank, brewery or merchant bank, when the operation is set up. A record of these investments and loans is kept in a form of journal entry, the entries are only made when the operation is set up. An example of this type of entry is shown in figure 2.25, linking it to the purchase of the fixed assets of the operation. Whilst these entries are infrequent it may be necessary from time to time to record any profits made that have been re-invested in the operation or to record the repayment of loans. Banks and other financial institutions issue periodic statements as to the current loan balance and these statements themselves can act as a record. Profits made are recorded in the profit and loss account for each year and added to the capital in the Balance Sheet (see figures 2.23 and 2.35) after a consideration has been made for any profits retained by the owner for his own personal use (Drawings). Therefore it may be said that the Balance Sheet is an up to date record of the capital investment.

Capital Expenditure

The main expenditure involving capital in any business will be when the operation is acquired or set up and would be recorded in a similar way to capital income, as shown in the following example.

Example

On 1st June 198__ C. Beeson started business as a guest house proprietor with a capital in cash of £55,000 and a bank loan of £20,000. He acquired the following assets:

Freehold Premises	£63,500
Equipment	£ 4,000
Furniture & Fittings	£ 2,500
China, Glass, Cutlery & Linen	£ 700
Food Stocks	£ 200
Liquor Stocks	£ 400

The opening journal type entry is as follows:

June 1.			
	Freehold Premises	63,500	
	Equipment	4,000	
	Furniture & Fittings	2,500	
	China, Glass, Cutlery & Linen	700	
	Food Stocks	200	
	Liquor Stocks	400	
	Cash At Bank	3,700	
	Capital		55,000
	Bank Loan		20,000
		75,000	75,000

Being Assets and Capital at June 1st 198__ or Mr C. Beeson on the acquisition of the Victoria Park Guest House.

Fig. 2.25 *Example of Opening Journal Entry showing the Capital Income & Expenditure*

This statement of the operation may be used as a basis of information when preparing the final accounts at the end of the first trading period. We must be aware however that the food and liquor stocks and cash at bank will be different at the end of the trading period, as they will fluctuate daily during normal trading. These elements of stock and cash at bank are the Working Capital of the business.

We must also consider any new fixed assets purchased for an operation during a financial period, as this type of transaction involves Capital Expenditure. This kind of transaction usually involves the purchase of small items of equipment such as china, glassware, cutlery and linen; these have to be regularly purchased because of breakages and normal wear and tear. A simple type of analysis sheet may be kept, recording the purchase of such items as and when they occur. An example of the type of record kept is shown in figure 2.26. Note that each type of asset has its own column for the purpose of analysing the frequency of purchases and when a total is calculated this may be transferred to the balance sheet. The 'details' column may be used to record any relevant details of the purchase, such as the supplier's name, invoice number etc. Details regarding payment may also be recorded in the cheque number column for cross reference purposes, in the case of petty cash purchases the voucher number may be entered in this column.

Date	Details	Cheque No.	Equipment	Furniture & Fittings	China	Glass	Cutlery	Linen
20 Jun 8__	Musitano	51147	36.40					
27 Jun 8__	Lawleys	51159				22.60		
15 Aug 8__		PC 46				2.40		
29 Aug 8__	Linen Supplies	51211						88.60

Fig. 2.26   *Example of an Analysis Sheet Recording Capital Expenditure*

Student Activity No. 2.32
Prepare the opening journal entry for J. Rockwell who commenced business on March 1st 198__ as a Snack Bar Proprietor with a capital in cash of £10,000 and a bank loan of £4,000. The assets purchased are as follows:

Leasehold Premises	£8,500
Equipment	£2,000
Furniture	£ 800
China, Glass & Cutlery	£ 650
Food Stock	f 250

154

Revenue Income

There are many ways of recording revenue income, the main source of revenue being sales. What must be considered is the amount of information the caterer wants when recording sales and how many departments in his operation make sales direct to the customer. Hotels often use a visitors tabular ledger for this purpose, which is fully explained at the end of this section on methods of recording transactions. In food and beverage operations sales may be recorded on either a daily basis or for each unit of sale (ie. meal or customer) depending on the type of operation. In figure 2.27 the example shows how a public house or an industrial catering operation, records sales on a session or daily basis where only cash transactions take place. Extra columns may be added to include VAT or other income, for example operations may wish to break down food sales into starters, main courses, vegetables, desserts, snacks etc. These columns may be totalled weekly or monthly, the results being transferred to the final accounts or master sheets (monthly or weekly analysis forms). A restaurant however may design a form to show a daily sales record using each table as the unit of sale, and recording details of payment. An example is shown in figure 2.28, the details being taken from the customer's bill, the bill number can be recorded onto the analysis sheet as a further means of food and cash control.

Date	Session	Total		Food		Beverages		Sundries	
01 Dec 8__	Morning	276	55	105	60	168	35	2	60
01 Dec 8__	Evening	418	50	74	20	341	20	3	10
02 Dec 8__	Morning	277	37	110	20	165	17	1	90
02 Dec 8__	Evening	438	30	73	60	362	30	2	40

Fig. 2.27   *Example of a Daily Cash Sales Record*

These analysis sheets give information of the separate areas of sales and details of cash received or credit given, the restaurant is also able to calculate the average spending per customer on food and liquor sales and record VAT collected.

There are a variety of billing machines, which are either mechanical or electronic and which may be used for recording sales details. These have the advantage of greater accuracy and speed of operation over manual systems. Many fast food operations have prices programmed into the machine, relating to the menu items, which not only increases accuracy and eliminates the chances of wrong prices being charged, but also gives a sales breakdown of menu items. Whilst we have mentioned in this section that systems may be designed to meet specific needs of caterers, this will also apply to programmes for billing machines.

155

'FOOD FOR THOUGHT' RESTAURANT

DATE: 17 Dec 8__

Table No.	Bill No.	Covers	Food	Liquor	Tobacco	VAT	Total	Cash Cheque	Access Barclay	Am. Exp Diners	Credit
6	1652	4	41.10	13.20		6.14	60.44		60.44		
5	1653	2	19.30	6.40	1.40	4.06	31.16	31.16			
8	1654	2	18.65	7.10		3.86	29.61		29.61		
3	1655	4	40.80	12.05	80	8.04	61.69			61.69	
1	1656	8	77.80	31.40	3.20	16.86	129.26				129.26
4	1657	1	8.50	3.00		1.72	13.22	13.22			
		21	206.15	73.15	5.40	40.68	325.38	44.38	90.05	61.69	129.26

Fig. 2.28 Example of a Restaurant Sales Analysis Sheet

Student Activity No. 2.33

(i) Draw up a Daily Sales Analysis Sheet for a restaurant with the following headings: Table Number, Bill Number, Number of Covers, Food Sales, Liquor Sales, VAT, Total Sales, Cash/ Cheque Paid, Credit.

(ii) Record sales and payment details for 6 tables.

(iii) Total each column, checking that the total sales balance with the cash and credit payments made.

Revenue Expenditure

When recording revenue expenditure it is important to separate the different types of payments that are made with a view to preparing final accounts. In the example shown in figure 2.29 the expenditure has been broken down into very broad categories. A caterer may break this down further if he so requires. Entries are made as and when they occur in the relevant column, including details of the transaction and how it is paid. A total column is usually necessary as some transactions include more than one entry eg. Cash and Carry, and also VAT is paid on some transactions. Cross checking may be carried out with the bank statement or petty cash vouchers to verify payment details. In the case of credit purchases details of the purchase are recorded with a note made of the supplier's name in the details column or a separate comments column.

At the end of the page the columns are totalled and carried forward to the first line of the next analysis sheet and at the end of the accounting period final totals are made and transferred to the trading and profit and loss accounts.

Cash and Bank Transactions

Although we have covered methods of recording income and expenditure in this section as well as in the first study book, the importance of controlling these aspects of a business operation cannot be over emphasised. The caterer must keep a record of all cash received and banked from sales or other income and a record of all expenditure made. These transactions may then be checked against the Petty Cash Book and Bank Statement. By using a Sales Analysis and Payments Record the caterer may check the appropriate columns with his bank statement if he adopts the procedure of paying all cash received into the bank. The same may be said for using the expenditure records if all payments are made by cheque. However some smaller operations make payments in cash straight from the till; there are many dangers if this is practiced as it is probable that some confusion will arise unless a very strict control is kept. All cash payments must be recorded together with amounts paid into the bank if they differ from sales receipts. An example of a double column cash book suitable for this type of practice is shown in figure 2.30. The principles followed are

Date	Details	Cash Cheque No.	Total	Food Pur.	Liquor Pur.	Wages	Fuel	Rent Rates Insur.	Laundry & Cleaning	Repairs Maint.	Admin Exp.	Sundry Exp.	VAT
April 10	Cash & Carry	111254	279.69	182.40	71.70				8.80			4.10	12.69
11	Wages	111255	446.30			446.30							
13	Greene King	Credit	260.09		226.40								33.69
14	LEB	111256	318.40				318.40						
15	Fruit	PC84	11.60	11.60									
16	R. Pollack	111257	77.82	77.82									
16	Water Rates	111258	87.20					87.20					
17	A. Builder	111259	48.30							42.00			6.30
18	British Telecom	111260	75.09								65.30		9.79
18	Light Bulbs	PC85	2.76									2.40	.36
18	Wages	111261	429.40			429.40							
19	B. Baker	Credit	71.30	71.30									
20	Postage Stamps	PC86	22.40								22.40		
21	Candles	PC87	8.05									7.00	1.05
21	Kneels Laundry	111262	115.69						100.60				15.09
	Total		2254.09	343.12	298.10	875.70	318.40	87.20	109.40	42.00	87.70	13.50	78.97

Fig. 2.29 An example of a Record of Revenue Expenditure suitable for a small Catering Operation

the same as for double entry book keeping. The balances shown on May 1st are the amounts held in cash and at the bank by the operation. All daily cash sales are recorded on the Debit side in the cash column, all bank and cash expenditure is recorded on the Credit side in the appropriate column. When cash is paid into the bank it should be noted that it is recorded as Cash going out of the operation on the Credit side and received into the operation as an income on the Debit side. This type of entry is known as a 'Contra Entry'. Any sales paid by cheque would be paid directly into the bank, as shown for the deposit received in the example. At the end of the accounting period the cash and bank columns are separately balanced and carried forward to the next accounting period.

DEBIT (INCOME)				CREDIT (EXPENDITURE)			
Date	Details	Cash	Bank	Date	Details	Cash	Bank
May				May			
01	Balance	260 00	1,500 00	02	Wages	305 10	
01	Sales	230 42		03	Cash & Carry		470 40
02	Sales	271 20		03	B. Baker	55 70	
03	Sales	260 30		03	Water Rates		105 00
04	Sales	301 20		04	Cash Banked	500 00	
04	Cash Banked		500 00	04	Greene King		220 30
05	Sales	288 70		05	A. Milko	82 60	
05	Sales (Deposit)		50 00		Balance C/F	668 42	1,254 30
		1,611 82	2,050 00			1,611 82	2,050 00
06	Balance B/F	668 42	1,254 30				

Fig. 2.30   *Example of a Double Column Cash Book*

Student Activity   No. 2.34
 (i)   Draw up a Double Column Cash Book with separate Cash & Bank columns for Debit and Credit.
 (ii)   Record the following transactions
     May 1st   Opening Balances DR Cash £75.00 DR Bank £700.00
     May 2nd   Cash Sales £225.40
     May 3rd   Paid Wages in Cash £232.40
     May 3rd   Cash Sales £236.70
     May 4th   Cash Sales £231.90
     May 4th   Paid Insurance by Cheque £210.00
     May 5th   Cash Sales £219.40
     May 5th   Paid £700 Cash into the Bank
     May 5th   Paid Rates £485.00 by Cheque
     May 6th   Cash Sales £255.70
     May 6th   Paid for Food Purchases £143.20 in Cash
     May 7th   Cash Sales £234.80
     May 8th   Cash Sales £252.60
     May 8th   Paid Wages in Cash £314.40
 (iii)   Balance the Cash and Bank columns of your cash book.

159

Debtors and Creditors

It is important in any business operation to keep a record of and control over debtors and creditors as they affect the financial stability of the operation. For example, if a business does not pay its suppliers regularly this may lead to an inability at some stage to pay huge debts. There will also be a lack of regard from the suppliers who will then not give their best service or prices because they do not know if and when they are going to be paid. It is equally important for a business to ensure that its debtors pay regularly and on time as failure to do so means that cash is being tied up which could be used elsewhere. The control of debtors and creditors is an important aspect of 'cash flow' in a business. This will be examined more closely in Study Book 3. It is therefore important to establish a system of recording debtors and creditors to enable a business to check the accuracy of invoices and statements and to maintain prompt payments. In hotel and catering operations the majority of sales are paid for by cash, which, to a degree, eliminates some of the problems. However, it may also be argued that because debtors are a minority they are not properly controlled. When credit is given to a customer it should be properly recorded in a debtor's ledger or book, when the credit is given.

All payments are recorded when they are made and the ledger is checked at the end of each month for the purpose of reminders being issued. Regular debtors should have a ledger card or page of their own, recording all details of credit given and payments received. Examples of an occasional debtor ledger and regular debtors ledger are shown in figures 2.31 and 2.32 respectively. The occasional debtors ledger may be totalled for credit given columns and payment received columns, the difference being the amount of debts outstanding. A regular debtor's ledger may take the same format as the statement sent to the customer and be kept in a loose leaf file or on index cards. Some operations will use this system for both regular and occasional debtors but this will probably be due to the amount of credit given and the number of debtors involved. Whichever system is used, the total debts must be available at all times for checking and at the end of accounting periods for recording in the final accounts.

Date	Name	Details	Amount	Payment Details	
				Date	Amount
10 May 8__	S. Francis	Hotel Sales	£ 55.20	11 Jun 8__	55.20
15 May 8__	C. Dyer Ltd	Hotel Sales	£ 30.50		
20 May 8__	P. Atkins	Wedding	£410.00		
21 May 8__	J. Marcus	Hotel Sales	£ 71.30	1 Jun 8__	71.30

Fig. 2.31 *Example of Occasional Debtor's Ledger*

Name:	CITY BIKES LTD		Credit A/C No: 17	
Address:	4 EASTHOPE WALK		Credit Limit: £1,000	
	LONDON SE1.			
Date	Details	DR	CR	Balance
5 Sep 8__	Restaurant Sales	68.20		68.20
26 Sep 8__	Restaurant Sales	52.15		120.35
02 Oct 8__	Hotel Sales	60.30		180.65
04 Oct 8__	Function Sales	325.80		506.45
10 Oct 8__	Cheque Received		120.35	386.10
24 Oct 8__	Restaurant Sales	61.70		447.80

Fig. 2.32 *Example of a Regular Debtor's Ledger*

The method of recording creditors has, in most small and medium sized operations, been to retain invoices until a statement from the supplier has been received, then check the invoices with the statement and make a payment as required. Most caterers have a procedure established with their regular suppliers, in that the statement arrives at the beginning of the month and payment is made in the second or third week of the month. It is the irregular creditor that is sometimes overlooked and more often than not these are for larger amounts. Creditors for smaller amounts are sometimes forgotten. We must therefore look at similar systems to those of recording debtors for an operation to control the amount of credit received and payment procedures. The example in figure 2.31 is easily adapted for occasional creditors, this may also be said for the example in figure 2.32 which can be adapted for regular creditors. Another method of recording regular creditors is shown in figure 2.33, using an analysis sheet where daily purchases are recorded under the appropriate supplier. If we assume that the caterer has a regular payment date for his creditors, each column may be totalled, the payment made can then be deducted and the new balance calculated. The example shows an analysis system for an operation which pays its accounts in the middle of the month for the previous month's purchases. The advantages of this system are that the total creditors can easily be calculated at any time and information regarding the purchases in these areas are also monitored to facilitate their control.

Computers are widely used to record debtors and creditors in larger operations; the information regarding purchases, returns and payments is easily keyed into the computer which in turn can give daily readings as to their analysis and totals. The computer may also be programmed to give daily reports of debtors who have exceeded their credit period and to print out reminder notices as and when necessary. A distinct advantage of computers in this area is that set accounting procedures are automatically carried out, giving the caterer greater control and financial efficiency.

Date	Details	B. Baker	S. Milko	F. Fish	V. Veg	M. Meat	C. Chill
Mar 1	Balance	120.20	160.30	110.40	205.60	226.30	170.70
1	Purchases	5.20	4.10			26.18	
2	Purchases	5.20	4.10		17.30		
3	Purchases	5.80	4.10	23.60		20.30	31.40
17	Purchases	5.20	4.10			31.60	23.70
	Total	200.30	251.70	180.90	319.55	350.35	260.80
17	Payment	120.20	160.30	110.40	205.60	226.30	170.70
18	Balance	80.10	91:40	70.50	113.95	124.05	90.10
18	Purchases	5.20	4.10		21.10		

Fig. 2.33   *Example of Regular Creditor Analysis & Control Sheet*

VISITOR'S TABULAR LEDGER

Keeping control over guests' expenditure, guests' payments and departmental income is an essential feature of any hotel operation and its accounting system. A hotel guest will, on average, make ten transactions a day with the hotel, in its different departments. This might include, being charged for the room, meals, drinks, telephone calls etc. For a hotel of 50 bedrooms this would involve recording 500 transactions each day. This is further complicated by guests checking out at different times, often unannounced and wanting their bill calculated at short notice. While most hotels of 30 bedrooms use billing machines or electronic data processing to record these charges, small operations will use a 'visitors tabular ledger', which is the manual system programmed into these machines. Small operations often simplify this system by charging guests rates inclusive of meals and some beverages such as early morning tea and after dinner coffee, or they might insist on cash payment for all expenditure over and above the room or inclusive rate.

The principles of the 'visitors tabular ledger' are that each room has its own column and charges are recorded as they are incurred, crediting the department where the expenditure was made. At the end of each day the room rates are recorded, each room is totalled and the balance outstanding carried forward to the next day. Each department's income is totalled for the day and recorded on a master sheet to give a break down of the hotel's sales over a period of time. When guests check out their account is totalled and the appropriate amount is entered as a Debit, according to how they pay, either by Cash (Cheque) or Credit. These cash or credit entries act as a cash received or debtor's ledger accordingly. An example of a 'visitor's tabular ledger' is illustrated in figure 2.34, which shows how a whole day's business is recorded and balanced for a small hotel with a bar and restaurant open to non-residents. All prices include VAT. The day's business is as follows for the 30th September 198__.

Residents	Balance B/F	Rate	Departure Date
Room 1	£170.30	£25	2nd Oct
2	£ 46.20	£15	30th Sept
3	£ 85.30	£25	2nd Oct
4	£ 41.10	£25	10th Oct
5	£216.40	£35	1st Oct

8.00am	All guests take early tea @ 50p each except Room 2.
9.00am	All guests take breakfast @ £3.00 each.
10.00am	Telephone Room 2 — 30p.
10.30am	Room 2 checks out paying in cash.
12.00	Mr Perry checks in. Rate £15 per night. Room 6.
1.15pm	Room 3 pays £100 on account.
1.30pm	Room 6 Bar charge £1.20.
2.30pm	Restaurant lunches @ £5.20 each. Rooms 1, 5 and 6. Chance takings £76.40.
4.00pm	Mr and Mrs Belton check into Room 7 — Rate £30.
4.30pm	Beverages. Room 7. £1.30.
6.00pm	Telephone charges Room 5. £1.10; Room 6 £2.40.
6.15pm	VPO — Flowers Room 4. £7.00.
9.00pm	Restaurant charges for Dinner at £7.20 each. Rooms 1, 3, 4 and 7. Chance takings £132.60.
10.00pm	Mr Edwards checks into Room 2 — rate £15.
11.00pm	Room 1 Beverages £1.20.
11.15pm	Bar charges, Room 1 £5.10; Room 2 £3.40. Cash Takings £261.60.
11.30pm	Control shows Room 1 overcharged yesterday by £1.80.
11.30pm	Post Room Charges and balance ledger.

The ledger is balanced by totalling each room to the first total line, the total being entered into the balance C/F line after any adjustments have been made for corrections and payments, as in the case of Rooms 1 and 3. The bar and restaurant columns are totalled and entered into the cash line. The Credit entires for Cash, Ledger, Adjustments and Balance carried forward, are then totalled. Each type of charge is then added across the page and the amount recorded in the daily total column. The total of the daily totals is then calculated for the debits (charges) and the credits (payments). These totals should be equal, as recording all the charges will be equal to amounts paid plus balances carried forward to the next day.

Whilst this system may seem complex the obvious advantages are that the hotel has a detailed record of all sales, guests' accounts and cash received and charges to ledger. There are other systems of keeping guest's accounts used in the industry but the 'visitors tabular ledger' and computerised or mechanical systems offer greatest control to management and proprietors alike.

MOUNTS BAY HOTEL

DATE: 30 September 198_

Room	1	2	3	4	5	6	7	2	Bar	Restaurant	Daily Totals
Name	Mr/s Bowden	Mr F. Alco	Mr/s Jordan	Mr/s Hurst	Mr/s Abbot	Mr Perry	Mr/s Belton	Mr Edwards			
No. of Guests	2	1	2	2	3	1	2	1			
Balance B/F	170.30	46.20	85.30	41.10	216.40	-	-	-			
Rooms	25.00		25.00	25.00	35.00	15.00	30.00	15.00			
Breakfast	6.00	3.00	6.00	6.00	9.00						
Lunch	10.40				15.60	5.20				76.40	
Dinner	14.40		14.40	14.40			14.40			132.60	
Early Tea	1.00		1.00	1.00	1.50						4.50
Beverages	1.20						1.30				2.50
Bar	5.10					1.20		3.40	261.60		3.80
Telephone		.30			1.10	2.40					
V.P.O.				7.00							7.00
Sundries											
Total	233.40	49.50	131.70			23.80	45.70	18.40	261.60	209.00	
Cash/Cheque		49.50	100.00						261.60	209.00	
Ledger											
Adjustments	1.80										1.80
Balance C/F	231.60		31.70			23.80	45.70	18.40			
Total	233.40	49.50	131.70			23.80	45.70	18.40			

Fig. 2.34 *Example of a Visitors Tabular Ledger*

164

Student Activity   No. 2.35

(i) Draw up a visitor's tabular ledger similar to the example in figure 2.34 for an 8 bedroom hotel with a bar and restaurant open to non-residents.

(ii) Enter onto the ledger the following details:

Guests in Residence — 15 October 198__

Room No	Name	No. of Guests	Balance B/F	Rate
1	Mr & Mrs Hankcock	2	£ 74.30	£27.00
3	Mr Rushton	1	£ 32.30	£18.00
5	Mr Alaster	1	£ 18.00	£18.00
6	Mr & Mrs Pryor	2	£ 89.70	£27.00
7	Mr & Mrs Speed	2	£104.80	£27.00
8	Dr Morris	1	£ 99.70	£18.00

(iii) Post the following transactions to the ledger:

7.45am	All rooms have early tea @ 45p each.
8.30am	All rooms have breakfast @ £2.90 each except Room 5.
9.00am	Room 7 checks out and pays in cash.
9.30am	Mr Rushton checks out and charges his account to ledger.
11.15am	Room 8 has morning coffee @ 40p.
12.30pm	Restaurant book shows: Room 1 lunch £10.30; Room 6 lunch £9.80; Chance lunches £65.40.
3.00pm	Afternoon tea. Room 5 @ £1.80
4.00pm	Mr and Mrs Evans check into room 7 and have afternoon tea @ £1.80 each (Rate £27.00).
7.00pm	Telephone charges. Room 8 £2.65; Room 7 £1.05.
9.15pm	Mr Sinclair checks into Room 4 (Rate £18.00) and asks you to pay his taxi £4.00.
9.15pm	Restaurant book shows: Room 4 £11.00; Room 7 £20.80; Room 6 £26.10; Room 1 £19.40; Room 8 £10.40; Chance Dinners £166.40.
11.00pm	Bar charges: Room 8 £5.80 Cash sales £152.60.
11.30pm	Dr Morris pays £100 in cash on account.
11.30pm	Post room rates and balance ledger.

FINAL ACCOUNTS

We have so far examined methods of recording business transactions with a view to preparing the final accounts of an operation. The final accounts are the Trading, Profit and Loss Accounts over a period of time, showing the profits made and a Balance Sheet showing the value of the operation at a given date. The information required to prepare these final accounts is recorded in the trial balance, together with any adjustments and provisions we may have to make to give more accurate results. We will cover the adjustments and any provisions made as this section progresses.

The Trading Account

The purpose of the trading account is to calculate the gross profit made. by an operation during the accounting period, by deducting the cost of sales from the sales. The cost of sales is calculated by adding the stock at the beginning of the period to the net purchases and deducting the stock at the end of the period. It is usual to calculate separate results for rooms, food and liquor because of their different gross profit margins as has been previously explained. The trading account for a restaurant selling food and liquor would be set out as follows:

Trading Account for Year ending 31st March 198__

		Food		Liquor		Total
Sales		20,000		10,000		30,000
— Cost of Sales						
Stock 01 Apr 8__	700		500		1,200	
+ Purchases	8,200		5,000		13,200	
	8,900		5,500		14,400	
— Stock 31 Mar 8__	800	8,100	600	4,900	1,400	13,000
Gross Profit		11,900		5,100		17,000

The restaurant is able to calculate the gross profit percentage for both aspects of its operation. The Total Gross Profit is carried on to the Profit and Loss Account.

Student Activity   No. 2.36

From the above example calculate the Gross Profit Percentage for Food Sales, Liquor Sales and Total Sales

The Profit and Loss Account

The purpose of the profit and loss account is to calculate the net profit or loss of the operation by deducting all expenses (ie. wages and overheads) from the gross profit calculated in the Trading Account. The Profit and Loss Account would be set out as follows:

Profit and Loss Account for Year Ending 31st March 198__

Gross Profit		17,000
less Wages	7,000	
Gas & Electricity	2,500	
Rent & Rates	2,000	
Administration Expenses	1,400	
Cleaning Materials	300	13,200
Net Profit		£ 3,800

The Balance Sheet

The purpose of the balance sheet is to reconcile the assets of an operation with the liabilities. The fixed assets are listed and totalled, the working capital is calculated by deducting from the short term assets (stocks held, cash and debtors) the short term liabilities (creditors and bank overdrafts). These short term assets and liabilities are referred to as current assets and liabilities. The fixed assets and working capital are added together and compared with the long term liabilities of the operation. The long term liabilities will be the capital after the net profit has been added and drawings taken away and any loans the operation has received. The balance sheet would be set out as follows:

Balance Sheet as at 31 March 198___

Fixed Assets			
	Premises (leasehold)	10,000	
	Equipment	3,000	
	Furniture & Fittings	2,000	
	China, Glass & Cutlery	400	15,400
Current Assets			
	Food Stock	800	
	Liquor Stock	600	
	Debtors	400	
	Cash at Bank	650	2,450
Current Liabilities			
	Creditors	850	1,600
			£17,000

Financed by:			
	Capital	12,200	
+	Net Profit	3,800	16,000
−	Drawings		1,000	15,000
	Bank Loan		2,000
			£17,000

When preparing final accounts it is important to note the following points of presentation.

(i)   The Trading and Profit and Loss Accounts are headed 'for the year ending' because they represent results over that period of time.

(ii)   The Balance Sheet is headed 'as at' because it is a statement of the business sitution at a particular point in time.

(iii)   To save space and emphasise the importance of certain figures, totals of certain categories are added and entered adjacent to the column with a line showing to what point the total has been made.

A full set of Final Accounts from a Trial Balance

Set out below is a full set of final accounts taken from the trial balance of a hotel and catering operation. The only additional information required are the food and liquor stocks taken at the end of the period.

The Pier House Restaurant
Trial Balance as at 30th September 198__

	DR	CR
Capital		55,090
Bank Loan		22,000
Premises (Freehold)	75,000	
Equipment	6,500	
Furniture & Fittings	4,200	
Food Stock 1.10.8__	760	
Liquor Stock 1.10.8__	1,100	
China Glass & Cutlery	780	
Food Purchases	23,200	
Food Sales		61,580
Liquor Purchases	14,050	
Liquor Sales		31,720
Rates	3,600	
Administration Expenses	3,910	
Creditors		3,260
Sundry Expenses	1,200	
Debtors	1,220	
Repairs & Maintenance	2,050	
Cleaning Materials	740	
Drawings	4,600	
Cash in Hand	150	
Cash at Bank	3,960	
Wages	21,080	
Gas & Electricity	5,550	
	173,650	173,650

NB: Food Stock 30.0.8__ £800
Liquor Stock 30.9.8__ £1,250

The Pier House Restaurant
Trading and Profit & Loss A/C for year end 30 Sept 8__

	Food		Liquor		Total	
Sales		61,580		31,720		93,300
— Cost of Sales						
Stock 01 Oct 8__	760		1,100		1,860	
+ Purchases	23,200		14,050		37,250	
	23,960		15,150		39,110	
— Stock 30 Sep 8__	800	23,160	1,250	13,900	2,050	37,060
Gross Profit		38,420		17,820		56,240

less Expenses		
Wages		21,080
Gas & Electricity		5,550
Rates		3,600
Administration Expenses		3,910
Repairs & Maintenance		2,050
Cleaning Materials		740
Sundry Expenses		1,200	38,130
Net Profit		£18,110

The Pier House Restaurant
Balance Sheet as at 30 Sept 8__

Fixed Assets			
Premises (Freehold)		75,000	
Equipment		6,500	
Furniture & Fittings		4,200	
China Glass & Cutlery		780	86,480
Current Assets			
Food Stock	800		
Liquor Stock	1,250		
Debtors	1,220		
Cash in Hand	150		
Cash at bank	3,960	7,380	
Current Liabilities			
Creditors		3,260	4,120
			£90,600
Financed By			
Capital	55,090		
+ Net Profit	18,110	73,200	
− Drawings		4,600	68,600
Bank Loan			22,000
			£90,600

Student Activity   No. 2.37

From the following Trial Balance as at 31 Dec 1985 for Winston's Restaurant prepare a Trading, Profit and Loss Account for the year ending 31 Dec 1985 and a Balance Sheet as at that date.

Trial Balance as at 31 Dec 8__

Capital		48,000
Bank Loan		15,000
Premises (Leasehold)	47,000	
Equipment	12,000	
Furniture & Fittings	10,500	
Stock 01 Jan 8__ Food	990	
Liquor	2,320	
Wages	24,600	
Creditors		4,100
Insurance	1,220	
Sales − Food	71,250	71,250
Liquor	33,820	33,820
Rent & Rates	8,200	
Admin. Expenses	1,590	
Debtors	370	
Gas & Electricity	4,880	
Maintenance	1,600	
Purchases − Food	24,530	
Liquor	17,050	
Cash at Bank	6,070	
Owners Drawings	9,250	
	£172,170	£172,170

Stock taken at 31 Dec 1985 was Food £1020; Liquor £2,470

169

Adjustments to Final Accounts
Whilst we have examined the preparation of final accounts for a hotel and catering operation from the trial balance, there is other information we have to consider in order to give a realistic breakdown of costs and an accurate net profit. The trial balance lists capital and revenue income and expenditure but does not show any provisions an operation may make for depreciation of its assets, bad debts or adjustments for expenses paid in advance or for those not yet billed. Each type of provision or adjustment needs individual consideration and treatment in the final accounts.

Provision for Depreciation
Depreciation constitutes writing off the value of the fixed assets used in a business operation due to wear and tear and the passing of time. It is necessary to charge depreciation against the profits of an operation by treating it as an expense in the profit and loss account and deducting the same amount from the value of the asset in the Balance Sheet. Whilst there are different methods of depreciating assets, a business will select the most suitable according to the type of asset and also to gain maximum tax benefits. The reason for treating depreciation as an expense is that the customer must pay for the use of the asset and the basis for calculating selling prices is to use the information contained in the profit and loss account. For example, if a business decides to depreciate an asset worth £5,000 by 20%, the depreciation charged in the profit and loss account would be £1,000 and the asset value in the balance sheet would be revalued at £4,000. Depreciation is not charged on Freehold Premises as property appreciates in value through the passing of time, however it would be charged for Leasehold Premises and is known as 'amortisation of leasehold value'. Small items of equipment (eg. china, glass and cutlery) are re-valued at the end of an accounting period, the depreciation being calculated as the difference between the inventory valuation at the beginning and end of the period. An example of depreciation and how it is recorded in the final accounts is shown in figure 2.35.

Provision for Bad Debts
Bad debts are debtors who do not pay their accounts. Whilst in the hotel and catering industry most transactions are made in cash some credit is given to customers and operations that give credit must make a provision against the profits, for debtors who do not pay. The provision is calculated as a straight percentage of the total debtors, the amount of provision is treated as an expense in the profit and loss account and is deducted from the debtors in the balance sheet. This has the effect of reducing the net profit so that customers are charged for any bad debts, when selling prices are calculated, and reducing the value of debtors in the balance sheet. For example, if a business has

debtors of £4,000 and makes a provision for bad debts of 5%, the net profit is reduced by £200, as would be the true value of the debtors, to £3,800. An example of provision for bad debts and how they are recorded in the final accounts is shown in figure 2.35.

Adjustments for Prepayment of Expenses

Prepayment of expenses usually occurs with the payment of fixed expenses such as rents, rates and insurances because of different accounting periods between the parties concerned. For example, if a hotel and catering operation has a financial year from January to December and it pays insurance for the coming year in April, the true insurance paid, which would relate to their financial year, is for April until December and would amount to 9/12ths of the total recorded in the Trial Balance. Therefore, if the amount shown in the Trial Balance is £1,200 the true value would be £900, the £300 difference would apply to the next accounting period of the operation. The £300 would therefore be deducted from the expense in the profit and loss account having the effect of increasing the net profit and would also be recorded in the balance sheet as a current asset. An example of prepayments and how they would be recorded in the final accounts is shown in figure 2.35.

Adjustments for Accrued Expenses

Accrued Expenses are charges which a hotel and catering operation have incurred but have not yet been billed for. The most common examples would be charges for gas, electricity and telephone services, where the supplier has a different accounting period to that of the operation. For example, a hotel could consume over two month's worth of electricity in a financial period but by the time the hotel is billed it would have to be recorded in the accounts of the next financial period. Therefore an adjustment is made to the final accounts by adding the accrued charge to the expense in the profit and loss account and treating it has a current liability in the balance sheet. This has the effect of reducing the net profit and increasing the liabilities of the operation, giving a more accurate indication of the true value of these figures. Accrued charges are either estimated or calculated from the meter readings of the services provided. An example of the entries for accrued charges in the final accounts is shown in figure 2.35.

When these adjustments and provisions are carried out in the final accounts we have a dual effect to consider for each transaction. These will be, the effect on profit in the profit and loss account and the effect on the value of the operation in the Balance Sheet. By making these adjustments and provisions we are able to calculate a more accurate profit, which relates to the accounting period under examination. A full set of adjusted accounts are illustrated in figure 2.35 showing how the provisions and adjustments that are listed at the end of a trial balance are recorded in the final accounts.

Final Accounts with Adjustments

In the previous example for The Pier House Restaurant the following notes have been recorded after the completion of the Trial Balance.

(i) Food Stock @ 30.9.8__ is £800; Liquor Stock @ 30.9.8__ is £1,250 (both these figures have already been considered in the cost of sales calculation).

(ii) Depreciate both the equipment and furniture by 20%, china, glass and cutlery are revalued at £600.

(iii) Create a provision for Bad Debts of 5%.

(iv) £600 of the rates have been prepaid for next year.

(v) Gas and Electricity charges accrued are £800.

Fig. 2.35   *A set of Final Accounts including Provisions and Adjustments*

The Pier House Restaurant
Trading, Profit and Loss Account for year end 30 Sept 8__

	Food		Liquor		Total	
Sales		61,580		31,720		93,300
— Cost of Sales						
Stock 01 Oct 8__	760		1,100		1,860	
+ Purchases	23,200		14,050		37,250	
	23,960		15,150		39,110	
— Stock 30 Sept	800	23,160	1,250	13,900	2,050	37,060
Gross Profit		38,420		17,820		56,240
Less Expenses						
Wages				21,080		
Gas & Electricity	5,550					
+ Accrued Charges	800			6,350		
Rates	3,600					
— Prepayment	600			3,000		
Administration Expenses				3,910		
Repairs & Maintenance				2,050		
Cleaning Materials				740		
Sundry Expenses				1,200		
Provision for Bad Debts				61		
Depreciation						
Equipment			1,300			
Furniture & Fittings			840			
China, Glass & Cutlery			180	2,320		40,711
Net Profit						£15,529

We are able to examine how these charges affect the profit and value of an operation by comparing the accounts illustrated in figure 2.35, with the final accounts shown in the previous example for the Pier House Restaurant. The changes we can observe are listed as follows:

(i) Net profit has been reduced from £18,110 to £15,529 by these adjustments.

(ii) The value of the fixed assets has been reduced by £2,320 due to the effect of depreciation.

(iii) Current Assets have increased by £539 due to the effects of the Bad Debt provision and the prepayment.

(iv) Current Liabilities have increased by £800 due to the Accrued Electricity Charge.

(v) The value of the business has changed from £90,600 to £88,019 in the balance sheet.

The Pier House Restaurant
Balance Sheet as at 30 Sept 8__

Fixed Assets		At Cost	Depreciation	Current Value
Premises (Freehold)				75,000
Equipment		6,500	1,300	5,200
Furniture & Fittings		4,200	840	3,360
China Glass & Cutlery		780	180	600
Current Assets				
Food Stock		800		
Liquor Stock		1,250		
Debtors	1,220			
— Provision for Bad Debts	61	1,159		
Prepaid Rates		600		
Cash in Hand		150		
Cash at Bank		3,960	7,919	
Current Liabilities				
Creditors		3,260		
Gas & Electricity Accrued		800	4,060	3,859
				£88,019
Financed by				
Capital		55,090		
+ Net Profit		15,529	70,619	
— Drawings			4,600	66,019
Bank Loan				22,000
				£88,019

In this section of the book we have covered the different methods that may be used by hotel and catering operations to record their financial transactions and how this information is treated in the preparation of final accounts. Whilst the assembly and presentation of financial information is an important aspect of the accounting procedures of a business organisation, the use and interpretation of this information must be considered as equally important. The information gained from historic accounts should be acted upon to improve the efficiency of the operation concerned, by way of reducing costs, increasing profits, fixing budgets and reviewing prices. In study book three we will examine information gained from the accounts of an operation with a view to achieving these objectives.

Further Reading

Book keeping In The Hotel and Catering Industry: *R. Kotas*
Accounting In The Hotel and Catering Industry:
   F. Wood and P. Lightowlers

Student Activity No. 2.38

(i) Repeat the Trading, Profit and Loss Account and Balance Sheet for Winston's Restaurant in Study Activity No 2.37 making the following provisions and adjustments.

(a) Depreciate Leasehold Premises by £2,500; Equipment and Furniture by 10%.

(b) Create a provision for Bad Debts of 10%.

(c) Insurance prepaid £150.

(d) Gas and Electricity Accrued £210.

(ii) Calculate the difference in Net Profit after these provisions and adjustments have been made.

Student Activity No. 2.39

From the trial balance set out below for the El Sombrero Restaurant as at 31 Dec 8__, prepare a Trading, Profit and Loss Account for the 3 months ending 31 Dec 8__ and a Balance Sheet at that date.

	DR	CR
Capital		30,000
Bank Loan		16,600
Food Purchases & Sales	6,100	17,350
Liquor Purchases & Sales	3,050	7,650
Rates	820	
Premises	33,000	
Administration Expenses	500	
Debtors & Creditors	1,400	1,140
Furniture	5,200	
Equipment	6,020	
Insurance	190	
Food Stock 01 Oct 8__	420	
Liquor Stock 01 Oct 8__	510	
Wages	7,090	
Bank Loan Interest	960	
China Glass & Cutlery	2,540	
Gas & Electricity	3,450	
Repairs & Maintenance	410	
Cash in Hand	65	
Cash at Bank	1,015	
	£72,740	£72,740

Take the following into consideration:

(i) Food Stock at 31 Dec 8__   £440
         Liquor Stock at 31 Dec 8__   £610

(ii) Rates prepaid £165

(iii) Gas charges accrued £190

(iv) Create a provision for Bad Debts of 5%.

(v) Depreciate furniture and equipment by 15%, china, glass & cutlery are revalued at £2,210.

174

ASSESSMENT QUESTIONS

1. Explain the purpose of keeping accounts.
2. Explain the meaning of Capital Income and list examples.
3. Explain the meaning of Revenue Income.
4. Explain the meaning of Capital Expenditure and list examples.
5. Explain the meaning of Revenue Expenditure and list examples.
6. Explain the meaning of Debit and Credit Entries in Ledger Accounts.
7. Explain the purpose of a Trial Balance.
8. From the following transactions, open up Ledger Accounts as appropriate, record the transactions listed below, balance off the Ledger Accounts and extract a Trial Balance.

   Tim Hornby sets up business as a Crêperie proprietor with a capital in cash £30,000 and a bank loan of £12,000 on May 1st 198__. His transactions are as follows:

   March

1st	Purchases Leasehold premises paying £25,000 in cash.
2nd	Pays cash for Equipment worth £6,800.
3rd	Purchases Furnishings and Fittings for £6,000.
4th	Purchases Food Stock for £960 by cash.
5th	Pays Rent in cash £600.
6th	Pays Insurance in cash £320.
7th	Purchases Equipment worth £1,500 on credit from H. James & Co.
8th	Cash Sales £425.
8th	Purchases Food Stock on credit from Youngs Seafood Ltd worth £230.
9th	Pays Wages in cash £185.
10th	Cash Sales £515.
11th	Purchases Food Stock on credit from H. Green worth £190.
12th	Purchases Food Stock for £220 cash.
13th	Returns Food Stock to H. Green worth £25.
13th	Cash Sales £550.
14th	Pays for Cleaning Materials in cash £65.
15th	Pays for Advertising in cash £230.
16th	Cash Sales £570.
17th	Purchases Food Stock on Credit from H. Green worth £210.
18th	Pays Wages in cash £355.
18th	Pays H. James £680 cash.

9. Explain the principles of the Visitors Tabulor Ledger.
10. Explain the purpose of the Trading Account.
11. Explain the purpose of the Profit and Loss Account.

12. Explain the purpose of the Balance Sheet.
13. Explain the meaning and purpose of Depreciation.
14. Explain the purpose of creating a provision for Bad Debts.
15. Explain how Prepayments are accounted for.
16. Explain how Accrued Charges are accounted for.
17. From the Trial Balance and Adjustments set out below for 'Looby's Bistro' prepare a Trading, Profit and Loss Account for 6 months ending 30 Sept 8__ and a Balance Sheet as at that date.

Looby's Bistro
Trial Balance as at 30 Sept 8__

	DR	CR
Capital		10,900
Bank Loan		4,000
Food Purchases & Sales	6,280	15,260
Liquor Purchases & Sales	2,900	6,640
Premises (Leasehold)	8,000	
Equipment & Furniture	5,600	
Rent & Rates	1,800	
China Glass & Cutlery	955	
Wages	4,435	
Food Stock @ 01 Apr 8__	400	
Liquor Stock @ 01 Apr 8__	420	
Advertising	400	
Administration Expenses	610	
Debtors & Creditors	240	940
Gas & Electricity	1,690	
Cleaning & Laundry	305	
Cash in Hand	145	
Cash at Bank	3,165	
Maintenance	210	
Sundry Expenses	185	
	£37,740	£37,740

Take the following adjustments and provisions into consideration.
(a) Food stock at 30 Sept 8__ £370.
   Liquor Stock at 30 Sept 8__ £405.
(b) Create a provision for Bad Debts of 5%.
(c) Depreciate Leasehold premises by £500; Equipment and Furniture by 10%; China, Glass and Cutlery are revalued at £905.
(d) Rent and Rates paid in advance £450.
(e) Gas and Electricity Accrued £95.
18. Explain the advantages of using electronic data processing systems in the preparation of accounts.

Purchasing Costing and Control

STUDY BOOK THREE

Purchasing Practice and Stock Management

In the previous studies we examined the principles involved in the purchasing and storage of materials for hotel and catering operations. The aim of this approach was to demonstrate the way in which efficient purchasing and storage procedures were implemented to ensure that the objectives set down by the business policy of the organisation were achieved. Whilst these principles have been of a practical nature in producing purchase specifications and providing adequate storage facilities etc., we must now examine the management skills necessary to maintain continuity in the supply and the price of materials used by the industry. We will therefore examine methods of purchasing research from the market information available to purchasing officers, to assist them in maintaining cost control and continuity of supply. Within the operation itself we will examine methods of stock management to assist them in achieving the same objectives.

PURCHASING RESEARCH

An important aid to management when planning for the future is a knowledge of the cost and availability of the materials they will need to meet the demands placed upon their organisation. Whilst in almost all cases it is impossible to predict future prices and availability of materials with any precision, the caterer often finds himself in a position of having to do this. Unlike manufactured goods, which in most cases rise in price, food prices will rise and fall in price, presenting further problems to the caterer. It may be argued that if future price increases were known the caterer could change his menus so as not to use these types of food in abundance, eg. fish. This would then have the effect of decreasing demand and consequently the price would not increase. The future cost of materials is therefore often open to guess work based upon past trends and to a degree on the caterer's intuition.

The caterer must therefore observe trends in prices and availability which are linked together by a basic economic principle, ie. supply falls therefore demand increases and prices go up and vice versa. For the caterer to be able to plan his menus and subsequent purchasing requirements he must assess from the market information available where he is going to get best value. Availability of most food products is now all the year round, due to much improved transportation services which allow fresh foods to be imported from world wide sources of supply. Improved technology has also contributed to better methods of food storage in transit, as well as increasing the range of frozen, dried and preserved foods available. We may therefore assume all year round availability, but if fresh foods are required the cost will vary according to availability. Since 1977 the caterer and hotelkeeper have published a Food Cost Index prepared for them by Richard Kotas and Bernard Davis of the University of Surrey. This index is based upon a computer analysis of 150 different food items with hundreds of catering establishments contributing information. The results are published monthly in the Caterer and Hotelkeeper, in addition to their weekly market price guide and are based on an index of 100 in 1977. Figure 3.1 shows a graph of the index from 1977 to 1984 of the average increases that have taken place in the 150 food items over this time. The index shows average food costs rose to over 170 during 1984 which indicates an average increase of over 70% since 1977. From this graph it is easy to observe that there is a seasonal variation to be considered, this is because lower than average food prices occur between August and February in most years. Whilst this index is concerned with the average food cost, there is also a detailed analysis of the individual food items published each month. Figure 3.2 shows a table of monthly price changes for the different commodity groups. From this table we are able to observe changes in food costs during the year and plan pur-

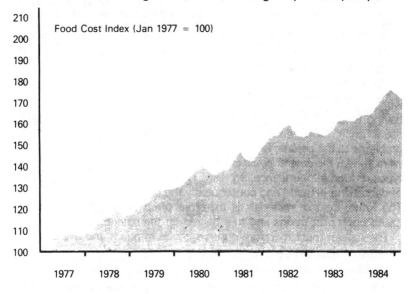

Fig. 3.1 *Caterer and Hotelkeeper Food Cost Index*

chasing and menus accordingly. By further research into the commodity group the caterer is also able to decide on the most economic cuts of meat, vegetables etc. There will, of course, be local variations to these prices which will involve the caterer doing his own research from his own sources.

From his observations of the information available to him the caterer is able to take appropriate action to control his food costs and maintain continuity of supply. Decisions regarding when to use fresh or frozen foods or to project certain dishes on menus are made easier by following and acting on trends that can be deduced from the information gained. We can therefore assume the caterer is able to have a more sophisticated approach to purchasing by observing long term trends in food costs from the sources we have examined.

The Caterer Food Cost Index
Base: 1st Jan, 1977 = 100.0

Commodity Group	Jan	Feb	Mar	Apr	May	June	July	Aug	Sept	Oct	Nov	Dec
Meat	165.4	164.7	163.0	169.4	175.2	179.6	179.9	173.4	178.5	173.4	173.5	176.3
Portion Controlled Meats	167.1	162.8	167.7	171.4	178.6	176.0	167.1	170.0	172.3	173.2	172.8	172.8
Offal	126.5	121.1	121.3	119.0	124.3	120.5	119.2	122.0	120.4	125.2	123.6	128.1
Processed Meats	149.9	145.3	145.8	143.6	145.0	147.4	145.4	144.5	148.5	147.5	149.8	151.0
Fish	136.5	137.5	139.2	138.7	138.5	133.0	131.3	135.5	131.0	135.0	141.1	135.3
Fresh Vegetables	123.5	123.3	119.5	121.5	127.1	143.0	136.1	133.8	135.0	133.3	131.0	138.4
Frozen Canned Veg	138.7	136.8	137.7	136.4	137.9	138.6	137.1	142.0	145.7	145.1	148.3	146.8
Fresh Fruits	157.9	146.4	152.3	158.9	156.8	160.5	174.0	157.3	143.9	150.5	144.9	147.7
Frozen Canned Fruits	152.4	154.7	154.2	152.6	159.0	156.3	155.4	160.6	161.4	164.7	164.4	165.3
Dairy Produce	193.6	187.4	191.9	200.8	203.1	196.1	202.3	195.6	202;9	207.2	202.8	205.8
Groceries	167.6	165.6	169.1	168.8	167.2	174.3	179.4	176.7	180.3	179.2	197.3	179.8
Overall Index	154.4	152.2	153.2	155.1	157.8	160.5	160.6	159.1	161.1	161.1	161.2	162.6

Fig. 3.2 *Table of Monthly Price Changes for Commodity Groups*

Student Activity   No. 3.1

(i)   From the Food Cost Index for 1984 prepare a graph comparing the price changes for the following commodity groups:
  (a) Fresh Vegetables and Frozen/Canned Vegetables.
  (b) Meat and Portion Controlled Meats.

(ii)   Make a list of the most economic months for each group of commodities.

(iii)   Discuss in your group the reasons for the changes in food cost for each commodity group.

Student Activity   No. 3.2

Research past editions of the Caterer and Hotelkeeper weekly food price lists the price of English and New Zealand legs of lamb for the past three months and draw a graph comparing their prices.

Make or Buy Decisions

The decision for a hotel and catering operation to make its own or buy in products involves comparing the advantages of one option against the other. The 'make' option is excluded for all items which cannot be made using existing equipment or skills subject to the work load of the department. The 'buy' option being excluded for all items which can be economically made within the operation by using existing equipment or skills, subject again to the work load of the department. In hotel and catering operations these decisions usually apply to the use of convenience foods, laundry and linen provision, maintenance and stationery requirements. Major areas of expenditure such as laundry or maintenance will require a detailed analysis of the capital and revenue expenditure involved as well as the various organisational problems. This will be balanced against the cost of contracting out to external organisations. For smaller areas of expenditure, such as the use of convenience and bought in foods, changing the use and repair of linen or printing requirements, the caterer will consider the advantages and disadvantages of 'make or buy' and how they may affect his operation. In some cases the following reasons may force his hand or greatly influence his decision.

(i)   Major price increases.
(ii) Service or delivery failures from suppliers.
(iii) Deterioration in the quality of service or product supplied.
(iv) Emergency supplies required due to unforeseen events.
(v)   Ecomomic pressure to reduce costs or retain staff during quiet periods.
(vi) Very specialised requests from customers.

With the increased range of convenience foods available to the caterer a 'make or buy' decision often has to be made and is now in many cases part of the catering policy of different organisations. The use of convenience foods will increase food costs against the use of raw materials, but it should have the effect of reducing labour costs because less skill is necessary when preparing foods and time is also saved. Therefore, apart from the catering policy when making 'make or buy' decisions the caterer should in the first instance compare the cost of buying in food against the cost of raw materials from a standard recipe and the cost of its production, ie. labour and overheads. The supplier of bought in foods will also have incurred these costs, though through batch production and other reasons they may be less. However, he will have additional costs in packaging and delivery as well as his profit. The caterer must also consider whether or not his staff have the skills to produce such products to the standard required, and whether the equipment provided is suitable to achieve the same standards. An additional consideration will be the capacity of the department concerned to absorb the extra work load without affecting existing production or efficiency. The image of 'home produced' food will already have been decided in the catering policy of the organisation but in some cases where a predominance of convenience foods are used this can be used to enhance sales or for special promotions.

Student Activity   No. 3.3

(i)   Compare the food cost of a 16 portion Mocha or Black Forest Gateau purchased from a frozen food supplier and one made from a standard recipe in your practical cookery text book.

(ii)   List the extra costs that would have to be considered when preparing this dish yourself.

(iii)   Discuss in your group which product would be preferable in the following establishments:

(a) Motel Coffee Shop.

(b) Privately owned Bistro.

(c) Department Store Restaurant.

STOCK MANAGEMENT

The principles of stock management involve making certain that sufficient levels of stock are held to ensure that the operation can function efficiently in relation to the financial and catering policies of the business concerned. Too little stock being held may result in commodities not being available when they are needed. Conversely, excess stock holdings will lead to unprofitable capital investment. It is therefore important that minimum and maximum stock levels are established by management and also a rate of stock turnover required to efficiently utilise capital investment. The rate of stock turnover will vary according to the type of establishment, the frequency of delivery from suppliers and the storage space available. Food stock turnover will usually be once every two weeks, although fast food operations located in city centres may have a turnover of stock every few days. In contrast more luxurious operations, situated in remote locations, will turnover their stock every three weeks or more. Liquor stock turnover will usually be every 4-6 weeks; variations will occur according to the range and type of liquor sold. Public houses or restaurants selling mainly real ale or house wine respectively, will turnover their stock more quickly than cocktail bars or high class restaurants who have a more extensive range of liquor available.

Rate of Stock Turnover Calculation
The formula used to calculate the annual rate of stock turnover is shown below:

Annual Cost of Sales ÷ Average Cost of Stock Held
= Stock Turnover per annum

Example:
A hotel's cost of food sales for a year is £46,000, the stock held at the beginning of the year was £1,600 and at the end of the year is £1,780.

Average Stock	=	£1,600 + 1,780 ÷ 2 = £1,690
Stock Turnover p.a.	=	£46,000 ÷ 1,690 = 27.2 times p.a.
Stock Turnover in days	=	365 ÷ 27.2 = 13.4 days (ie. 2 weeks)

Buffer Stock Levels
A buffer stock level is the minimum level of a stock item which should always be held to prevent establishments running out of supplies of that specific item. The formula for calculating buffer stock levels is as follows:

Average Stock Held − ½ Normal Ordering Quantity

The average stock held for each item is also the re-order level and is determined by:

(i) Perishability and availability.
(ii) Maximum and minimum amount used during the period concerned, according to the sales volume anticipated.
(iii) Regularity of delivery and ordering time.
(iv) Proper storage space available.
(v) Economic ordering quantity.

The normal ordering quantity will be the difference between the maximum stock level and the minimum ascertained by taking the above points into consideration. This assumes that normal conditions prevail in the supply of a demand for that particular stock item. The purpose of the buffer stock is to absorb any unusual conditions that might prevail. The buffer stock should also relate to the average usage of a stock item between deliveries. For example, if average usage is 50 units per week and deliveries are weekly, then the buffer stock should be able to absorb the weekly usage in the event of non delivery.

Example of a Re-order Stock Level Calculation
The average weekly consumption is 25 units of a stock item which is delivered weekly and which requires 3 days ordering time. The maximum stock level would be 3 week's stock of 75 units, the minimum level would be 1 week's consumption of 25 units and the average stock would be 50 units. The re-order stock level would be calculated as follows:

Buffer Stock + ½ Weekly Usage (3 days order time)
25 + 12.5 = 37.5 units

The normal ordering quantity would be 50 units (the difference between maximum and minimum stock levels). The buffer stock may be checked by using the following formula:

Average Stock Held − ½ Normal Ordering Quantity
ie. 50 − (½ × 50) = 50 − 25,

the buffer stock would be adequate at 25 units.

Economic Ordering Quantity

To ascertain economic order quantities for stock items we must consider the following points:

(i) Usage of the stock item.

(ii) Cost of the stock item per unit at different quantities of purchase.

(iii) Budget available for purchasing stock.

(iv) Storage space available.

(v) Rate of stock turnover required.

(vi) Shelf life of stock item.

Whilst it is often cheaper to buy in bulk, the caterer must consider the points we have mentioned to gain the most economic price for his operation. For example, a small hotel may find it more economical to purchase domestic sizes of certain stock items which he rarely uses from a supermarket rather than bulk purchase from a wholesaler or cash and carry. At the other end of the scale a large hotel may find it more economical to purchase its house wine by the cask and then bottle it for themselves. Each type of establishment must therefore consider the points mentioned earlier in relation to their own financial and purchasing policies to create their own economies of stock.

Pareto Analysis of Stock Holding

Pareto analysis involves placing stock items into different categories according to their usage-values. If this analysis is applied to stock control in three different values it will categorise them into groups. Group A is for high usage value items which would qualify for special treatment in their ordering and control. Group C is for low usage-value, which will probably account for over half of the stock items held getting routine treatment in their ordering and control. Group B is for intermediary usage-value items with various policies in their ordering and control. To put a value on each group for hotel and catering operations is difficult because expenditure and sales volume varies according to the establishment and its size. For small operations Group A would be in the range of £3,000-£5,000 and Group C in the range of £50-£200 per annum. Large operations would, however, categorise Group A items as £60,000-£100,000 and Group C as £100-£2,000 per annum. The value of these groups may also be expressed as unit value of stock items, in which case Pareto Analysis for Group A stock items would have a value of £50-£100 per unit and Group C items a value of 50p-£5. An example of Group A may be a hind quarter of beef against a steak for Group C. The advantage of preparing a Pareto Analysis of stock is that high value items can be given more rigorous control procedures than standard systems used for lower value items.

Student Activity No. 3.4
Prepare a Pareto Analysis on a unit value basis for food stock items that may be found in the stores of your college department or your own place of work.

Further Reading
Caterer and Hotelkeeper Food Cost Index   *(Monthly)*
Purchasing Principles and Management   Chapter 7   *Baily and Farmer*
Food and Beverage Control   Chapter 7   *Kotas and Davis*

ASSESSMENT QUESTIONS

1. List the sources of market information available to the caterer.
2. Explain the action you may consider when past trends indicate you are faced with imminent price rises.
3. List the reasons that may influence caterers to make their own products rather than buy them in.
4. Explain how you would compare costs with a view to recommending 'make or buy' decisions.
5. Explain the principles of stock management.
6. A fast-food restaurant's cost of food sales are £89,800. Stock held at the beginning of the year is £1,450 and at the end of the year is £1,670.
   (a) Calculate the rate of stock turnover in days.
   (b) Comment on the result.
7. Explain the points you would consider when deciding on buffer stock levels.
8. Explain the considerations made when ascertaining economic order quantities.
9. Explain Pareto Analysis of stock holding.
10. Prepare a Pareto Analysis on a unit value basis for stock items you would expect to find in a cleaning materials store.

Budgetary Control

Budgetary Control is an important management technique. It is used for controlling income and expenditure by preparing budgets relating to the business activities of an operation and provides a basis for comparison with actual results. In this section we will examine the roles for forecasting, budgeting and variance analysis as part of the budgetary control procedure.

The forecasting of future activities involves preparing details of estimated sales and related costs, planning capital expenditure on assets to meet these future demands and planning future cash requirements for the business to function. A budget is a planned statement of the future financial affairs of a business organisation for the purpose of achieving given objectives set down in the policy of that business organisation. The difference between forecasting and budgeting is best described by saying that a budget is prepared from the estimated future results ie. the forecast. Variance Analysis is a study of the reasons for changes that may occur between budgeted and actual results.

BUDGETING

There are different types of budget that may be prepared for all kinds of business organisations and which are also used for hotel and catering operations. In this study we will examine these budgets. We must be aware that budgets are prepared from forecasts made by the departments of an operation in relation to estimated income and expenditure. As this is the case, it is regarded as being fair to have some consultation in their preparation and the way they may affect the operation as a whole. Therefore, budget committees are formed from staff who are involved in budget preparation or may be affected by them. Before we examine the role played by budget committees, we will, first of all, look at the structure of budgeting and the budgets that are prepared for hotel and catering operations. Figure 3.3 shows a typical budget structure that may exist from the formation of a company policy through to the preparation of a budgeted balance sheet at the end of the budget period. The 'budget period' may vary from one month to five years depending on the type of budget. For hotel and catering operations it is preferable to budget over a period of six months or a year, sub-dividing the budget into monthly periods to

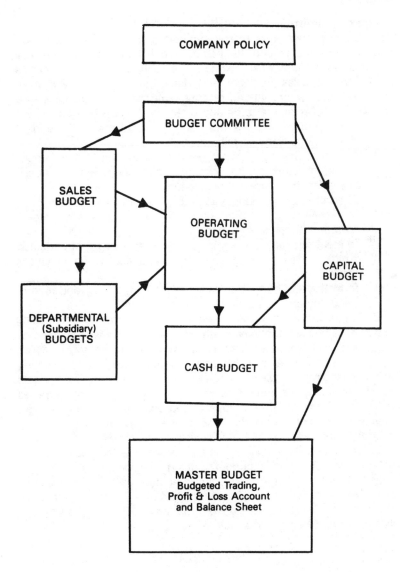

Fig. 3.3 *A Budget Structure*

permit comparison with actual results and thereby increasing control. Seasonal operations should budget for high and low periods separately.

Budget Committees

The budget committee is an advisory body to a business organisation and not an executive one. Its membership will consist of the General Manager who will act as chairman, the accountant who will act as secretary, the sales manager and departmental heads who have responsibilities for capital and revenue expenditure. In some cases a budget controller may also be appointed but it is generally accepted that the accountant also fills this role. The functions of the budget committee may be listed as follows:

(i) To ensure that budgets are prepared according to the organisational structure of the operation and clearly define responsibilities for the budgeted expenditure.

(ii) To administer the budget according to company policy.

(iii) To receive and consider departmental budgets and prepare operating budgets from them.

(iv) To meet regularly and compare actual results against budgeted results, recommending any remedial action when variances occur.

(v) To review the budget as and when it is necessary and recommend any amendments that may be required.

The budget committee will prepare a 'budget manual' containing details of all budgets that have been prepared; this will ensure that they are satisfactorily followed. The manual will set out the way in which budgets and accounts are classified, detailed procedures concerning review periods and a calendar of dates for budget reports. The budgets which are set by the committee are essentially for planning purposes and are known as 'fixed budgets' because they do not change, irrespective of increases or decreases in the volume of sales. However, it is also necessary to prepare 'flexible budgets' which are usually calculated when the actual results are known. The 'flexible budget' is an extension of the 'fixed budget' in that it considers the effect that a change in sales volume has on the budgeted results. This will then assist the budget committee in their analysis of any variances that have taken place. We will examine the preparation of a flexible budget in the section on variance analysis later in this study.

TYPES OF BUDGET

In this section we will examine how the different subsidiary budgets are prepared and the contribution they make to the master budget. The master budget is better explained as a budgeted trading, profit and loss account and a budgeted balance sheet. Subsidiary budgets may also be known under the headings of sales budgets, departmental operating budgets, capital and cash budgets.

Sales Budgets

The sales budget is regarded by some as the most important budget, because all other budgets are based upon it. The budget is guided by the company's sales policy and is dependent upon the following areas of information:

(i) Sales figures and statistics from previous years for all departments of the operation.
(ii) Accurate forecast of future sales.
(iii) Spare capacity that the operation has for expansion.
(iv) The anticipated reaction from any sales promotion and advertising that is taking place.
(v) The economic climate and the way in which it might affect business demand, employment and disposable income.
(vi) The effect any local or regional events may have.
(vii) Competition that exists locally.
(viii) Changes in prices and tariffs.

Example of a Sales Budget
Set out below are sales details for the Sandpebbles Hotel for the month of September 198__. The hotel has 30 bedrooms with a restaurant open to the public and a restaurant and residential licence.
Rooms: 700 room nights at an average rate of £17 per room per night.
Food Sales: 1,800 covers at an average spending of £5.40 each.
Liquor Sales: £4,850.
For the forthcoming year prices have been increased as follows: The average room rate to £18 per person per night, the average spending in the restaurant to £5.60 and bar prices by 5%. It is anticipated that sales will increase by 5% for rooms and food, liquor sales are not expected to increase. The sales budget for September would be set out as shown in figure 3.4, note that the increase in sales has been calculated on the new prices.

SANDPEBBLES HOTEL			Sales Budget for Sept. 198__	
Department	Sales Last Year (£)	No. of Covers/Rooms	Average Price	Total This Year (£)
Rooms Food Liquor	11,900 9,720 4,850	735 1,890	£18.00 £ 5.60	13,230 10,584 5,093
Total	26,470			28,907

Fig. 3.4 *Example of a Sales Budget*

Student Activity   No. 3.5

From the information and forecasts set out below prepare a Sales Budget for next year.

	LAST YEAR			NEXT YEAR	
	Units Sold	Average Price	Total	Price Change	Sales Forecast
Rooms	11,860	£20.00	£237,200	£21.50 per room	2% Increase
Food	13,650	£ 6.10	£ 83,265	£ 9.40 ASP	20% Decrease
Liquor			£ 80,940	5% Increase	10% Decrease

A decision has been made to improve the hotel restaurant operation by changing its theme and menu, consequently prices have been increased and seating capacity reduced. Comment on the effect this has had on the budgeted sales figure.

Departmental Operating Budgets

Departmental budgets may also be known as subsidiary budgets and are prepared for each department of an operation. They form part of the master budget in the contribution they make to the overall budget of an operation. Their main source of information, in the first instance, would be from the sales budget, if they are a revenue earning department eg. rooms, banqueting etc.

Non-Revenue Earning Departments

Non-revenue earning departments eg. maintenance, laundry and advertising would be given a budget total to work from, this total would be linked to total turnover of the operation. Consequently, this figure will vary but, as the costs are linked to the rise and fall in sales, problems should not occur, providing they have been properly considered in the first instance. The budget should be prepared after considering the previous year's expenditure and the antitipated expenditure in the budget period. There should also be consideration given in a maintenance budget to any capital expenditure involved in the budget period, which may affect the department, in addition to that linked directly to expenditure. For example, if the expenditure on maintenance is budgeted at 3.5% of sales from past accounts, then the budget would be adjusted from the sales budget accordingly. Any additional work such as installing new equipment or services would be budgeted for from the Capital Budget. This may also be said of marketing budgets, whilst there is the normal marketing expenditure in selling a hotel and its services, the marketing of a new project, eg. a bar or a restaurant, would be budgeted for in the capital cost of that project. We are therefore able to distinguish between budgeting for capital expenditure and budgeting for revenue expenditure. Capital expenditure budgets are involved in the cost of improving existing facilities (assets) or setting up new facilities whereas the operating budget is involved with costs maintaining the existing services or facilities. An example of a non-revenue earning department's budget is shown in figure 3.5. From this budget, we can notice a general increase in budgeted expenditure of 10% with the exception of depreciation and hire charges. As these charges are fixed, they do not change unless more equipment is purchased or hired. We are therefore able to understand the affect of fixed and variable costs on budgeting. Different operations may have various approaches to the treatment of shared overheads. In the example, we have assumed fuel charges are charged directly to the laundry but we must be aware that this is not always the case, we will study this further in the next section of the book.

DEPARTMENT: **LAUNDRY**		BUDGET PERIOD: 19__8
19__7 Actual	Expenditure	19__8 Budget
£ 29,860 4,120 2,040 5,142 420 360 550	Wages & Staff Expenses Materials Hire Charges Fuel (Electricity) Sundry Charges Maintenance & Repairs Depreciation	£ 32,846 4,532 2,040 6,756 462 396 550
£43,492	Total	£47,582
PREPARED BY:	APPROVED BY:	DATE:

Fig. 3.5 *Departmental Operating Budget*

Revenue Earning Departments

Where revenue earning departments are concerned the budgets are prepared from the costs involved, relating to the sales budget. These costs will include materials (food and drink), direct labour and overhead charges, and are based on the previous year's cost and adjusted to take account of cost increases as well as any forecasted sales increase. For example, in the sales budget for the Sandpebbles Hotel, illustrated in figure 3.4, liquor sales are forecasted to be £5,093 for the month of September. If the hotel adopts a liquor gross profit of 55%, the cost of

SANDPEBBLES HOTEL BAR OPERATING BUDGET for Sept. 198__			
	%	£	£
Budgeted Sales Cost of Sales	100 45		5,093 2,292
Gross Profit	55		2,801
Labour Cost Cleaning Materials Net Operating Profit	15 1 39	764 51	815 1,986

Fig. 3.6 *Departmental Operating Budget*

sales may be calculated as 45% of £5.093 which is £2,292. Other direct costs such as labour may also be calculated as a proportion of the sales figure. Indirect costs such as fuel and administration expenses, are budgeted for in the overall operating budget for the establishment. Therefore, the bar will have a budgeted operating profit as shown in figure 3.6.

Indirect Labour and Overheads Budgets
The indirect elements of labour and overheads are, to a greater degree, fixed expenses, although there is a variable element to be considered. Indirect labour costs cover management salaries, security staff etc. and the amount budgeted for them will not vary provided it is properly considered by the budget committee. The variable elements will increase or decrease in line with sales and will include part time and casual staff, it is also important to include labour costs other than wages such as staff meals, transport and national insurance costs. Overhead costs are also of a fixed nature, and will include: Rents, Rates and Depreciation, as well as the main proportion of fuel costs. Variable overheads will be elements of fuel, cleaning and laundry expenses, which will move in line with sales. Whilst it is easy to budget costs which do not change, it is more difficult to budget the variable element of them. It is generally regarded that unless costs are easily apportioned to a department they are charged to the operation overall.

Operating Budget
The operating budget will be an amalgamation of all the sales departmental budgets, showing the budgeted operating profit for each

SANDPEBBLES HOTEL – OPERATING BUDGET
Budget Period September 19__6

Department	Rooms		Food		Liquor		Total	
	%	£	%	£	%	£	%	£
Sales	100	13,230	100	10,584	100	5,093	100	28,907
Cost of Sales			40	4,234	45	2,292	22.5	6,526
Gross Profit	100	13,230	60	6,350	55	2,801	77.5	22,381
Labour (Direct)	15	1,984	22	2,328	15	764	17.5	5,076
Expenses (Direct)	20	2,646	5	529	1	51	11.0	3,226
Operating Profit	65	8,600	33	3,493	39	1,986	49	14,079
Indirect Expenses — Labour Costs					3.4	1,000		
Rates & Insurance					3.7	1,060		
Fuel					5.0	1,442		
Maintenance					3.0	867		
Laundry					4.0	1,160		
Marketing					3.0	867		
Admin. Expenses					3.0	867		
Sundry Expenses					1.3	400		
Depreciation					2.0	600	29	8,263
BUDGETED NET OPERATING PROFIT							20	5,816

Fig. 3.7 *Example of an Operating Budget*

department and the net profit for the whole operation, after shared labour and overhead costs have been deducted. An example of the operating budget for the Sandpebbles Hotel is shown in figure 3.7, using the information already shown in figures 3.4 and 3.6 for the month of September 198__.

Student Activity   No. 3.6
From the sales budget you have prepared in Activity No. 3.5, prepare an operating budget considering the following forecasts and information:

	Rooms	Food	Liquor
Gross Profit	—	68%	60%
Direct Labour	16%	24%	14%
Direct Expenses	11%	10%	2%
Indirect Expenses			
Rates & Insurance	£16,200		
Management Salaries	£10,500		
Administration	3% of Sales		
Depreciation	£6,000		
Marketing	3% of Sales		
Maintenance	3.5% of Sales		
Fuel — Fixed	£19,000		
Variable	0.5% of Sales		

Capital Budgets
Capital Budgets deal with the Capital and Assets of the operation, the most important of these being capital expenditure and cash budgets. The capital expenditure budget usually extends over longer periods of time normally based on a five or ten year plan and includes the expenditure on fixed assets during that time. Some business organisations will prepare separate budgets for equipment, furniture and fittings and smaller items of equipment. The budgets are prepared allowing departmental expenditure on equipment over the budget period, depending on the availability of cash. Control over capital expenditure is easily applied, because the budgeted figure may not be exceeded without authorisation from the budget committee. The committee, when preparing capital expenditure budgets, will have to set aside a proportion of their budget in the case of emergencies, due to equipment failures or other events. An important aspect of capital budgeting is the availability of cash to fund any projects, as well as providing sufficient cash for the day to day operation of the business.

Cash Budgets
The cash budget is usually the last to be prepared, as it will forecast the incoming and outgoing of cash, based on the operating income from

sales and the expenditure of cash on materials, labour and overheads. It will also show the budgeted expenditure on assets and other incomes the business may have through raising capital or interest and rents received.

The cash budget is usually broken down into monthly periods to accommodate delays in cash income and expenditure which occur through the giving and receiving of credit. It is also necessary to prepare a monthly breakdown of all income and all expenditure. This should be carried out bearing in mind those which involve immediate income and expenditure and those which are delayed. The majority of sales in the hotel and catering industry are cash transactions; it must however be decided what the proportions of cash and credit sales are and the period of delay in payment by debtors. Expenditure involves a majority of credit being received in the purchase of materials and the payment of overheads. Wages, however, involve the immediate outflow of cash, as do a small proportion of purchases (ie. petty cash transactions). Some expenses such as Rents, Rates and Insurances are paid in advance. This involves an outflow of cach prior to the budget period it relates to in calculating profits. The actual payment, as and when it occurs, is recorded in the cash budget. The principle involved in the preparation of a cash budget is that of establishing the cash balance at the beginning of the budget period, adding on income received in the period and deducting expenditure made during the same period. The difference between these figures will be the balance of cash carried forward to the next period. If budgets are prepared on monthly periods covering the whole budget period it is possible to ascertain the amount of debtors, creditors, accruals and prepayments at the end of the period. These figures will be transferred as current assets and liabiities to the balance sheet.

Preparation of a Cash Budget Exercise
The Budget Committee of the Cutty Sark Restaurant have prepared the following forecasts for inclusion in the Master Budget.

Month	Sales	Purchases	Wages	Overheads	Depreciation
May	17,000	9,600	5,600	2,100	200
June	19,000	8,000	5,800	2,000	200
July	20,000	10,000	7,200	2,200	200
August	24,000	11,000	7,400	2,400	200
September	30,000	15,600	7,600	2,800	200

Additional Information:
  (i)   10% of the sales will be on credit, debtors will be expected to settle their accounts in the month after the transaction.
 (ii) All purchases are on credit, creditors will be paid two months after the transaction.
(iii) Wages will be paid in cash.
(iv) Annual Rates of £1,200 are paid in March for the year starting April 1st 198__.

(v) Fuel charges for quarter ending 30th June amounting to £300 will be paid in July; this quarter's will be paid in October.

(vi) All other overheads are paid when incurred in cash.

(vii) The balance of cash at the bank on 1 July is £2,000

The Cash Budget for quarter ending 30th September 198__ is shown in figure 3.8 was prepared after considering the information given as follows:

Cash Budget for the CUTTY SARK RESTAURANT Quarter Ending 30 Sept. 8__

	July	Aug	Sept	Notes
Cash Incoming				
Opening Balance	2000	2800	8800	
Cash Sales	18000	21600	27000	
Credit Sales	1900	2000	2400	Debtors: £3,000
Other Income				
Total	21900	26400	38200	
Cash Outgoing				
Purchases	9600	8000	10000	Creditors: £26,600
Wages	7200	7400	7600	
Rates	300			Prepaid: £600
Other Overheads	2000	2200	2600	Accrued: £300
Other Expenditure				
Total	19100	17600	19200	
Balance C/F	2800	8800	19000	

Fig. 3.8 *Example of a Cash Budget*

(i) The actual cash sales for each month are recorded after deducting the 10% credit sales, this 10% credit figure is recorded in the following month showing the cash received for credit sales. (ie. £1,900 cash received from credit sales in July is 10% of the total June sales of £19,000). The £3,000 credit sales for September are recorded as debtors in the notes column for transfer to the balance sheet at a later stage.

(ii) The actual cash outgoing for purchases each month is recorded as the purchases for two months previous to the payment date. (ie. May's purchases are paid in July). The total of purchases owing at the end of the budget period is recorded in the notes column as creditors for later transfer to the balance sheet. (ie. £11,000 (Aug) + £15,600 (Sept) = £26,600).

(iii) Wages are recorded as forecasted because there is no time delay.

(iv) Rates were paid for the whole year in advance before the budget period, therefore no outgoing of cash is recorded for them. Because this transaction was made in March for the financial year commencing 1st April, the amount prepaid is recorded in the notes column as it stands at the end of the budget period for later transfer to the balance sheet.

(v) The previous period's fuel charges have been recorded as being paid in July, the fuel charges for the budget period are totalled and recorded as accrued in the notes column for later transfer to the balance sheet.

(vi) Other overheads paid during the budget period are calculated by deducting £200 from the forecast figure to cover the rates already paid and the fuel charge for each month which will be paid in October.

(vii) The opening bank balance is recorded as the opening balance on the budget.

Other points to note when preparing cash budgets are that depreciation is not recorded, because it does not involve any cash expenditure. The closing cash balance carried forward at the end of the budget period is transferred to the balance sheet in the master budget. In this particular exercise there has been no other income or expenditure, however, when this occurs it would be recorded in the appropriate space. Examples of other income would be rents or interest received and other expenditure would be purchasing assets or repaying loans etc.

Student Activity No. 3.7

From the following forecasts and information for the Dracena Hotel prepare a Cash Budget for budget period quarter ending 31 Dec 198__

Month	Sales	Purchases	Wages	Overheads
August	2,600	1,150	600	550
September	2,500	1,100	600	500
October	2,200	950	500	600
November	2,200	1,200	500	500
December	2,600	1,200	600	550

Additional Information
(i) Sales are 90% in cash, the remainder is paid after 5-8 weeks.
(ii) Purchases are 90% on credit, accounts being paid within 2 months.
(iii) Wages are paid when incurred.
(iv) Overheads include £50 per month depreciation and are paid 50% in cash and 50% after a delay of one month.
(v) The hotel is repaying a loan at a rate of £150 per month.
(vi) The opening bank balance at 1st October will be £1,300.

Student Activity No. 3.8

Simon Francis is setting up business as a restaurant owner in March with the intention of starting business on April 1st. After purchasing the necessary assets his bank balance will be £1,000 on April 1st. He forecasts his sales will be £3,000 for April and will increase by 10% on the previous month for May and June. He estimates 20% of his sales will be on credit, his debtors are expected to pay their accounts after two months. He will operate on a 40% food cost replacing his stock on a daily basis, he will purchase all his stock on credit and he has agreed to settle his accounts on a monthly basis. Wages are estimated to be £680 per month and will be paid in cash. He estimates his overheads will be £580 per month, of which rent is £150 and which will be paid for six months in advance on April 1st. The remaining overheads are paid as follows: 50% after one month and 50% after two months. Mr Francis has a loan which he has agreed to repay at £200 per month, commencing in April. He also expects to receive £1,000 from a life insurance policy in May which he will pay into the business, he plans to spend this amount on carpets in June. Prepare a Cash Budget for Mr Francis for the first 3 months of his operation.

Master Budgets — Budgeted Trading and Profit and Loss Accounts
The master budget of a business operation is a budgeted set of final accounts ie. Trading and Profit and Loss Accounts and a budgeted Balance Sheet, different operations will refer to them under either title. They are prepared from all subsidiary budgets and forecasts within the operation and present a synopsis of the budgeted results. In this section we have so far examined the preparation of these subsidiary budgets, we must now examine how they would be presented in the master budget. We are able to prepare a budgeted trading, profit and loss account from the departmental forecasts and operating budgets. These are usually set out showing revenue earning department's sales and gross profits in a budgeted trading account. The budgeted profit and loss account, showing operating expenses and non-revenue earning department's budgets, the difference between the budgeted gross profit and total expenses being the budgeted net profit. An example of the budgeted trading and profit and loss account for the Sandpebbles Hotel is shown in figure 3.9, all the information being

SANDPEBBLES HOTEL
Budgeted Trading, Profit and Loss Account for month end 30 Sept 8__

	Rooms	Food	Liquor	Total
Sales	13,230	10,584	5,093	28,907
— Cost of Sales		4,234	2,292	6,526
Gross Profit	13,230	6,350	2,801	22,381
Less Expenses				
Wages & Salaries			6,076	
Rates & Insurance			1,060	
Fuel			1,442	
Maintenance			2,481	
Laundry			2,772	
Marketing			867	
Admin. Expenses			867	
Sundry Expenses			400	
Depreciation			600	16,565
Net Profit				5,816

Fig. 3.9 *Example of a Budgeted Trading and Profit and Loss Account*

taken from the budgeted operating statement in figure 3.7. Note the different way of presenting this information and compare it with the trading and profit and loss accounts illustrated in study book 2 figure 2.35. The direct labour costs have been added together, whilst direct expenses have been added to the relevant cost area (in this case they have been equally shared between maintenance and laundry).

Master Budgets — Budgeted Balance Sheets
Whilst we have been able to prepare budgeted trading, profit and loss accounts from forecasts and budgets for the budget period. To prepare a budgeted balance sheet we must consider the balance sheet at the beginning of the budget period and any changes that will take place in the value of the assets and liabilities during the period. We will consider the four main areas of the Balance Sheet and how the budgets may affect them.

Fixed Assets
Planned changes in the value of fixed assets will be budgeted for in the Capital Budget and any additions or reductions will be transferred to the Balance Sheet from there. The adjustments to fixed assets for budgeted depreciation will take place in the budgeted balance sheet by using the normal method practiced in final accounts.

Current Assets
The value of debtors and prepayments will be taken from the notes made on the cash budget, as will the final cash balance, this being the cash in hand or the bank balance at the time. Stock will be recorded as the anticipated stock value at the end of the budget period, it will usually be higher at the end of the period due to inflation affecting its value.

Current Liabilities
The value of creditors and accrued charges will be taken from the notes made on the cash budget. In the event of the cash budget showing a minus cash figure (ie. an overdraft) at the end of the budget period this would be recorded as a Current Liability.

Financing — Long Term Liabilities
Any changes in long term loans or new capital arranged during the budget period will be detailed in the capital budget and adjusted accordingly on the budgeted balance sheet. The net profit will be transferred from the budgeted profit and loss account and treated by the normal method for a balance sheet, as will the treatment for drawings. An example of a budgeted balance sheet is shown in the next section, covering the preparation of a master budget from given data regarding forecasted and budgeted results.

Master Budgets — A Full Example

On 01 April 198__ The Balance Sheet of the Lobster Pot Restaurant was as follows:

Balance Sheet as at 01 April 8__

			(£)
Fixed Assets			
Freehold Property		110,000	
Fixtures & Equipment		32,000	142,000
Current Assets			
Food Stock	1,500		
Liquor Stock	2,300	3,800	
Debtors		1,200	
Cash At Bank		2,750	7,750
Curent Liabilities			
Creditors (Trade)	5,050	5,050	2,700
			£144,700
Financed By:			
Capital		104,700	
Bank Loan		40,000	£144,700

(i) The budget committee has provided the forecasts and budgets of the restaurant for the period of 3 months from 1st April.

	Food Sales	Liquor Sales	Wages	Overheads
April	7,400	3,700	2,400	2,100
May	7,600	3,800	2,450	2,150
June	8,100	4,100	2,650	2,300

(ii) The cost of food sales is budgeted to be 40% of sales and liquor costs at 50% of sales.

(iii) 90% of sales are for cash, the remaining 10% being on credit, debtors are expected to pay in one month.

(iv) All purchases are made on one month's credit, the stock levels are maintained throughout the year, stock being replaced on a daily/weekly basis as appropriate.

(v) Wages are paid weekly in cash.

(vi) A breakdown of the overheads expenditure is as follows:
   (a) Depreciation on fixtures and equipment is £300 per month.
   (b) Rates of £2,400 pa are paid in advance on 1st April.
   (c) Fuel is paid quarterly at the end of March, June, Sept and December. The budgeted figures for April, May and June are £380, £400 and £440 respectively.
   (d) Other expenses are treated as cash.

(vii) It is anticipated that £5,000 of the bank loan will be repaid in June.

(viii) It is planned to purchase £2,000 worth of equipment in May, payment being £1,000 in cash and the remainder will be paid in July.

From this information we are able to prepare a budgeted trading and profit and loss account, a cash budget for the budget period and a budgeted balance sheet showing the value of the restaurant at the end of the period.

LOBSTER POT RESTAURANT

Budgeted Trading and Profit and Loss Account for Quarter End 30 Jun 8__

	Food	Liquor	Total
Sales	23,100	11,600	34,700
Cost of Sales	9,240	5,800	15,040
Gross Profit	13,860	5,800	19,660
less expenses			
Wages		7,500	
Rates		600	
Fuel		1,220	
Depreciation		900	
Other Expenses		3,830	14,050
Net Profit			5,610

Notes on the preparation of the Budgeted Trading and Profit and Loss Account

(i)   Cost of Food and Liquor Sales are calculated at 40% and 50% of total period sales respectively.

(ii)   Rates charged cover the budget period only.

(iii)   Other expenses are calculated by deducting depreciation, rates and fuel from total overheads forecasted.

Cash Budget for the Quarter Ending 30 Jun 8__

Cash Income	April	May	June	Notes
Opening Balance	2,750	2,870	4,730	
Cash Sales	9,990	10,260	10,980	
Credit Sales	1,200	1,110	1,140	Debtors: £1,220
Total	13,940	14,240	16,850	
Cash Expenditure				
Food & Liquor Purchases	5,050	4,810	4,940	Creditors: £5,290
Wages	2,400	2,450	2,650	
Rates & Fuel	2,400		1,220	Prepaid: £1,800
Other Overheads	1,220	1,250	1,360	
Capital Expenditure		1,000	5,000	Equipment: £1,000
Total	11,070	9,510	15,170	
Balance C/F	2,870	4,730	1,680	

Notes on the preparation of the Cash Budget

(i)   The Opening Cash Balance has been taken from the balance sheet as at 01 April. Other figures taken from this balance sheet are the debtors of £1,200 which is the credit sales income from March and the creditors £5,050 which are the purchases for March, both of which affect the inflow and outflow of cash during April.

(ii)   Food and Liquor Sales are added together for each month, 90% of this figure is recorded as a cash income for the month and the remaining 10% is recorded as an income in the following month.

Credit sales for June will be transferred to the balance sheet as a debtor.

(iii) Monthly Food and Liquor Purchases are calculated as 40% and 50% of sales respectively and added together, the amount will be recorded in the following months column when the accounts are actually paid. Purchases for June will be transferred to the balance sheet as a creditor.

(iv) Rates are paid for the whole year and are recorded in total as a cash expenditure for April. A note is made of the 9 months prepayment for transfer to the balance sheet as a current asset.

(v) Fuel Expenses are totalled and recorded as an expenditure in June when the account is paid.

(vi) Other Overheads for each month are calculated by deducting the depreciation, rates and fuel charges allocated for that particular month from the total monthly expenditure.

(vii) Capital Expenditure for equipment and loan repayments are recorded when they occur, a note being made as to the outstanding equipment creditor for transfer to the balance sheet.

LOBSTER POT RESTAURANT

Budgeted Balance Sheet as at 30 June 8__

				(£)
Fixed Assets				
Freehold Premises				110,000
Fixtures & Equipment		32,000		
+ Additions to Equipment		2,000	34,000	
− Depreciation			900	33,100
				143,100
Current Assets				
Stock — Food	1,500			
— Liquor	2,300	3,800		
Debtors		1,220		
Rates Prepaid		1,800		
Cash At Bank		1,680	8,500	
Current Liabilities				
Creditors (Trade)		5,290		
(Equipment)		1,000	6,290	2,210
				£145,310
Financed By:				
Capital			104,700	
+ Net Profit			5,610	£110,310
Bank Loan			40,000	
− Repayment			5,000	35,000
				£145,310

Notes on the preparation of the Budgeted Balance Sheet

(i) The equipment additions are added to the existing figure in the balance sheet and depreciation charged for the period is deducted to give the new value of equipment.

(ii) Current Assets and liabilities are taken from the notes on the Cash Budget, the stock figures are taken from the levels determined by the budget committee for the end of the budget period.

(iii) The new capital is calculated by adding the budgeted net profit to the capital in the balance sheet as at the 1st April. The bank loan is adjusted to account for the repayment to be made in June.

Student Activity   No. 3.9

Jason Small plans to open a Vegetarian Restaurant on 1st July 198__. His balance sheet prepared at the end of June is as follows:

Jason Small — Balance Sheet as at 30 Jun 8__

Fixed Assets			(£)
Premises (Leasehold)			10,000
Furniture & Equipment			28,000
Current Assets			
Food Stock	2,000		
Cash at Bank	2,000	4,000	
Current Liabilities			
Trade Creditors		2,000	2,000
			40,000
Financed By:			
Capital			35,000
Bank Loan			5,000
			40,000

Jason has prepared the following forecasts:

(i) Sales are expected to be £5,000 per month for the first three months and £6,000 per month thereafter. 10% of his sales will be on credit, debtors paying in one month.

(ii) Cost of Sales are planned to be 35% of sales, the food stock being replaced during the month in which the food is sold, one month's credit has been agreed with suppliers.

(iii) Monthly wages and overheads of £1,650 will be paid out in cash. This does not include rent and insurance of £3,500 for the first year which will be paid in July or initial advertising of £650 for the first six months, to be paid out in August.

(iv) Depreciation of 10% per annum is to be charged on the leasehold premises and furniture and equipment.

Prepare a monthly cash budget, a budgeted trading, profit and loss account and a budgeted balance sheet for the budget period ending 31st December 198__.

VARIANCE ANALYSIS

Variance analysis is the comparison of actual results with the budgeted figures of a business operation. As we explained earlier in this section, it is the final part of budgetary control and must be regarded as an essential part of budgeting procedures. The function of the budget committee will be to analyse any variances that may occur, suggesting possible reasons for such variances and recommending remedial action according to the type of variance. There are two types of variance we must examine, these are sales variances and cost variances, in most cases they will be related. For example, an increase or decrease in sales will in most cases result in an increase or decrease in costs, the question being, are they relative? In this section we will examine methods of calculating variances and their possible causes.

Sales Variances

Sales variances occur for three reasons, either because of a change in the number of customers or the amount they spend or a combination of both. For example, an increase in actual sales volume over the budgeted figures may be due to more customers spending the same amount, or less customers spending more, or more customers spending more per head. The opposite may be said for a decrease in the actual sales volume over the budgeted figures. The budget committee should then evaluate why any differences have occured. The variances shown in figure 3.10 of £630 in total sales volume may be explained as follows:

No of Covers Variance: 100 covers at £3.00   = £300
Average Spend Variance: 1100 covers at 30p   = £330

∴ increase of total sales volume   £630

Both these variances would be known as favourable variances.

	Budgeted	Actual	Variance
No. of Covers	1,000	1,100	+ 100
Average Spend	£3.00	£3.30	+ 30p
Sales Volume	£3,000	£3,630	+ £630

Fig. 3.10 *Example of Sales Variances*

The use of a flexible sales budget, as shown in figure 3.11, show the sales volume variances as £330, this being the change in average customer spend, the increase in number of covers being accounted for in the flexible budget.

	Budgeted	Flexible Budget	Actual	Variance
No. of Covers	1,000	1,100	1,100	—
Average Spend	£3.00	£3.00	£3.30	30p
Sales Volume	£3,000	£3,300	£3,630	£330

Fig. 3.11 *Example of a Flexible Sales Budget*

An unfavourable or adverse sales variance is shown in figure 3.12, where the number of covers has been increased but the average spend has dropped. Whilst results show a drop in sales volume of £85, comparison of the actual results with the flexible budget figures show an adverse average spend variance of £385. This may be explained as follows:

No. of Covers Variance: 100 Covers at £3.00   = £ 300
Average Spend Variance: 1100 Covers at −35p   = £(385)
Sales Volume Variance   = £(85)

On examining these results the budget committee would ascertain the reason for the drop in average spending of 35p per cover, which might, for example, be due to poor sales promotion by waiting staff and attempt to rectify it.

	Budgeted	Flexible Budget	Actual	Variance
No. of Covers	1,000	1,100	1,100	—
Average Spend	£3.00	£3.00	£2.65	— 35p
Sales Volume	£3,000	£3,300	£2,915	— £385

Fig. 3.12   *Flexible Budget showing Adverse Sales Variance*

Causes of Sales Variances

We have examined the methods of calculating sales variances from forecasted results and shown that they are caused by, either a change in the number of covers, or by a change in the average customer spending. When there is a decrease in the number of covers from the forecasted figure the budget committee must attempt to find a reason for this and recommend remedial action. The objective of the action will be to increase the number of covers sold by either using promotional methods, such as advertising, or making the establishment more attractive to customers. The option open to the operation will be to ascertain why it is not attracting the anticipated market, either through their prices, menu, service given or image etc. and then take the appropriate action. When variance analysis shows that customers are spending less than the anticipated amount, then once again reasons for this should be ascertained. A common cause is a lack of salesmanship by service staff in selling dishes or extra courses and drinks to customers. Other reasons may be that the prices of extra courses or drinks are too high, or in some cases the customers may not be aware of their availability. Remedial action may take the form of training staff in selling, merchandising through sweet trolleys etc. or more imaginative pricing.

Student Activity   No. 3.10

The sales forecast for the Edgecumbe Park Restaurant was 1,200 covers with an average spend per head of £4.50 on food and £1.70 on liquor for the month of May. The actual results were 1,100 covers spending £4.70 per head on food and £1.45 per head on liquor.

(i)   Prepare a statement showing the variances that have occured.

(ii) Explain possible causes for variances and suggest remedial action.

Cost Variances

Cost variances with regard to materials, occur for three basic reasons. These may either be because of a change in the forecasted cost of materials or because of a change in the quantity used or a combination of both. These variances are known as material cost variances (ie. food

206

and drink) or usage variances. Other cost variances may be considered in the difference between budgeted and actual labour and overhead costs. It would be reasonable to assume that a change in the volume of sales would also lead to a change in the cost of these sales. By carrying out variance analysis we are able to assess changes in material costs against changes in sales, as well as being able to show other variances which occur through changes in costs and usage. The use of flexible budgets will establish which variances are due to sales changes and which are due to other reasons. The example of a flexible budget in figure 3.13 shows an increase in costs of £800, however the increase in sales accounts for £400 of these costs as shown in the flexible budget column. The increase between the actual results and the flexible budget highlights a variance of £400 which would need investigation. If this investigation reveals that there has been a rise in the cost of materials of £200 over the budgeted cost, the remainder would be known as a usage variance. The change in gross profit and the effects of the variances are summarised in a reconciliation statement as shown below:

	Budgeted Gross Profit		*6,000*
Add	*Favourable Variances*		
	Increase due to Sales		*600*
			6,600
Less	*Adverse Variances*		
	Increases due to Food Cost	*200*	
	Increase due to Usage	*200*	*400*
	Actual Gross Profit		*£6,200*

Fig. 3.13 Example of a Flexible Budget showing Cost Variances.

	BUDGET	FLEXIBLE BUDGET	ACTUAL	VARIANCE
SALES	10000	11000	11000	
C.O.S	4000	4400	4800	400
G.P.	6000	6600	6200	(400)

Student Activity No. 3.11

The budgeted and actual results of The Bullring Steak House for the month of September are shown below:

	Budgeted	Actual
Sales	£16,500	£19,200
Cost of Sales	£ 5,775	£ 7,720
Gross Profit	£10,725	£11,480

(i) Prepare a Flexible Budget to indicate the variances that are due to the change in sales volume and those due to a rise in the cost of materials or usage.

(ii) Investigation shows that food prices were £480 higher than anticipated for September. Using this information prepare a statement reconciling the budgeted and actual gross profits showing all the variances that have occurred.

Causes of Cost Variances

We have examined methods of calculating and investigating cost variances from budgeted figures and ascertained that they are due to changes in sales or the cost of materials or the amounts of materials used. With regard to changes of costs due to sales variances, we are obviously aware that these should be relative and therefore expected. However, we must be aware of the cost behaviour regarding semi-variable costs, such as labour and overheads and take care that these costs do move with sales in their relative proportions. We should also be equally aware of decreases, as well as increases, in costs. A decrease may indicate that the customer is not getting proper value for money, either through poor service or quality. As a consequence, future sales may be affected. When this situation arises the reasons for the cost decreasing should be closely scrutinised and it should be ensured that standards are not affected. If this is not the case then the budget should be adjusted accordingly. With regard to increases in costs, these should be thoroughly investigated and reasons for them ascertained. Increases in the cost of materials should be investigated with the supplier in that he is supplying the correct goods as per the purchase specification and agreed prices. If these costs are unavoidable then the budget must be adjusted after checking alternative sources of supply or using different materials, recipes or portion sizes, if they do not affect the standard required. When usage variations occur, thorough investigation of internal activities should take place with regard to wastage at all stages of production ie. from the stores through to the portion that is actually served. Any variations from the standards or procedures set down should be rectified, if the usage variance is established as unavoidable then the budget should be adjusted accordingly. In some cases variance analysis and subsequent investigation may show that increases in the costs of materials may cause a decrease in usage and vice versa because a different quality or grade of food has been used due to availability. For example, more expensive vegetables of a higher quality are used and consequently the yield will be greater. At the other end of the scale a cheaper lower grade may have a lesser yield.

Increases in labour costs may be due to two reasons; either due to an increase in the wages paid to staff or because of over staffing. It would be reasonable to say that wage rises should be budgeted for. However, some rises may be unavoidable due to increases by the government in National Insurance contributions. In such cases the budget should be adjusted accordingly. Overstaffing may necessitate reorganising working rosters and controlling the use of casual staff, or, in severe cases, laying staff off, being careful not to affect the standard of service given. Labour Cost variances consisting of rate and efficiency variances are illustrated in the following example.

Example of Labour Cost Variances
The budgeted labour cost for a particular function was at a standard rate of pay of £3.50 per hour with a standard time of 3 hours for 6 staff.

The actual results show that 6 staff were employed for 4 hours at £3.25 per hour. The overall variance shows:

Standard time (3 hrs) × Standard Rate (£3.50) × 6 = £63
Actual time (4 hrs) × Actual Rate (£3.25) × 6 = £78

Unfavourable Variance = £15

This variance is due to:

(i) Rate variance of the difference between the standard rate of pay (£3.50) and the actual rate of pay (£3.25)
= 25p × 24 hours = £6 (favourable).

(ii) Efficiency variance of the difference between the standard time (18 hours) and the actual time (24 hours)
= 6 × £3.50 = £21 (unfavourable).

(iii) Reconciliation of variances show
(unfavourable variance) £21 − (favourable variance) £6 = £15.

Overhead variances are not a common occurence because they are usually considered as a fixed cost. However, they do occur and are generally attributed to increased charges by external services eg. gas, electricity etc. Usually sufficient notice is given for budgets to be adjusted accordingly. If usage is found to be a cause of overhead variance then economies can be made by tighter controls over lighting and heating or, in the case of telephone charges, by restricting use to off peak periods.

In this section we have considered variance analysis as the calculation and investigation of the differences between budgeted and actual results. It is possible to carry out variance analysis to a greater depth, but it is regarded as being beyond the scope and level of this study book. Further reading for students who wish to consider applications of variance analysis in greater depth to higher diploma or HCIMA Part B levels is therefore recommended. The author recommends Harris and Hazzard, 'Accounting and Financial Management in the Hotel and Catering Industry', Vol. 2. Chapter 10.

Further Reading

Food and Beverage Control: *Kotas and Davis* Chapter 4
Management Accounting for Hotels and Restaurants: *Kotas* Chapters 10 and 11.

ASSESSMENT QUESTIONS

1. Describe the difference between Forecasting and Budgeting.
2. List the different types of budgets that are prepared for the industry.
3. Describe the functions of a budget committee.
4. Explain the purposes of preparing a budget manual.
5. Define the term 'budget period' listing appropriate periods for different budgets.

6. During the first quarter of last year the Spaghetti Junction Restaurant served 11,430 customers who spent an average of £4.20 per head. The forecasts for next year are for a 5% increase in customers and prices are being increased by 7% which is not expected to affect the average spending per customer. From this information prepare a Sales Budget for the same period next year.

7. Explain the difference between fixed and flexible budgets.

8. Explain the difference between revenue earning and non-revenue earning departmental budgets.

9. Explain the considerations that would be made when preparing non-revenue earning budgets.

10. The house manager of the Palace Hotel has forecasted accommodation sales of £2,630,000 next year. Prepare a departmental operating budget considering the following budgeted costs. Labour 14% of sales, direct fuel and heating 9% of sales, accommodation marketing budget of £38,000 and cleaning materials etc. 1.5% of sales.

11. List the types of income and expenditure that would be included in a Capital Budget.

12. Explain the purpose of a cash budget.

13. The Grecian Taverna started business on October 1st with £5,000 cash after purchasing, equipping and furnishing the operation. The forecasts for the first six months show:

	Sales	Purchases	Wages	Overheads
October	6,500	4,200	1,500	1,350
November	7,000	3,200	1,500	1,350
December	8,500	4,000	1,800	1,350
January	7,500	3,400	1,600	1,350
February	7,000	3,200	1,500	1,350
March	7,000	3,200	1,500	1,350

Sales are expected to be 75% Cash, 25% Credit. Purchases are expected to be 80% Credit, 20% Cash. Creditors and Debtors are on monthly terms. Wages are paid weekly. Overheads include the following expectations:
Depreciation — £120 per month. Fuel — £360 per month paid in November and February. Rates — £200 per month paid six months in advance in October. The remaining overheads will be paid in cash during the month of expenditure. New carpets fitted in September will be paid in November costing £2,830.
Prepare a cash budget for the Restaurant for the first six months of operation.

14. You have been asked to prepare a master budget for 6 months ending 30 Sep 8__ for a friend of yours who owns the Silver Dollar Diner. He presents you with last years accounts set out below and the following information.

Trading Profit & Loss A/C for year ending 31 Mar __6

Sales		36,600
— Cost of Sales		16,800
Gross Profit		19,600
Wages	7,800	
Overheads	4,300	12,100
Net Profit		7,500

Balance Sheet as at 31st March __6

Fixed Assets			
Premises (Leasehold)		14,000	
Equipment & Furnishings		6,800	20,800
Current Assets			
Stock	800		
Rates Prepaid	200		
Cash at Bank	750	1,750	
Current Liabilities			
Creditors	700		
Electricity Accrued	150	850	900
			£21,700
Financed by:			
Capital	13,500		
+ Net Profit	7,500	21,000	
— Drawings		3,300	17,700
Bank Loan			4,000
			£21,700

In preparing the master budget for the Silver Dollar Diner for the next 6 months the following information must be considered.

(a) It is forecast that all sales and costs will increase by 10% on last years figures.

(b) All sales and costs accrue evenly over the period and the level of stock is maintained.

(c) All sales are cash and purchases are 50% cash, the remainder being paid after one month.

(d) Wages are paid weekly in arrears.

(e) Of the Overheads; Rates of £400 are paid in January and July for 6 months in advance; provision for depreciation is £50 per month; all other overheads are paid in cash the month after they are incurred.

(f) The owner plans to repay £1,000 of the Bank Loan in September.

(g) Drawings of £400 each month are to be budgeted for in this period.

Prepare a budgeted trading, profit and loss account, cash budget and a budgeted balance sheet for the six month period 1st April 19__6 to 30th Sept 19__6.

15. Explain the types of variance that occur between budgeted and actual results.

16. Explain the causes of sales variances.

17. Explain the causes of cost variances.
18. The budgeted and actual results of the Spare Part Factory Canteen for April are shown below:

	Budgeted	Actual
Sales	8,200	9,100
Cost of Sales	5,740	6,670
Gross Profit	2,460	2,430

(a) Prepare a statement showing the variances that are due to the change in sales and those due to a rise in the cost of materials or usage.

(b) It is discovered that price rises in vegetables have accounted for an increase in purchases of £500 during the month. Draw up a reconciliation statement showing all the variances that have occurred.

Statements of Costs and Expenses

In this section we will expand on the costs and expenses that are involved in the preparation of operating statements which we have previously studied. It is important to establish realistic figures of costs and profits by using operating departments with a view to monitoring the performance of a business operation. We will therefore have to analyse labour costs and overhead expenses, place them into their different categories and examine how these costs behave in a variety of situations. Whilst we are able to break down certain cost areas that are relevant to specific departments, a consideration must also be made to the treatment of expenses that apply to the overall operation and which can not be specifically identified and allocated to the departments. We must also consider the application of these costs and expenses when preparing Trading and Profit and Loss Accounts.

OPERATING STATEMENTS

In Study 2 we examined the use of operating statements and how they are prepared, setting out all departmental sales, costs and profits and comparing them with budgeted results in both £ p and percentages for trading periods. Operating statements are used to control costs by departmental heads and managers. The method of control used is the departmental comparison of budgeted with actual expenses during the control period covered. This control period will vary according to the type of income or expenditure.

Departmental sales and cost of sales are compared and checked on a daily basis with cash and credit sales records and, on both a weekly and monthly basis, with food and beverage control summaries. The purpose of this close control is to establish any deviances and variances as they occur. Immediate action may then be taken to correct the differences, in order to avoid unnecessary losses or wastage that may lead to a fall in profits. The appropriate departmental manager will make a comparison between the budgeted and actual results for the departmental gross profit, the net margin after labour costs and the operating profit after expenses have been deducted. Service department managers then compare their budgets with the actual results on a monthly basis. The hotel or catering manager will then review the gross operating profit on a monthly basis by using the same process.

He will also compare the budgeted and actual net profit of the operation on a quarterly and annual basis after adjustments have been made for plant and accommodation depreciation. Provisions for plant and accommodation depreciation and capital expenditure are usually of a fixed nature and are controlled by the policy decisions of the business organisation. The feedback which is obtained by using operating statements to compare budgeted and actual results is important because, by establishing control levels and responsibility for results at different stages, a business operation is able to closely monitor its results. They will therefore assist the operation to be more cost effective and profitable.

Preparation of Operating Statements

The preparation of an operating statement showing any deviations between budgeted and actual results must involve the use of the budgeted trading profit and loss account and the actual results for the same trading period. This is best explained by following the example set out below:

Luke Kemp operates a hamburger restaurant in a medium sized provincial town. His budgeted results for July 198___ are set out below.

		£	%			£	%
	Food Sales	7,500	100		Liquor Sales	3,500	100
less	Cost of Sales	2,625	35	less	Cost of Sales	1,575	45
	Gross Profit	4,875	65		Gross Profit	1,925	55
	Labour Costs	1,875	25		Labour Costs	525	15
	Net Margin	3,000	40		Net Margin	1,400	40
Overheads						2,420	22
Net Operating Profit						1,980	18

His results for July 198___ were:

Food Sales	7,800
Liquor Sales	3,450
Cost of Food Sales	2,574
Cost of Liquor Sales	1,587
Food Labour Costs	1,833
Liquor Labour Costs	535
Gas & Electricity	730
Rent, Rates & Insurances	900
Repairs & Maintenance	180
Administration Expenses	360
Sundry Expenses	230

The operating statement for July 198___ may now be prepared using the information we have been given.

Food Operation	Budgeted £	Budgeted %	Actual £	Actual %
Sales	7,500	100	7,800	100
less Cost of Sales	2,625	35	2,574	33
Gross Profit	4,875	65	5,226	67
less Labour Costs	1,875	25	1,833	23.5
Net Margin	3,000	40	3,393	43.5
Liquor Operation				
Sales	3,500	100	3,450	100
less Cost of Sales	1,575	45	1,587	46
Gross Profit	1,925	55	1,863	54
less Labour Costs	525	15	535	15.5
Net Margin	1,400	40	1,328	38.5
Food Net Margin	3,000		3,393	
Liquor Net Margin	1,400		1,328	
Total Net Margin	4,400	40	4,721	42
less Total Overheads	2,420	22	2,400	21.3
Net Operating Profit	1,980	18	2,321	20.7

The operating statement for Luke Kemp's Hamburger Bar shows that profitability has been increased above budgeted expectations, by increased sales, higher gross profit and reduced labour costs in the food operations. The liquor operation, however, causes some concern, with a reduced proportion of sales compared to the increase in food sales. Gross profit for liquor is slightly below the budgeted figure and wages are slightly increased. The actual overheads show only a minute variation from the budgeted figure and·should be regarded as satisfactory. Mr Kemp, after analysing the results, should therefore attempt to increase his liquor sales by internal sales promotion and be aware of any further developments in the liquor operation's gross profit. It can therefore be said that the feedback obtained from preparing an operating statement will help maintain and improve profitability for this operation.

Whilst it may be regarded as easier for operations which have more than one operating department to control directly related material costs to achieve set targets, it is equally important to control other cost centres. The proprietors of many operations do not achieve profit targets because they are not aware of the true labour or overhead costs involved in the operation. Failure to understand and treat these costs properly may lead to mis-leading results regarding a department's efficiency or profitability. We must therefore consider labour and overhead costs in greater detail, with regard to their calculation, how they behave and their treatment in different types of operations.

Student Activity No. 3.12

Home Counties Caterers has a budgeting system in operation, the budgeted results for October to December 198___ are set out below:

Sales	£170,000
Cost of Sales	40%
Labour Costs	21%
Overhead Costs	20%
Net Profit	19%

The Actual Results for the same period are as follows:

Sales	£162,400
Cost of Sales	£ 66,100
Wages	£ 31,400
National Insurance	£ 2,750
Fuel Charges	£ 8,150
Rent & Rates	£ 4,700
Hire Charges	£ 4,450
Administration	£ 5,800
Disposable Materials	£ 3,200
Sundry Charges	£ 2,400
Depreciation	£ 2,500

(i) Prepare an operating statement showing a comparison of budgeted and actual results.

(ii) Briefly explain reasons for any variances that are shown by this statement.

LABOUR COSTS

Labour costs represent the second largest area of expenditure in most hotel and çatering operations and indeed, in more labour intensive operations, such as luxury hotels and restaurants, they can be the greatest area of individual expenditure. The constituent costs of labour in addition to actual wages paid to employees are listed as follows:

• National Insurance Contributions

• Staff Meals and Accommodation

• Holiday, Pension Fund and Sickness Payments

• Bonuses and Other Benefits

• Recruitment and Training Costs

• Staff Uniforms and Transport

Once an operation has established its true labour cost ie. the total cost of employing staff, then it should determine this cost in relation to sales turnover for purposes of control. The operation should also determine how it will share these costs amongst its operating departments and how these departments are going to control their individual labour costs to keep within their budgets.

Labour Costs in Relation to Sales
The labour cost percentage as we have previously studied is calculated by:

Labour Costs ÷ Sales × 100

Labour Costs are calculated as a percentage of total sales to give a yardstick for the overall operation. Each department will also calculate its individual labour cost percentage, giving the departmental yardstick. Preparation of these calculations will enable labour costs to be monitored and controlled for all aspects of an operation. In figure 1.30 we analysed the labour cost percentages for different types of establishment and operations and we were able to observe certain differences between them. We must also be aware that the departments in a hotel and catering operation will have different labour cost percentages. Each department or operation is individual in its proportions of labour costs because of the levels of service offered to customers, the physical layout of the building, the amount of labour saving equipment used and the use of convenience foods and materials etc. In a hotel we may expect the following labour cost percentage from revenue earning departments: the preparation and service of food in a coffee shop using convenience foods and plate service will have a cost percentage of 17-19% against a silver service restaurant using fresh foods of 22-24%. Bars will have a labour cost ranging from as low as 9% for a public bar to 15% for a cocktail bar. Rooms will expect a labour cost of 12-18%, which will cover housekeeping, reception and porterage costs. We can therefore see that the overall labour cost will depend on the proportions of sales from operating departments. For example, an accommodation biased operation will have a smaller labour cost percentage than a food and beverage biased operation. We must also consider the treatment of ancilliary staff labour costs as well as those of management.

Treatment of Labour Costs
We have examined labour costs and the percentages that may be expected from different types of operation and the departments of an operation. Whilst we have attempted to categorise labour costs into departments, in many cases this may be impractical because operating departments rely on other aspects of the overall operation to function efficiently. We are therefore able to say that there are two types of cost behaviour where labour costs are concerned.

Direct Labour Costs are those which can be attributed to a specific area of sales. For example, a chef's wages can be directly related to food sales. Direct costs are therefore easily apportioned to the department concerned.

Indirect Labour Costs may also be referred to as 'common or joint costs' and are incurred by the overall operation in the provision of services to all departments. For example, in a hotel, the manager's salary would be difficult to relate to individual departmental sales. There is no accurate method of showing these types of costs amongst operating departments. Although a manager's salary can be apportioned by using the sales mix, according to departmental profits, or on the basis of the labour cost for each department, none of these methods can be regarded as being totally satisfactory. The treatment of indirect labour costs therefore needs careful consideration.

Departmental Labour Cost Statements
In order to provide effective control over departmental labour costs each department must prepare a weekly labour cost statement. The purpose of this statement will be to compare the weekly labour costs for each department against last year's cost for the same period and the budgeted figure for that week. Each department head will be responsible for keeping his labour costs within the set targets to ensure that any increase or decrease in costs will be relative to charges in sales, by manipulating part-time or over-time staff costs. By preparing a weekly labour cost statement, department heads will quickly be able to detect any increase in labour costs, away from the previously set down norm, after taking into consideration any seasonal fluctuations. In order to be able to compare results properly, such items as holiday and sickness pay are not included in the weekly statement, because no two years will be the same. Whilst these figures must be included in labour cost, for the purpose of this exercise they are not; the figures included will be the regular costs involved, such as wages and staff meals. For comparative purposes, only percentages for last year and this year are used, as it would be inaccurate to compare actual figures, due to increases in wages paid and possible sales fluctuations.

Labour cost statements are prepared from last year's results for the same period, the budgeted results and the actual results for the period in question. Figure 3.14 shows a weekly labour cost statement for the housekeeping department of a 120 bedroom hotel in a provincial town. The statement is prepared from last year's figures shown below and the departmental budget was prepared by adding 10% to these figures, to cover increases in turnover and labour costs in line with inflation. The actual results are as shown on the statement illustrated.

Last Years Room Sales: £14,250
Last Years Labour Costs:
2 Supervisors @ £125 per week; 1 Linen Keeper @ £120 per week
400 Chambermaid hours @ £2.50 per hour
67½ Cleaning hours @ £2.40 per hour
72 Laundry hours @ £2.50 per hour

218

QUEEN'S HOTEL — Weekly Labour Cost Statement

Department: *Housekeeping* Week Ending *24 Sep 8__*

Last Year Actual		Details	This Year Budget		This Year Actual		Variance	
£	%		£	%	£	%	£	%
14,250	100	Room Sales	15,675	100	15,050	100		
250	14.6	Supervisors	275	14.6	275	14.7	—	(0.1)
1,000	58.5	Chambermaids	1,100	58.5	1,120	59.9	(20)	(1.4)
162	9.4	Cleaners	176	9.4	158	8.4	18	1.0
120	7.0	Linen Keeper	132	7.0	132	7.0	—	—
180		Laundry	198	10.5	187	10.0	11	.5
1,712	100	Total	1,881	100	1,872	100	9	—
	12	Labour Cost As % Total Sales		12		12.4		(0.4)

Fig. 3.14 *Example of a Weekly Labour Cost Statement*

From an analysis of the weekly labour cost statement the housekeeper, as the head of department, will be able to analyse her labour costs by comparing budgeted with actual results for the period in question. From the statement we are able to observe that, whilst labour costs are below the budgeted figure, sales are also below forecasted results in a greater proportion, which gives an overall labour cost increase of 0.4% of room sales. Further examination will show that the fixed elements of labour cost ie. supervisors and linen keeper, are according to budgeted results. Expenditure on chambermaid's wages are above the budgeted results, whereas those for cleaners and laundry staff are below. As a result of the changes in cost proportions there will obviously be some slight fluctuation in the percentage of fixed labour costs of supervisor staff. The housekeeper, on studying these results, will be able to make the slight adjustments in her work rosters to bring her labour costs in line with budgeted futures.

Student Activity No. 3.13
Set out below are the sales and labour costs for the Park Royal Hotel Food Department for week ending 30th January 19__5 and the budgeted and actual results for the same period in 19__6.

	Wk/End 30 Jan __5 Actual Results	Wk/End 31 Jan __6 Budgeted Results	Wk/End 31 Jan __6 Actual Results
Food Sales	£9,600	£10,800	£11,600
Head Chef	£ 200	£ 210	£ 210
Head Waiter	£ 160	£ 168	£ 168
Chefs	£ 940	£ 990	£ 1,100
Waiters	£ 620	£ 700	£ 950
Still Room Hands	£ 180	£ 204	£ 255
Kitchen Porters	£ 160	£ 168	£ 190
Wash Ups	£ 140	£ 160	£ 180

(i) Prepare a weekly labour cost statement for this department.

(ii) Comment on the results shown.

Use of Part-Time and Casual Labour

As we discovered in the previous section, controlling labour costs is a continuous problem for managers and supervisors in hotel and catering operations. If we observe the trends shown in both figure 3.14 and the student activity no. 3.13, labour costs behave in two ways, those which are fixed, such as department heads and supervisors and those which are variable, such as chambermaids and service staff, key personnel generally come under the category of fixed labour costs, as they will be employed regardless of the level of turnover, in almost all cases they will be full time employees. Variable labour costs however, cover the employment of staff that are related to the level of turnover. The number and cost of staffing will rise and fall according to the volume of sales. While, in most cases, the majority of staff employed in these positions will be full time employees, to assist in the control of labour costs, there is also a great reliance on part-time and casual labour. This will help departmental heads and management to keep within their budgets when planning manpower levels to accommodate fluctuations in sales.

Fluctuations in sales not only occur over weekly or monthly periods but also hourly in day to day operations. Customer demand may either be concentrated into short periods of time, or extended over very long periods of time, this will increase organisational problems. The industry therefore relies on the use of part-time and casual staff to cope with these problems. There is a large section of the population available and suitable for this type of employment, there are two main reasons for this. Firstly, the majority positions available are those in low skill types of jobs, for which unskilled persons can be easily trained. The caterer can take advantage of the availability of staff of this type by recruiting locally and using less expensive methods of recruitment and selection. Employment of local staff will also reduce transportation costs for staff who may have to work extrordinary hours and who may require transport late at night. Secondly, the hours of employment are generally for short periods during the daytime and for longer periods outside normal working hours. Therefore, we can utilise the demand of housewives or mothers with school children, seeking 4 hours work during the day, as a second income to the household, without disrupting the normal family routine. Positions suitable for this category of part-time worker would be chambermaids, canteen servery staff, lunchtime bar and restaurant staff. Evening casual work is usually more suitable for students, secondary employment, or for working adults with families. There are many positions in public houses, food operations and banqueting to utilise this source. Part-time positions are often available for only 3-4 nights a week either during weekends or at other peak periods, satisfying the needs of both the employer and the emplolyee. It is up to the department head concerned to employ part-time and casual staff who are sufficiently flexible in their availability to satisfy his particular requirement.

We have examined the advantages of using part time staff to control labour costs, in addition we must also consider some of the disadvantages of using this type of employment. Part time staff tend to be less reliable than full time staff in that their part time employment may not be their primary source of income, either for them personally, or for their household. It could also be argued that they may not gain as much job satisfaction as full time employees may gain because they may feel alieniated from the full time staff or because they are part time they feel that they do not have an important role in the organisation. These problems however, should be overcome by supervisory staff who must be aware of the problems and be able to motivate staff and give them a feeling of job security. Administratively, the employment of part time staff increases the organisational load for management. Therefore, communication systems must be developed to maintain links with staff, regarding when they are required to work and of equal importance, when they are not required. The employment of many part time staff will also increase the work load of personnel and wages departments, this will also need organisational consideration.

Although we have examined the advantages and disadvantages of employing part time and casual staff, the arguments in favour of their employment would seem to be stronger. The main arguments against this must be purely communicative and organisational and which any effective organisation should be able to overcome. The gains to be enjoyed by business operations are the control they exercise over labour costs, by using part time labour in addition to the full time work force, thus maintaining standards of service and increasing profitability.

Student Activity   No. 3.14
(i)   Draw up a list of jobs in the following hotel and catering operations that would be suitable for part time and casual employees.
   (a) Public House.
   (b) School Meals Canteen.
   (c) Fast Food Operation in Londons West End.
   (d) Motorway Service Station.
(ii)   State the hours you may expect them to work in each operation.
(iii) List the advantages and disadvantages of employing part time and casual staff.

OVERHEAD EXPENSES

In the previous study areas we defined overheads as expenses incurred in the running of an operation other than material and labour costs. We also studied overheads in so much as they have three different types of behaviour. Fixed overheads are those which accrue through the passing of time and do not fluctuate with sales, they are a set figure for an accounting period. Variable overheads are those which change directly in relation to the volume of sales during an accounting period. The third category is semi-variable overheads (also known as semi-fixed) which are a combination of fixed and variable. This means that whilst there is a fixed element to them there is also an element which will fluctuate according to changes in sales volume.

Classification of the Behaviour of Overheads

We have established that, as an element of cost, the behaviour of overheads is in three categories; fixed, variable and semi-variable. We will now consider the many different types of overhead expenditure and examine their behaviour more closely.

Rents

These accrue with the passing of time and in all cases are regarded as a fixed expense. Under this classification will be rents for property and hire charges for equipment, leasing of motor vehicles, radio and TV rentals. Rents and hire charges are subject to external influences and may be said to be uncontrollable. The only control exercised by a hotel and catering operation will be in the selection of who to hire or rent from. The exception to this will be in the case of premises.

Rates

These cover property rates levied by the local authority and water rates from the appropriate statutory body, they accrue with the passing of time and are therefore treated as a fixed cost. In operations which are serviced by metered water it would be regarded as a semi-variable cost. All rates are set by external authorities and are regarded as uncontrollable because the business must pay them by law; projected increases must therefore be budgeted for.

Fuel Charges

These cover gas and electricity costs and are treated as a semi-variable. They have, however, a greater fixed element than variable because operations have to be heated and lit regardless of the volume of business. Operations that have oil-fired heating would treat oil charges as a fuel cost.

Business Expenses

These cover costs that relate to the direct business expenses, such as insurance charges on the building, contents and liabilities, loan interests, credit card charges, licence fees and professional fees. Certain costs in this group will be fixed by their very nature, these are insurances and licence fees. The other costs are variable according to the amount of interest paid on financing, volume of credit card sales and the number of times professional people are consulted. All business expenses, however, should be accurately budgeted for and treated as a fixed cost.

Administration Expenses

These cover costs that relate to the day to day administration of the operation and must not be confused with business expenses. These costs are telephone costs, printing, stationery materials, travelling expenses and postage. They are treated as a semi-variable cost because aspects of administration take place regardless of the sales turnover. There is an increase in these costs as turnover increases. Telephone costs are a good illustration of fixed and variable costs because rental charges are fixed and charges for calls are variable. It can be said that telephone costs are also a good example of prepaid and accrued costs, rents being paid in advance (prepayment) and call charges being paid in arrears (accrual).

Laundry and Cleaning

This covers costs that are involved in purchasing cleaning materials, laundry costs, specialist cleaning services and waste disposal. These costs are semi-variable in nature with a high proportion of them being fixed. The one exception to this being laundry, which will have a very low fixed element and a very high proportion of variable, especialy in hotels and restaurants which use linen, table cloths and serviettes etc.

Miscellaneous Expenses

These cover any irregular costs that an operation may incur. Examples of these costs may be garden expenses, tips to deliverymen etc. They must be regarded as semi-variable because some types of miscellaneous cost will be regarded as fixed whilst others will be variable. These costs are sometimes referred to as sundry expenses.

Motor Expenses

These cover the costs involved in maintaining and running motor vehicles used by the operation. They are regarded as semi-variable costs, the fixed element covering vehicle insurance, vehicle taxation and certain maintenance costs. The variable element will cover maintenance, servicing and fuel costs which may be attributed to the use of vehicles. Whilst these costs are variable motor expenses are usually budgeted for as a fixed cost, in which case they would be treated as such.

Repairs, Renewals and Maintenance Costs

These cover regular and irregular costs involved in repairing and maintaining furnishings, equipment and premises. Regular costs will include maintenance contracts for such things as equipment and lifts. In order to maintain the fabric of the building and for equipment to function efficiently the majority of repairs, renewals and maintenance costs are fixed. There is an element of variable costs in repairs to and renewal of equipment, due to increased use or damage through rising sales volume. Although it may be argued that adequate maintenance

223

should prevent this, there should be a contingency for emergencies, such as breakdowns in hot water systems. The maintenance budget should be fixed to cover emergencies which involve smaller amounts of expenditure. In the event of larger amounts being required a contingency plan should be prepared. Proprietors of operations should not confuse expenditure on repairs and renewals with that of capital expenditure on renewing or replacing fixed assets.

Specialist Expenses
Outdoor catering and fast food operations will have costs covering disposable crockery, glassware, cutlery and packaging involved in serving and selling their products. These costs are essentially variable in their nature and should be costed and budgeted as such. Other specialist costs should be analysed and appropriated accordingly.

Depreciation and Amortisation Provisions
Provisions for depreciation of furniture, fittings and equipment and for amortisation of leases are treated as fixed costs. They are set in advance as part of the financial policy of the organisation in reducing and writing off the value of fixed assets. Depreciation is an expense to an operation because it is charging the use of the assets against the profits. This will be further reflected in the prices charged to customers by the calculation of profit required before fixing profit margins and prices. Depreciation should therefore not be confused with capital expenditure.

Bad Debts Costs and Provisions
Bad debts should be regarded as an expense and written off against profits in the profit and loss account. A percentage of debtors should also be calculated and a provision made in the event of them not paying. Bad debts are a variable cost as they will relate directly to the volume of sales and amount of credit given. This will also mean a reduction of the value of debtors in the balance sheet. Some operations will include bad debts in their business expenses.

Student Activity   No. 3.15
Prepare a list of overheads you would expect to find in a hotel under the following headings:
  (i)   Fixed Overheads.
 (ii)   Semi-variable Overheads.
(iii)   Variable Overheads.

Apportionment of Overhead Expenses
We have examined overheads as an overall cost of an operation however, we must also be aware that some of these expenses may be attributed directly to revenue earning departments; Expenses which are of a more general nature to an operation have to be shared amongst the departments if they wish to prepare departmental

accounts or operating statements. This procedure is known as apportionment of expenses. The way in which these expenses are apportioned will depend on the accounting policy of the operation and the type of expense involved. It would be fair to say that the different policies used by operations will have varying effects on departmental operating profits, in some cases turning losses into profits and profits into losses if a different method was used. If we take accounting policies aside, in this section we will put a greater emphasis on the type of expenses and where there are alternative methods these will be mentioned. Apportionment methods will therefore vary according to the type of expense and for this study we will split them into broad based groupings as shown below.

Rents, Rates and Depreciation
These costs are usually apportioned by the amount of floor space occupied by each department, although in the case of certain equipment it would be possible to charge depreciation provisions directly. An example of using apportionment of these costs by floor space occupied is shown as follows: A hotel has annual rates of £50,000, the space occupied by rooms is 70%, provision of food departments 20% and bars 10%. The rates for the accommodation operation would be calculated in this way:

$$£50,000 \times 70 \div 100 = £35,000$$

By the use of the same method of calculation, the food aspect of the operation would contribute £10,000 and the bars £5,000. The formula for this calculation would be:

Total Expense × % of Space Occupied ÷ 100

Fuel Costs
In operations where departments are not individually metered for fuel directly consumed, the total expenses for fuel are usually apportioned on floor space occupied, using the same method as for rates. Some operations may apportion these costs on a basis of sales mix or, as a proportion of departmental contribution to gross profit, an example of this calculation is shown later in this section (see Net Margin Apportionment).

Administration and Business Expenses
This type of expense may be said to be relative to sales, the expenses being apportioned to the sales mix of the operation because as sales increase so would these costs. For example, if the total administration and business expenses of an operation are £30,000 and the sales mix is Rooms 55%, Food 28% and Liquor 17%. The formula used for calculation would be:

Total Expense × % of Sales Mix ÷ 100

The apportionment of the expenses being Rooms £16,500, Food £8,400 and Liquor £5,100. An alternative method may be to share expenses of this nature equally among the departments but this is regarded as unfair on low revenue earning departments.

Marketing Costs

These expenses are usually shared according to the sales mix because of their direct relationship (ie. marketing and promotion generate sales). In cases where there has been direct promotional costs for a specific department of an operation then such costs would be directly allocated.

Repairs, Renewals, Maintenance and Miscellaneous Costs

It is probable that these costs will be directly allocated to departments according to their individual expenditure. Although in some cases they may be shared equally or according to the sales mix.

Laundry and Cleaning Costs

These expenses are usually costed directly to the departments concerned and will therefore be termed 'allocated expenses'.

Specialist and Other Expenses

In specialist cases expenses for such items as disposable crockery and cutlery are usually attributed to a particular area of sales and would be allocated accordingly.

We can see from the treatment of overhead expenses that they fall into two categories with each category having its own treatment. Direct costs are allocated to the user department and indirect costs are apportioned to the user department. In selecting methods of apportionment, operations must be aware that departmental heads will have little or no control over expenditure of most overhead expenses. In many cases this will include those expenses that can be directly allocated. A hotel and catering operation must, therefore, select a method of apportionment which gives a fair representation of the costs that apply to departments and not give a wrong impression of profits. It can also be argued that the various methods of apportionment will either penalise departments which have high sales or show improved efficiency through increased gross profits or net margins. Restaurant proprietors need to be aware that costs should not be loaded onto one aspect of their operation, as food and liquor sales and their respective costs complement each other. This also may be said for a majority of other catering operations.

Examples of Overall Apportionment of Overheads

The information set out below shows the annual sales, departmental net margin and floor area for a hotel with three revenue earning departments.

	Sales		Net Margin		Floor Area	
	£	%	£	%	sq. m.	%
Rooms	52,800	60	45,900	76	45,000	75
Food	22,000	25	8,800	15	12,000	20
Liquor	13,200	15	5,600	9	3,000	5
Total	88,000	100	60,300	100	60,000	100

Total overheads of £27,500 are to be apportioned.

(i) *Sales Mix Apportionment*
Formula : Overheads × Sales Mix % ÷ 100

Rooms Share	= £27,500 × 60 ÷ 100 =	£16,500
Food Share	= £27,500 × 25 ÷ 100 =	£ 6,875
Liquor Share	= £27,500 × 15 ÷ 100 =	£ 4,125
		£27,500

(ii) *Net Margin Apportionment*
Formula : Overheads × Net Margin % ÷ 100

Rooms Share	= £27,500 × 76 ÷ 100 =	£20,900
Food Share	= £27,500 × 15 ÷ 100 =	£ 4,125
Liquor Share	= £27,500 × 9 ÷ 100 =	£ 2,475
		£27,500

(iii) *Floor Space Apportionment*
Formula : Overheads × Floor Space % ÷ 100

Rooms Share	= £27,500 × 75 ÷ 100 =	£20,625
Food Share	= £27,500 × 20 ÷ 100 =	£ 5,500
Liquor Share	= £27,500 × 5 ÷ 100 =	£ 1,375
		£27,500

(iv) *Equal Share Apportionment*
Formula : Overheads ÷ No. of Departments
£27,500 ÷ 3 = £9,167

To summarize; we can observe from the above results that the share of overheads for each department can reflect greatly varying results as is also shown in the different operating profits set out below. This information confirms that the apportionment of overhead expenses needs very close consideration with regard to the type of cost and its behaviour.

Department	Rooms (£)	Food (£)	Liquor (£)
Sales Mix Method	36,300	1,925	1,475
Net Margin Method	25,900	4,765	3,125
Floor Space Method	25,275	3,300	4,225
Equal Share Method	43,633	(367)	(3,567)

Fig. 3 14 *Table Showing Operating Profits After Different Methods of Overhead Apportionment*

227

Student Activity   No. 3.16
The Dormy House Hotel has sales of £143,500 per annum with departmental sales as follows: Rooms £97,500, food £28,700, Liquor £17,300. The total floor area of the hotel is 62,000 sq. m. which, when split up departmentally, shows that rooms occupy 49,600 sq. m., food operations occupy 9,300 sq. m. and bars occupy 3,100 sq. m.

(i)   Calculate the departmental share of overheads totalling £38,875, after the following methods of apportionment have been decided.

(a) Rates, Depreciation and Fuel Charges according to floor space.

(b) Administration and Marketing Costs according to sales mix.

(c) Laundry, Cleaning, Repairs and Maintenance Costs are allocated.

(d) Remaining Costs are shared equally.

The accounts of the operation show the following overheads:

Rates	£5,270
Gas and Electricity	£9,700
Laundry and Cleaning — Rooms £5,630; Food £1,200; Liquor £205	
Administration Costs	£2,100
Business Expenses	£1,900
Repairs and Maintenance — Rooms £4,910; Food £1,800; Liquor £450	
Marketing Costs	£2,870
Miscellaneous Expenses	£ 840
Depreciation	£2,000

(ii)   Discuss in your group the methods of apportionment that have been used in this example and the way in which they affect departmental profitability.

Student Activity   No. 3.17
The Dormy House Hotel's departments provide the following net margins on the sales shown in Activity No. 16.

Rooms	£84,108
Food	£10,906
Liquor	£ 8,610

(i)   Prepare an operating statement to show individual overhead costs and operating profit for each department from the information given and calculated by yourself in Activity No. 16.

(ii)   Show the percentage overheads for each department.

Further Reading
Hotel and Catering and Budgets: Chapters 10 and 11   *Boardman*
Catering Costs and Control: Chapter 14   *Paige*
Food and Beverage Control: Chapter 11   *Kotas and Davis*

ASSESSMENT QUESTIONS

1. Explain the importance of establishing costs and profits to give feedback of business performance.

2. (a) Construct monthly operating statement showing the relationship between costs as percentages using the following information:

	Budgeted Results		Actual Results	
	Food (£)	Liquor (£)	Food (£)	Liquor (£)
Sales	4,200	1,450	4,550	1,400
Cost of Sales	1,470	653	1,590	690
Wages	924	232	995	230
Direct Overheads	420	145	440	140
Indirect Overheads	452		450	
Business Expenses	200		195	
Depreciation	100		100	

    (b) Comment on the results that are shown by the operating statement.

3. Define the terms 'Direct Labour' and 'Indirect Labour'.

4. List costs of employing staff that would be included in the overall labour cost.

5. Prepare a weekly labour cost statement from the following information:
    The weekly labour costs for last year and this year for the Micro-Chip Factory are

Staff	Last Year	This Year
Manager	£190	£202
Cooks	£420	£495
Catering Assistants	£480	£582
Cleaners	£210	£223

    Budgeted labour costs were a 6% increase on last years results. Sales last year were £8,200. The forecasted increase was 6% and actual results were an 8% increase.

6. List operational situations that would require the employment of casual and part time staff from a cost view point.

7. List the advantages and disadvantages of employing casual and part time staff.

8. Define the term 'overheads' and explain the meaning of 'fixed', 'variable' and 'semi-variable' overheads.

9. Prepare a list of overhead expenses under the following categories.
    (a) Fixed Overheads
    (b) Variable Overheads
    (c) Semi-Variable Overheads

10. Explain the effects depreciation has on the net profit of an operation and the value of its fixed assets.

11. Explain the principles of apportionment of overhead expenses and the methods that may be used for different types of expenses.

12. Explain how different methods of apportionment of overheads can affect departmental operating profits.

13. (a) Calculate the overhead expenses for each department of an operation from the information given below.

    (b) Prepare a departmental profit and loss account from the information given and your calculations of departmental overheads in part (a).

	Rooms	Food	Liquor
Sales	106,500	34,700	16,900
Gross Profit	106,500	20,200	7,100
Allocated Repairs & Maintenance	16,100	2,080	700
Allocated Wages	21,350	8,140	1,650
Allocated Cleaning & Laundry	9,280	1,050	210
Shared Expenses			
Rates	11,000		
Depreciation	4,000		
Administration Expenses	6,200		
Sundry Expenses	1,050		
Marketing Costs	2,900		
Business Expenses	4,800		
Management Salaries	22,600		
Gas & Electricity	13,900		

The above expenses are shared out on the basis for Rates, Depreciation and Fuel Charges according to the floor space occupied of Rooms 2/3rd total floor area, food preparation and service 2/9th of total floor area and bars 1/9th of total floor area. Administration, sundry expenses and management salaries are apportioned according to the sales mix of the operation. Business expenses are showed equally amongst the operating departments.

14. Explain the principles of the apportionment of overhead costs to operating departments.

Section D   **MARGINAL COSTING**

Marginal costing is a method of costing where overheads are not shared or apportioned between operating departments. The difference between the selling price and the variable or direct cost of sales (ie. the marginal cost) is calculated and is referred to as the contribution.

ie. Sales − Variable Direct Costs = Contribution

The 'Contribution' made by sales will contribute towards the fixed costs and the total contribution must exceed these costs before a profit is made. We previously examined contribution on a unit basis (ie. rooms and meals) in that each unit sold will make an individual contribution towards the fixed costs of an operation. When sufficient rooms or meals have been sold to cover the fixed costs (ie. the break-even point) then each unit will contribute to the profit. Marginal costing treats the contribution made by sales in total, as illustrated below:

Banqueting Sales	£77,500	(100%)
less Banqueting Costs	£42,625	(56%)
= Contribution	£34,875	(44%)

Therefore, if the fixed costs of the operation are £29,000 the net profit would be £5,875. If, however, the fixed costs were £39,000, the contribution made would not cover the fixed costs and a net loss of £4,125 would occur. The contribution made by sales towards the fixed costs is, therefore, important to the operation in that they are covered during the financial period. However, with individual banquets or units of sale it is important that the 'contribution' made covers some of the fixed costs of an operation. This will ensure that overall loss is reduced when there is no alternative sales to be gained during off peak periods.

Contribution Pricing
Contribution pricing may also be known as Direct Cost Pricing or Marginal Cost Pricing. This method of pricing is concerned with fixing a price to maximise the total contribution made towards the fixed costs and net profit of an operation. The objective of this is to fix a price, using the variable or direct cost as the minimum and, to a degree, what the customer is prepared to pay as a maximum. To enable operations to use this method of pricing the fixed costs are treated as period costs during the accounting period, the fixed costs will be written off against profits at the end of the period.

Accommodation Sales
In order to maximise sales in hotel during off peak periods such as, weekends in city hotels, or, outside the main holiday periods in seasonal operations, it is better to make some contribution to the fixed costs than none at all. Unlike material goods, an empty hotel bedroom is a sale lost forever. This method of pricing may also be used during peak periods. If, for example, a hotel has 10 vacant rooms at 6 o'clock in the evening it is better to sell them at a reduced price, which covers the variable cost and makes a small contribution towards the fixed costs, than not at all. By sticking to a rigid pricing policy where each unit of sale covers the total cost plus a net profit margin, the hotel may well end up with 10 empty rooms, making no contribution at all.

Room Sales Example of Contribution Pricing
A hotel has fixed a price for bed and breakfast per person per night of £22.00, which covers the variable costs of £6.50 and makes a contribution sufficient to cover fixed costs and net profit margin.

Selling Price	£22.00
less Variable Costs	£ 6.50
Contribution	£15.50

The price range is therefore £6.50 to £22.00, a contribution will be made towards fixed costs and profits, providing the rooms is sold for more than £6.50.

Banqueting Sales
The regular method of pricing banqueting sales, as we examined in study two, is to calculate the variable costs (ie. food and labour costs) and other costs directly related to the function, such as flowers or disco hire, before increasing these costs by a percentage to cover fixed cost and a net profit margin. The total cost plus net profit method will be used to fix a selling price. There may be certain circumstances in a banqueting operation which justify selling banquets or functions at a price which is below the total cost, in order to obtain prestigious business or, to utilise facilities during periods of low demand. Contribution pricing methods are suitable for fixing the price of functions in these circumstsnces, where the variable and direct costs to the function are used as a minimum price. The maximum price will be what the customer is prepared to pay, so long as it is in excess of the minimum. This will have the effect of reducing the loss that will be incurred if the facilities are not utilised at all.

Banqueting Sales example of Contribution Pricing
The banqueting department of an operation has quoted the price of a function for 100 covers at £11.50 per head. A breakdown of the sales and costs of the function are as follows:

Sales	100 covers @ £11.50	=	£1,150	(100%)
less Variable Costs	100 covers @ £ 6.50	=	£ 6.50	(56.5%)
Contribution		=	£ 500	(43.5%)
less Fixed Costs		=	£ 300	(27%)
Net Profit			£ 200	(16.5%)

NB: The fixed costs have been calculated by totalling all fixed costs apportioned to the department which is then divided by the number of days the department functions during the accounting period eg. £109,500 ÷ 365 = £300. If there is no other business available that day, it may be necessary to cut the price in order to reduce the loss of £300 that would be made if the facilities were not used. With the minimum price being £6.50, a price of £8.50 may be offered and if it was accepted we would have the following situation:

Sales	100 @ £8.50	=	£ 850
less Variable Costs	100 @ £6.50	=	£ 650
Contribution		=	£ 200
less Fixed Costs		=	£ 300
Net Loss		=	£(100)

Although the net loss to the banqueting department is £100, it is better than the loss of £300 if no business was done at all. It may also be argued that this will help to enhance the goodwill of an operation if pricing of this nature is used for charitable functions or other worthwhile activities, thus enhancing the operation's reputation. However, care must be taken when reducing the prices of functions because it may lead to adverse reaction when normal prices are charged.

Contribution pricing leads to imaginative pricing in order to maximise sales in a market which is highly elastic. It is also particularly suitable for hotel and catering operations which have a high degree of fixed costs. Although this method of pricing can be used to generate sales, it should not be considered as the primary method because there is a danger that it may not cover fixed costs in total over a period of time. Caterers should be aware of their costs and the behaviour of these costs in order to utilise this method of pricing effectively.

Student Activity No. 3.18

The banqueting department of The Windsor Hotel operates all year round and has the following fixed costs apportioned or allocated to it:

Salaries & Wages	38,500
Rates & Depreciation	18,200
Repairs & Maintenance	4,600
Administration & Business Costs	9,300
Miscellaneous Costs	1,900

A net profit of 20% is required from the department. The local Rotary Club has asked for a menu with a food cost of £3.90 for its ladies' night for 200 covers, extra costs for this function will be £240.

(i) Fix a selling price per head for this function to cover the total cost and net profit required.

(ii) State the minimum price that may be quoted.

(iii) Quote a price allowing a £1 per head contribution towards the fixed costs.

(iv) Show how the quoted price will affect departmental profit or loss.

ASSESSMENT QUESTIONS

1. Explain the definition of marginal costing.
2. Explain what 'contribution' must cover.
3. Explain the nature of fixed costs on a unit 'contribution' basis.
4. Explain the 'contribution' to fixed costs on a period basis.
5. Explain the advantages of pricing accommodation by using the 'contribution' method of pricing.
6. Explain the advantages of pricing banquets and functions by using the 'contribution' method of pricing.
7. Explain the uses marginal costing has when preparing tariffs for seasonal operations.

Computers and Accountancy Information Systems

We examined in study books one and two the basis of computer systems and programmes that may be used for purchasing and stock control, linking it to the food and beverage control procedures used in hotel and catering operations. In this section we will examine the uses of computers for hotel and catering operations and the systems that apply to and which may be used in food and beverage control and accounting information procedures. The computer itself is made up of five basic parts, these are:

(i)   An Input Unit.
(ii) A Memory Unit.
(iii) A Calculation Unit.
(iv) An Output Unit.
(v)   A Control Unit.

Programmes and systems are recorded and information is stored on cassettes or floppy discs and results are printed out either onto Visual Display Screens, or through a Printer, Word Processer or both. Information is fed into the computer through a keyboard to the central processor unit which will have a memory capacity, measured in kilobytes. The capabilities of the computer will be according to its storage capacity; one kilobyte stores one character of information. An important feature of computers that are suitable for hotel and catering operations will be the number of inputs they have through point of sale and control terminals. This is due to the many departments and functional control sections that these operations have.

Some of the uses a computer has in a hotel and catering operation are listed below:

(i)   Reservations, Check-in and Check-out Procedures.
(ii)   Customer Billing/Sales Ledger.
(iii) Financial Accounting.
(iv)   Food and Beverage Control/Stock Control.
(v)   Wages and Salaries.
(vi)   Telephone Logging.
(vii) Administration Records/Personnel/Sales.
(viii) Word Processing/Secretarial Functions.

Since the beginning of the 1980s the use of computers in hotel operations has been growing rapidly. A survey conducted by the

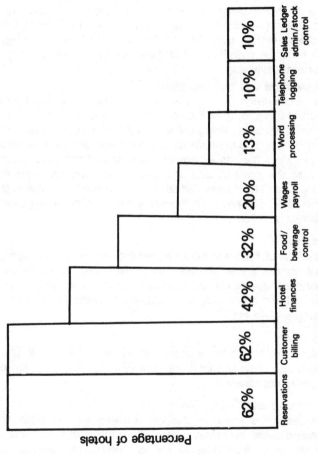

Percentage of hotels

Reservations	Customer billing	Hotel finances	Food/ beverage control	Wages payroll	Word processing	Telephone logging	Sales Ledger admin/stock control
62%	62%	42%	32%	20%	13%	10%	10%

(Caterer and Hotel Keeper/Gallup Survey 1983)

Fig. 3.15 *What Hotels use Computers for*

235

Caterer and Hotel Keeper at the end of 1983 in 3 star and above hotels showed that 35% of them used computers with a further 50% likely to use them by 1985. We can therefore see a growth rate from 8% in 1980 to 80% (approx) by 1985. The most common application (62%) was in front office reservations and guest billing, with 42% using them for accounting purposes and 32% for food and beverage control. Of the hoteliers surveyed, 25% said they were planning to introduce financial and control systems by 1985 and of those planning to use computers, many were considering using them for this purpose. In this section we will examine in closer detail the use of computers for food and beverage control and accounting information. When considering the sort of package which may be suitable for hotel and catering operations it must be mentioned that there are over 2,000 software packages currently available.

Food and Beverage Control Systems
There are a whole range of software packages that cover food and beverage control systems, from the compiling of basic stock records to recipe composition/menu pricing systems that analyse contribution to profits for each dish. The principle used in food and beverage control systems is to follow the movement of stock items from purchasing requirements to the point of sale and reconciling these results with budgeted forecasts. The design and structure of a food and beverage control system should be based on 5 levels of control information, each level is explained as follows:

Ingredient Analysis
The specifications of food and liquor ingredients covering purchasing specifications in the areas of: unit size, cost, yield, stock levels, ordering quantities, availability and sources of supply. This information should be stored with the facility for updating information with regard to price changes, yield etc.

Recipe Data Bank
A bank of standard recipes for all dishes served should be stored. This should be kept up to date so that it will be possible for the computer to sort and store as necessary.

Requisition Costing and Stores Control
Requisitions should be based on recipes, enabling the computer to prepare standard costings. Stores control, from the receiving of stock through to its issue, according to kitchen requistions, leading to inventory control; this being the first stage of audit reconciliation of purchases and sales.

Sales Analysis
Information regarding sales should be posted to the computer from points of sale. Analysis of previously recorded historic and forecasted

sales should take place, showing variances in budgeted and actual results and illustrating trends in historic and actual results, both in units, unit groups and total sales.

Management Information
This should show variance analysis, the control of stock levels and stock reconciliation and indices of cost and selling prices from the input and analysis of the previous four stages.

Programme menus for food and beverage control systems will include the following operations, assuming historic and forecasted results are already programmed:

(i) Set control dates and periods.
(ii) Input stock items in units and unit groups.
(iii) Input recipes/bar lists.
(iv) Input purchases.
(v) Inventory costs.
(vi) Stock take input.
(vii) Stock transfers and issues.
(viii) Input issues.
(ix) Input selling prices and variations (eg. happy hours and discounts).
(x) Input sales.
(xi) Input re-stocking lists.

Programmes will naturally vary according to the size, complexity and type of operation and to the control information required.

Accounting Information Systems
Accounting information systems are an extension of the food and liquor systems and, it may be said, that one would not adequately function without the other, for overall control. The major input of food and beverage control information forms the basis of the accounting function in the preparation of trading statements and departmental gross profits. Financial packages will also be considered at different levels, which are listed and further explained below.

Storage and Maintenance of Ledger Accounts
Keeping records of transactions in sales, purchases, debtors, creditors, cash, expenses, capital income and expenditure and asset value. Historic accounts (ie. previous years) forecasts and the master budget should also be stored in this data base.

Preparation of Financial Statements
From the data base operating statements, trading and profit and loss accounts would be calculated for each department and the business overall, together with a balance sheet and cash flow statements. The system must be capable of breaking down each cost centre, showing departmental and unit costs and variances between budgeted and

actual results, in fixed and variable costs and direct and indirect costs. These results and analyses would be available on a daily basis for operating statements, if required, and on a more periodic basis or analysis of overall costs and reporting profit and loss accounts and balance sheets.

Management Information

This should show debtor and creditor control, cash reconciliation on a daily basis, giving close control of working capital. Variance analysis of labour and overhead cost centres is carried out on a regular basis (weekly). Projections are made on capital income and expenditure as well as taxation.

Budgeting

By drawing on the data base and receiving an input of sales and cost projections the system prepares sales forecasts, operating budgets, subsidiary budgets and a master budget. Different projections and policies are analysed by using spread sheets which are further explained in the next section.

The information required by hotel and catering operations, to assess financial performance, is prepared by using data based systems, with operational inputs recording all types of income and expenditure. Programmes and systems will be used to sort out and organise the information. These then produce statements and reports that are required by the operation, with variance analysis of these results by the use of extended or additional programmes.

Report Generators

Report generators are a system being developed for data based programmes, which will allow the 'end user' (ie. the accountant or food and beverage controller) to assess his own data in the format that he requires. Information produced by the different systems available has in the past been rigid and set according to the programme requirement and design. Accountants and controllers will be able to use the data stored in the computer, to produce reports to their own requirements and needs, without re-programming systems. This development will increase the flexibility of data based systems and the speed of preparing specific reports or analysis of information.

Electronic Spread Sheets

Spread sheets can be applied to virtually all accounting and control functions and have a particular orientation towards cost analysis and budgeting. They are designed to cope with changes in cost and selling prices and the effects on forecasts if cost centres change, or if changes are projected without having to feed in historic information. For example, if an operation is considering menu changes or wage increases, the end result and effect on operational profitability is calculated and presented within minutes, whereas, originally, it would have taken an accountant hours, or even days, to prepare these results with a calculator. Spread sheets have the capabilty to integrate separate data files when recording a single transaction, to show the effect of the transactions on the ledger accounts involved, through to the operating statement and balance sheet. For example, the payment of a creditor would be shown in the appropriate ledger accounts, through to its effect on the working capital of the operation. Previously, this may have taken up to six separate inputs. Input operations will also be simplified by the spread sheet protecting data being entered into the wrong data file, by automatically moving in sequence from one input entry to the next. Spread sheets, in some cases, are able to present data in the form of graphs and charts for more visual information and projections. The benefits of using spread sheets are obvious; they save time in preparing information required for operations and give more detailed feedback. They also assist the caterer in giving projections on any new ideas or plans he may have, without laborious calculations being necessary, which gives him the opportunity to be more adventurous and experimental in his plans and thoughts about the development of the operation.

In this section we have explained the role computer systems may have in food and beverage control and accounting functions. There are many packages available for all sizes and types of operation, both in hardware and software, which will accomplish all that we have mentioned and more. There are regular reviews in the trade press on computers systems available to and suitable for the industry. The Caterer and Hotel Keeper produces an annual review of systems available, in conjunction with 'HOTEC' an annual computer exhibition for the industry, held each September/October.

Whilst is is impossible in this book to show practical applications, students should interact with computers and programmes available to them, especially in the use and application of spread sheets. New systems come onto the market every month and therefore it should be said that if any statistics were quoted or if any systems were reviewed in detail it is likely that they would be out of date before this book is published. This point demonstrates the speed of technology within this aspect of the industry.

Student Activity   No. 3.19
Prepare a specification for a computer system which will cover food and beverage control and accounting functions for either:
   (i)   A hotel with 200 bedrooms, a restaurant, coffee shop and 2 liquor outlets,   *or*
   (ii)   A restaurant of 100 covers with a banqueting suite.

239

Bibliography and Further Reading
Implications of Microcomputers in Small and Medium Hotel and Catering Firms: *HCITB Research Report*
Hard Facts About Software: *Restaurant Hospitality* June 1984
Computers — Systems on the Market for Hotels:
Computers — Gallup Survey; both *Caterer and Hotel Keeper* September 22nd 1983

ASSESSMENT QUESTIONS

1. List the basic parts of a computer.
2. List the uses of computers in hotel operations.
3. Explain the levels of control that can be used as a basis for food and beverage control systems.
4. Explain the levels of control that can be used as a basis for accounting information systems.
5. Explain the use of report generators.
6. Explain the application of electronic spread sheets for control accounting and forecasting.

Case Study Applications

The purpose of a case study is to carry out a detailed analysis of a hotel and catering operation from given data and information. This analysis should then be evaluated against budgeted figures or compared with previous results and normal operating yardsticks. From any evaluations made it would then be possible to make recommendations in order to either maintain or improve the results of the operation. In this section we will examine case study applications for food and beverage operations using the three stages already mentioned and within the parameters of the information given in this book. We will also link it to other subjects you have studied to a similar level, these subjects being, Food and Beverage Operations, Sales and Marketing and Behavioural and Supervisory Studies. It may be said, therefore, that a case study should not be just a financial analysis but that a more investigative approach being used to solve a problem. This may often prove difficult due to a lack of information, which may be limited to a series of accounts or operating statements, a brief outline of the operation or problem and perhaps a menu or layout plan of the operation. Therefore we may wish to include in our answer requests for further information to enable us to investigate our evaluations in greater detail before making any recommendations, or, base our recommendations on assumptions we make from the evaluation.

The case studies we will be using are taken from the HCIMA Part B Food and Beverage Management Examinations. Although this is an examination to a higher level than that for which this book is intended, the case studies used cover all aspects of intermediate level study. Therefore they are suitable to use outside examination conditions and obvious time limitations. The case studies have been modified slightly from the originals to give students the opportunity to carry out analysis techniques and calculations which may be regarded as time consuming in examination conditions.

Analysis of Information
When considering the analysis of accounting information we must examine the types of calculations necessary to give a complete breakdown of the data given, with a view to measuring efficiency and any trends or variances that occur between two or more sets of figures.

241

The types of calculation used will depend on the information given, therefore from the lists of calculation shown below, not all will be able to be calculated for every case study carried out. Analysis of accounting data to give profitability and efficiency ratios and percentages will include the following calculations we have studied in this book:

(i) Departmental/Total Gross Profit %.
(ii) Departmental/Total Labour Costs %.
(iii) Departmental/Total Overhead Costs %.
(iv) Departmental/Total Net Profit %.
(v) Departmental Sales Mix %.
(vi) Food and Liquor Stock Turnover Ratios.
(vii) Increases in Sales and Costs between accounting periods.
(viii) Sales for each staff member.
(ix) Profit earned by each staff member.

Analysis of operating statements will include the following calculations we have studied in this book.

(i) Departmental/Total Sales Variances.
(ii) Departmental/Total Cost Variances.
(iii) Average Spending per customer.
(iv) Average Daily/Weekly/Monthly Sales.
(v) Marginal Cost and contribution per customer.
(vi) Unit Cost per customer of Labour and Overhead Costs.

Evaluation of Information

The evaluation of information gained from the analysis of accounting data or operating statements will take place by comparing the results obtained with other results available and given in the case study. If these results are not shown then comparison must take place using standard yardsticks that may apply to particular types of operation. When evaluating the analysis of an operating statement we are considering the difference between budgeted and actual results of an operation and it is necessary to carry out forms of variance analysis. The first stage will be to consider sales variances and cost variances that may be related to them by an increase or decrease in sales volume, number of customers or average customer spending. Other reasons for variances will then be considered with regard to price of materials, usage or efficiency. When evaluating labour and overhead variances consideration will be given to the fixed, variable, direct and indirect nature of the costs.

When evaluating the analysis of accounts for different periods we consider them in two ways; firstly in percentage values with regard to any charges in the elements of cost and their respective proportions. It is often best to start with any changes in the net profit % and then to ascertain the reason from changes in gross profit % or labour and overhead cost %. It is often possible to identify reasons for changes in the net profit % by using this process. For example a 4.5% drop in net profit may be due to a 3.5% drop in gross profit due to an increase in food costs and a 1% increase in labour costs. We should also evaluate increases or decreases in the volume of sales between periods and the fact that costs have changed respectively. For example a 7% increase in sales should produce a 7% increase in the cost of sales but not necessarily in other costs unless they are variable. Stock turnover between periods should also be compared, as a low of turnover will indicate that stock levels are too high which in turn will in most cases affect the cost of sales and consequently gross and net profits. Consideration must also be made as to the type of operation and the types of commodities used because this will have a strong bearing on the stock turnover. When there are no figures available for comparison purposes it will be necessary to evaluate the results analysed against normal operating yardsticks. This is not a reliable method of evaluation because proportions of cost will vary according to the type of operation (see figure 1.30), the individual needs and financial policy of the operation concerned.

An equally important part of any evaluation will be to check 'what is missing' from financial information, which may have the effect of not giving a true representation of costs and profits eg. depreciation. Omitted items or areas of unusually low expenditure may give an indication as to the root cause of problems an operation may be having. Examples of this are low advertising or maintenance expenditure being a reason for not achieving sales forecasts or deterioration in the condition of the property respectively. Evaluation should also be made as to whether sales increases are due to increased customer spending or daily sales totals through price increases or if the increase is due to customers spending more, giving an indication of successful marketing or selling techniques. The two aspects of external and internal marketing may be evaluated in this way, an increase in the number of customers may be related to good sales promotion through advertising whereas an increase in customer spending may be credited to internal sales promotion. The evaluation of accounting information may therefore be summarised as identifying the reasons for variations between budgeted or historic results against the actual or current results of an operation.

Evaluation of other information given in the text of a case study will depend on the amount of information given. In some cases where this information is not obvious it may be a case of 'reading between the lines' and looking for supportive results in the analysis of accounting information. Statements showing staff discontent or customer dissatisfaction can be evaluated as organisational problems or the need to review the product or service sold. Each of these indications will have a contributory effect to either problem or in some cases be identified to one specific problem area. Analysis of menu items will show on evaluation the types of materials used, their purchasing and forecasting requirements, storage requirements and control procedures necessary. Evaluation of this type can often only be carried out effectively if further information is available.

Further Information Requirements
To expand on certain evaluations will often require further information, in some case studies students will be asked to list the further information they require in order to give an indication that they understand points raised in their evaluation. Further information should therefore be identified with the problem areas raised in the analysis and evaluation of the case study. To put this information into the broad categories of management techniques at this stage would be more sensible, although when looking at an actual case study it is better to be specific.

The analysis and evaluation of financial information will show variances in costs of materials, labour and overhead expenses, in which case further information will be necessary to identify any reasons. High cost of sales may be due to a variety of reasons such as wastage through bad buying, storage conditions or lack of control, therefore information on this aspect may be necessary. The cost of materials can rise necessitating more detailed information in this area and so on. Labour costs may be investigated more thoroughly through the examination of job descriptions and comparing staff rotas with peak periods of demand. Overheads may be closely examined in certain areas to pin point problems either through lack of, or, over expenditure. Sales may be analysed in greater detail for customer preferences, periods of demand and other trends. A balance sheet will show many aspects of the financial details of an operation, although much of the analysis of balance sheets is beyond the scope of this study it will inform us of depreciation aspects, stock levels, cash available and the financing of the operation.

Further information in other management areas of personnel, organisation and marketing may also be requested according to the problems observed. Staff problems can be further investigated by examining job specifications and descriptions, training programmes, work rosters and schedules, general working conditions and environment such as wages, uniforms, facilities and welfare. Market research information and customer profiles will give some insight into sales and promotional activities such as opening hours and whether or not the operation is making full use of customer demand with regard to the dishes, menu and serviced offered. Where other problems have been highlighted more information will be required as to company policies and organisational systems appertaining to the problem in question.

The use of further information to expand problems raised or shown by the analysis and evaluation of the information given in a case study will enable the student to make more detailed recommendations for improving the results of the operation in question. In real terms this information is usually available however for case study purposes it is unlikely. Therefore recommendations will be based on the information gained through the analysis and evaluation of the facts available.

Recommendations

The purpose of making recommendations is to show that the student understands the techniques and procedures available to correct any deficiencies an operation may have or to improve existing results. When problem areas have been identified a recommendation should be made to solve the problem by applying the techniques and procedures shown in this book and other areas of study. The type of recommendations that may be applied will vary according to the specific problem and the information available, some general examples are shown below.

Failure to achieve sales targets would result in recommendations being made to increase sales by changing the menu to suit customer demands, improving service and if necessary the image of the establishment, external advertising, internal selling and by restructuring prices to stimulate increased spending.

Failure to achieve gross profit targets may be rectified by making recommendations to improve or implement procedures in purchasing, costing and control throughout the whole cycle of the operation from the preparation of standard recipes and purchase specifications to cash control. Other recommendations can be to review pricing policies, make or buy decisions, methods of food preparation and stocks held.

Failure to achieve labour cost targets will result in recommendations being made regarding staff organisation in home work, job descriptions, work rosters and schedules in order to use labour more efficiently.

Failure to achieve overhead cost targets would result in recommendations being made to control areas of expense more closely by economising in fuel consumption, using telephones at off peak periods, introducing planned maintenance, make or buy decisions and more efficient uses of resources etc.

Labour problems may be eliminated or reduced by recommendations in organisational aspects, improved recruitment, selection and training procedures, improved working conditions and environment.

Whilst we have examined recommendations to improve results generally some case studies may require students to prepare menus, purchasing, costing and control procedures, job descriptions and other policies or procedures. When considering these questions, the answers should be related to the problem or operation concerned because it is easy to go off at a tangent into detailed theory and ignore the information that is requested. Recommendations and ideas for improvement should relate to the problem that has been discovered during the analysis and evaluation stages of the case study.

Presentation
Presentation of the answer to a case study is usually in a report form, this may be carried out in two ways. The first method being to take each problem individually showing the analysis, evaluation, further information required and the recommendations to solve that particular problem. This method, whilst isolating each problem, does tend to be disjointed and in many cases problems are inter-related which can lead to confusion or over complication of the report. The second method where the information is fully analysed, followed by a complete evaluation of this analysis and recommendations being made will eliminate any confusion and complications. The analysis of information may be presented in tabular or similar form alongside the results given for this purpose. The evaluation may be in a series of notes from this analysis with each problem area being separated, those which are interrelated may also be highlighted in this way. Recommendations may then be made separately for each point highlighted in the evaluation giving as much detail as necessary to cover the scope of the problem or question. Finally a summary of the recommendations stating what will be achieved if they are carried out. Students must be aware that presentation is an important part of any case study answer and that it should be a logical flow for the reader.

EXAMPLES OF CASE STUDIES

In this section we will cover the complete answer for one case study and examine the structure of an answer for another. The purpose being for students to understand the scope and depth of two different types of case study and the considerations that are made when answering them. These case studies are used with the approval of the HCIMA for which the author is grateful.

Case Study 1
Jim Haddock owns and operates a 60 seat licensed sea-food restaurant in Oldtown High Street. Since he opened up in 1978, the business has provided a modest return for Jim, and he judges his restaurant's success has been largley due to the maintenance of consistently high standards in food production and presentation. The menu and beverages lists have remained fairly static over the five year period and he feels that this fact, more than any other, will guarantee continued success. Staff are familiar with their work and standards are easy to control.

The restaurant provides a good level of table service and the tariff attracts shoppers and local business people for lunch between

12.15pm and 2.30pm; passing tourists are also attracted during the summer months. Evening meals are available from 7.00pm and last orders are taken at 10.30pm with trade coming from local people and some tourists. The restaurant closes on Sunday.

Six months ago Jim Haddock was told by his doctor to take work a little easier, so he appointed a full-time manager to handle the day to day running of the restaurant. Jim calls in once a week or so to keep an eye on the business; however the manager feels that he is not given sufficient scope for developing the business. The number of staff leaving, and staff absenteeism has risen significantly.

In order to remedy the situation, Jim Haddock has approached you with a view to your suggesting what should be done to put the restaurant back on its feet again. In your preliminary discussions with Jim, you discover that he has not been spending much each year on refurbishing the premises and the level of maintenance and hygiene has given rise to an informal warning from the Environmental Health Officer. Jim does have resources available for remodelling and refurbishing the premises, and he does recognise that some of the existing catering equipment needs to be replaced.

You have talked to some of Jim's customers and the impression gained is that whilst his restaurant is conveniently situated in the town, reasonably priced and the food of a good and consistent standard, the menu offered has become rather stale and unimaginative.

The restaurant uses fresh foods extensively (especially fish) and these are obtained daily from the local market. However, failure to forecast demand adequately often leads either to over-production or to items on the menu being discontinued.

Jim Haddock's financial year ends on 30th April, and the operating statement for the past three years is as follows:

	1982-83			1983-84			1984-85		
	£	£	%	£	£	%	£	£	%
Food									
Sales	82,000			85,600			88,500		
less food costs	34,500			35,100			39,000		
Gross Profit (food)		47,500			50,500			49,500	
Drink									
Sales	23,500			24,900			29,500		
less drink costs	14,000			14,300			17,100		
Gross Profit (drink)		9,500			10,600			12,400	
Total Gross Profit (food & drink)		57,000			61,100			61,900	
Labour & staff costs	31,400			34,800			39,700		
Overheads & operating costs	9,000			8,300			10,400		
Maintenance	1,700			1,500			1,200		
Total costs & overheads		42,100			44,600			51,300	
NET OPERATING PROFIT		£14,900			£16,500			£10,600	

The menu used in the restaurant comprises:

Starters
Honeydew Melon
Florida Cocktail
Mackeral Pâté
Shrimp Cocktail
Smoked Trout
Herring Platter
Deep Fried Scampi

Soups
Soup of the day
Minestrone
Cream of Asparagus
Clam Chowder (as available)

Hot Dishes
Dish of the day
Scampi — fried
Scampi — provencale
Trout grenobloise
Fillets of sole mornay
Fillets of sole veronique
Deep fried fillets of plaice
Grilled halibut steak
Skate with black butter
Whole Dover sole (as available)
    cooked to suit your requirements

Salads
Lobster (as available)
Scotch Salmon (in season)
Fruits de mer salad

Vegetables
Potatoes — boiled, french fried,
        croquette, baked
Garden peas
Whole french beans
Baby carrots
Brocolli

Sweets
Peach Melba
Pear Belle Helene
Cream Caramel
Apple pie and ice cream

Cheeseboard
Full selection available.   Coffee

The staffing position as at 15th May 1985 comprised:

Manager

2 full-time waiters	2 cooks
1 part-time waiter	2 wash-up/odd-job men
2 part-time waitresses	1 cleaner
1 chef supervisor	1 barmaid

You are required to submit a *Report* to Jim Haddock. Your report should include:

(i) An analysis of evaluation of *six* main problem areas.

(ii) An outline of *six* additional pieces of information you would require in order to obtain a fuller understanding of the situation in the restaurant.

(iii) Your recommendations for management implementation.

Case Study 1   Answer

From: Penny Pilling

To: Jim Haddock

Report on Haddocks Sea Food Restaurant

From the information available at present and my preliminary enquiries I am able to submit the following report on the trading situation and operation of your Sea Food Restaurant in Oldtown High Street.

Analysis of Trading Results for period 1982-85

	1982-83	1983-84	1984-84
Food Cost of Sales %	42	41	44
Food Gross Profit %	58	59	56
Liquor Cost of Sales %	60	57	58
Liquor Gross Profit %	40	43	42
Labour & Staff Cost %	30	31	34
Overheads & Operating %	9	8	9
Maintenance %	2	1	1
Net Operating Profit %	14	15	9

(NB: % Rounded to nearest whole number)

Evaluation of Six Main Problem Areas

(i) Food Gross Profit has decreased to 56% which is below the normal operating yardstick for an operation of this nature. It is also observed that costs have not increased in proportion to sales. Indications are that prices have not been increased in proportion with the rising cost of materials and the failure to forecast demand and consequent over-production will have led to high wastage.

(ii) Liquor Gross Profit is well below the normal level expected for an operation of this type. The reasons for this will either be due to lack of control or inefficient pricing methods or most probably a combination of both.

(iii) Labour Costs, despite the manager's salary, are showing a steady increase over the periods analysed which gives an indication of overstaffing. This is supported by high staff turnover and absenteeism levels, together with the impression gained from customers that the operation has become stale, which will have a spin off effect on the staff, who in turn may be contributing to the stale image.

(iv) The informal caution from the Environmental Health Officer causes greatest concern because of his powers to close the restaurant and more important the dangers inherent therein to both customers and staff. This is further supported by the low amount spent on maintenance each year and the owner's comments to this effect. It is also a further indication as to the state of the restaurant regarding furnishings and is a contributory factor to its stale image.

(v) Customers have indicated that the menu has become stale and unimaginative which has obviously affected sales. Other indications of this have already been mentioned. The increase in food sales over the last three years has been from £82,000 to £88,500 which represents an overall increase of £6,500 or 7.9% which would be well below the average price increases for the period. This indicates a substantial drop in real sales.

(vi) The manager feels he does not have sufficient scope for developing the business which indicates he has a control problem through lack of authority due probably to interference from the proprietor. This will also be a contributory factor to the staff problems already indicated.

Further Information Required

To understand the six problem areas in greater detail the following information would be required:

(i) Information of the food and liquor costing, pricing and control procedures and systems, purchasing records and details of volume forecasting methods to enable a thorough investigation of the increasing food cost percentage and low liquor gross profits.

(ii) Details of staffing information for 'all employees' to include job descriptions, work rosters and schedules, employee records and details of past employees with their reasons for leaving in order to identify the reasons for high staff turnover, absenteeism and labour costs.

(iii) Details of Environmental Health Officer's informal warning and details of the kitchen and equipment's age, maintenance and general condition to establish a development programme.

(iv) The Balance Sheet to show the value of furniture and fittings and their depreciation, stocks held and the financial structure of the restaurant with regard to future developments.

(v) Details of the market served to include customer profile, popularity of menu items, occupancy details and turnover with the intention of establishing a better product and service for the customer in keeping with their current demands.

(vi) Breakdown of all overhead expenditure with the intention of analysing areas of expenditure such as advertising and maintenance with a view to establishing operating budgets.

Recommendations

It is obvious that the fabric and image of the operation has been allowed to deterioriate over the last three years, probably being due to the owner's complacency and poor health. In order to carry out the proposals outlined below I recommend that the operation closes down for a period of time. The recommendations are as follows:

(i) Give increased control and responsibility to the manager, involving him in the planning and development of the re-organisation of the restaurant's activities. Making staff and other parties aware of his responsibilities and role within the organisation and giving him some form of incentive (eg. share of operating profits) to maximise sales and profits.

(ii) The restaurant *must* be brought up to a high standard of hygiene which more than complies with legal requirements. This will involve refurbishing and equipping food preparation areas.

(iii) Whilst maintaining the overall theme and high standards of the restaurant, the menu and wine list should be brought more in line with current trends and customer demands. This will involve the introduction of a wider range of dishes, possibly to include a variety of menu items other than seafoods. A more flexible approach should also be made towards the menu, giving the opportunity to change its content according to the availability of food products and to generally utilise materials.

(iv) The restaurant itself should also be refurbished and changed to promote its new menu and show a new image, thus putting its stale image in the past.

(v) Food and liquor control procedures must be introduced or existing procedures improved. These procedures must include costing and pricing systems which are easily maintained, standard recipes, purchase specifications, volume forecasting, ordering and stock control systems.

(vi) Job descriptions must be prepared for all staff, a training policy must be established and carried out, working conditions improved and the supply of new uniforms to blend in with the new image of the restaurant should be introduced.

(v) Prior to re-opening the restaurant must carry out an advertising promotion to make existing and new customers aware of the new menu and image of the operation.

(vi) Budgets for all aspects of sales and expenditure must be prepared to control material costs and allow for proper maintenance and marketing programmes to be implemented and carried out.

(vii) Throughout this whole exercise it must be emphasised that high standards of food and liquor sold, hygiene and control must be implemented and maintained.

Case Study 2

The menu shown in Appendix A has been devised for the Chiltern Restaurant, a sixty-seat eating house located in a town centre shopping precinct. The unit aims to cater for a wide cross-section of customers who visit the town for shopping, tourist and business purposes. Waitress service is used and all food is plated.

(i) You are required to show draft proposals for:
   (a) Methods of food production and its organisation.
   (b) Purchasing information for food and beverage commodities.
   (c) Storage requirements for food and beverage commodites.

(ii) Trading results for the Chiltern Restaurant for the sixth month of trading are shown in Appendix B. Identify the main features shown by these results and suggest remedial action to be taken by management.

(iii) At the end of the first year's trading, an analysis of food sales was undertaken as shown in Appendix C. Identify significant features shown by this analysis and propose, giving reasons, changes in the composition and pricing of the menu items and any further action that you might take.

Appendix A
Menu and Wine List for the Chiltern Restaurant

Appetisers

1	Fruit Juices	.15p
2	Florida Cocktail	.40p
3	Egg with Anchovy Sauce	.45p
4	Tuna Fish Salad	.60p
5	Prawn Cocktail with Brown Bread and Butter	.85p
6	Home-made Pâté with Toast	.90p
7	Soup	.20p
8	Corn-on-the-Cob	.35p

Hot Dishes (all served with Chips and Vegetables)

10	Deep Fried Scampi	£1.95p
11	Fried Fillet of Haddock with Lemon	£1.25p
12	Bacon, Egg, Sausage and Tomato	£1.30p
13	Lamb Cutlets with Mint Jelly	£1.70p
14	Grilled Pork Chop with Apple Sauce	£1.80p
15	6oz Sirloin Steak with Garlic/Parsley Butter	£2.70p
16	10oz Sirloin Steak with Garlic/Parsley Butter	£3.50p

Salads, etc.
21 Chicken Salad £1.75p
22 Pork Pie Salad £1.30p
23 Welsh Rarebit .... .75p
24 Roll and Butter .... .20p

Desserts
31 Apple Pie with Cream or Ice Cream .... .45p
32 Fruit Tart with Cream or Ice Cream .... .45p
33 Cheesecake .... .65p
34 Banana Split .... .50p
35 Fresh Cream Gateau .... .75p
36 Vanilla, Strawberry and Chocolate Ices .... .35p
37 Cheese and Biscuits .... .45p

Beverages
41 Pot of Tea .... .25p
42 Coffee with Cream (per cup) .... .40p
43 Milk (per glass) .... .20p

Wines
51 Carafe of House Red or White Wine (70cl) £2.40p
52 Le Piat — Beaujolais £3.70p
53 La Flora Blanche (White, medium sweet) £3.20p
54 Tanab Reisling £3.20p
55 Anjou Rosé £3.20p
56 Glass of House Red or White Wine .... .55p

Appendix B
Chiltern Restaurant
Trading Results for the Sixth Month of Trading

	Target/Budget Figures £	Actual Trading Results £
Sales		
Food	9,500	8,802
Liquor	1,500	1,378
Cost of Sales		
Food	3,325	3,300
Liquor	600	572
Gross Profit		
Food	6,175	5,502
Liquor	900	806
Total	7,075	6,308
Labour Costs	2,860	2,699
Overheads		
Fixed (rates, rent, etc.)	550	550
Variable (fuel, replacements, etc.)	925	890
Net Profit	2,740	2,169

Value of Stock held at the end of the sixth month (at cost price)
Food   £1,560
Liquor   £ 650

Food Sales Analysis — Chiltern Restaurant

Menu Items ranked by Income

	Item	Income £	Percentage income of total
16	10oz Steak	14,941	11.6
42	Coffee	14,882	11.5
15	6oz Steak	14,855	11.5
11	Haddock	11,585	9.0
31	Apple Pie	7,029	5.5
12	Bacon, Egg	6,511	5.1
6	Pâté	6,233	4.8
33	Cheesecake	5,861	4.5
5	Prawn Cocktail	4,839	3.7
21	Chicken Salads	4,347	3.4
24	Roll and Butter	4,244	3.3
14	Pork Chop	3,961	3.1
10	Scampi	3,933	3.1
35	Cream Gateau	3,780	2.9
13	Lamb Cutlets	3,692	2.9
32	Fruit Tart	2,837	2.2
7	Soup	2,203	1.7
36	Ices	1,928	1.5
23	Welsh Rarebit	1,921	1.5
34	Banana Split	1,731	1.3
22	Pork Pie Salad	1,566	1.2
41	Tea	1,560	1.2
2	Florida Cocktail	1,326	1.0
4	Tuna Salad	1,272	1.0
1	Fruit Juices	519	0.4
3	Egg and Anchovy	405	0.3
37	Cheese and Biscuits	371	0.3
8	Corn-on-the-Cob	308	0.2
43	Milk	249	0.2
	TOTAL	£128,889	100.00

Menu Items ranked by contribution to profits*

	Item	Profit Contribution £	Percentage of total contribution to profits
16	10oz Steak	10,108	16.1
15	6oz Steak	9,972	15.9
42	Coffee	7,896	12.7
11	Haddock	5,700	9.1
6	Pâté	3,307	5.3
33	Cheesecake	3,297	5.3
5	Prawn Cocktail	3,193	5.1
35	Cream Gateau	3,013	4.8
31	Apple Pie	3,009	4.8
7	Soup	1,964	3.1
36	Ices	1,772	2.8
34	Banana Split	1,142	1.8
32	Fruit Tart	1,072	1.7
12	Bacon, Egg etc.	1.047	1.7
14	Pork Chop	1.034	1.7
24	Roll and Butter	822	1.3
21	Chicken Salad	800	1.3
10	Scampi	615	1.0
13	Lamb Cutlets	536	0.9
23	Welsh Rarebit	467	0.7
4	Tuna Fish Salad	457	0.7
2	Florida Cocktail	451	0.7
22	Pork Pie Salad	442	0.7
1	Fruit Juices	342	0.5
43	Milk	102	0.2
51	Tea	19	0.0
3	Egg and Anchovy	-27	0.0
37	Cheese and Biscuits	-52	-0.1
8	Corn-on-the-Cob	-102	-0.2
	TOTAL Contribution to profits	£62.398	100.0

* In determining profit conbribution, raw material costs and directly related labour costs are deducted from the income received for each menu item.

Case Study 2   Answer Outline

(i) (a) Analyse the menu to indicate methods of production ie. canned foods, pre-prepared dishes, assembling of salads and grills. Showing the organisation necessary for quick response to orders by mis en place, flow of materials, equipment layout etc.

  (b) The purchasing information should be based on the methods of production shown in part (a) by preparing purchase specifications. Other information should include considerations made in the selection of sources of supply.

  (c) The methods of storage should be based on the types of commodities purchased and the amounts of stocks held.

(ii) The analysis of the Trading results should include the comparison of budgeted and actual results, comparison of profits, stocks, and costs with normal operating yardsticks. Recommendations for remedial action should be based on these calcualtions.

(iii) The analysis of food sales to show:

  (a) High income dishes where sales are high and they make a good contribution to profits.

  (b) Low income dishes where sales are low and they make a low contribution to profits.

  (c) Dishes where sales are high but they make a lower contribution to profits.

  (d) Dishes where sales are low but they make a higher contribution to profits.

Recommendations based on this analysis would be categorised as follows:

Group (i)   Maintain sales and profitability.

Group (ii)   Abandon menu items where practical or increase prices to increase contribution on essential menu items.

Group (iii) Reduce costs if possible or increase prices on popular items to increase contribution.

Group (iv)   Increase sales of high contribution menu items.

Students should list the dishes they propose to change, give examples on replacement dishes, give examples of where costs may be cut and how sales may be promoted.

ASSESSMENT QUESTION

Trading results for the Food and Beverage Department of the Icham Hotel are shown below. The hotel has bedroom accommodation for 100 guests and two food outlets — the Janus Restaurant and the Gateway Grill each with seating for 60 diners. The Restaurant offers à la carte meals six evenings per week and is closed on Sundays. The Grill is open from 7.30am until 10.00pm every day.

	Year ending 31 May 1984			Year ending 31 May 1985		
	£000	£000	%	£000	£000	%
Restaurant						
Sales	105.0			113.0		
Food Cost	35.0			40.0		
Gross Profit		70.0			73.0	
Wages	35.0			39.0		
Overheads	25.0	60.0		27.5	66.5	
Dept Profit		10.0			6.5	
Grill						
Sales	255.0			282.0		
Food Cost	115.0			125.0		
Gross Profit		140.0			157.0	
Wages	58.0			63.0		
Overheads	36.0	94.0		41.5	104.5	
Dept Profit		46.0			52.5	
Bar						
Sales	85.0			96.0		
Beverage Cost	34.8			43.0		
Gross Profit		50.2			53.0	
Wages	17.0			18.9		
Overheads	10.0	27.0		11.0	29.9	
Dept Profit		23.2			23.1	
Meals served:						
Restaurant		9,350			9,149	
Grill		48,000			52,000	
Average Salary per employee		£5,000			£5,500	

Prices and salaries were raisedby 10% on 1 June, 1984

(i) Submit an analysis and evaluation of the data given concerning the Food and Beverage Department.

(ii) Illustrate, with worked examples, *three* yardsticks by which staff utilisation in food areas can be measured.

(iii) List *six* pieces of additional information which would enable you to evaluate the food operation more accurately.

(iv) On the basis of your analysis and evaluation, make proposals for management action.

Index

Behavioural and Supervisory Studies for Hotel and Catering Operations

Ken Gale BA(Hons). Cert. Ed.

A companion series of study books to Purchasing, Costing and Control for Hotel and Catering Operations by Peter Odgers. These are designed to cover the BTEC Diploma and Certificate, Higher Diploma bridging levels and Part B HCIMA courses and examinations in the areas of Behavioural and Supervisory Studies for Hotel and Catering Operations.

There are three study books in the series, all incorporating a similar approach to this volume. The first study book is an analysis of aspects of human behaviour relevant to hotel and catering operations. The areas covered by this analysis are, therefore, individual differences, interpersonal and group influences on behaviour, social and situational skills and an introduction to the field of supervision. The second study book is an analysis of the role of the modern supervisor in hotel and catering operations. The analysis embraces supervisory techniques and approaches, principles of manpower management and relationships to other management grades in a range of hotel and catering operations. The third study book expands the areas covered in book two and through a range of tasks, activities and assignments assesses the supervisor's role in evaluating staff, organisational and employer's needs, in each case emphasising practical supervisory skills and techniques.

The major advantage of the books is that they are not designed merely as text books; by incorporating a wide range of student activities, assessment questions, practical exercises and recommendations for further reading the study books emphasise the role of the student in the learning process. The books will enable an assessment of understanding to be regularly monitored and checked and at the same time provide a detailed, relevant and comprehensive text which can be used for reference and research through the duration of the courses in question.